ᐁ THE POWER OF THE LAMB ᐁ

The
Power
of the
Lamb

∇

Revelation's
Theology of Liberation
for You

Ward Ewing

Wipf & Stock
PUBLISHERS
Eugene, Oregon

Wipf and Stock Publishers
199 W 8th Ave, Suite 3
Eugene, OR 97401

The Power of the Lamb
Revelation's Theology of Liberation for You
By Ewing, Ward
ISBN: 1-59752-589-8
Copyright©1990 by Ewing, Ward
Publication date 3/1/2006
Previously published by Cowley Publications, 1990

To the Students of Tianamen Square

Their witness revealed the beast.
May their sacrifice be a powerful force for peace.

Table Of Contents

Preface

This book is about power, or to be more precise, about the experience of being without power. It results from a journey which began with the experience of powerlessness: the world is out of control and doing hurtful things to me, to those I care about, to our society, to millions in other countries and cultures—just possibly the world is on a course for self destruction—and no one is able to do anything to change what is happening. Within the experience of powerlessness, I discovered the Book of Revelation, the record of God's people in their experience of powerlessness in the first century.

This book derives from the correlation between my experience and the experience of those first–century Christians.[1] In a working class community in the early 1980s, I experienced something of what it means to be without the power needed to acquire the basics of food, shelter, and transportation. That experience opened my eyes to see the universal experience of powerlessness. I began to examine Scripture, looking for insights about this aspect of the human condition. In Revelation I found symbols responding to the experience: the "four horsemen of the Apocalypse," whose glorious beginning leads to death and hell; "the beast," a multi-headed, conglomerate monster that overpowers everyone; and "the Lamb," an image of a vulnerable, unprotected Christ. These symbolic figures, as images of power and vulnerability, relate to our experience of impotence. Members of our congregation whose futures were uncertain and whose security and welfare were in jeopardy responded with a sense of identification to these images. I began to study Revelation to learn what its images and its theology might tell us about God's power for our vulnerable human condition.

Today most Christians do not share the perspective of those first readers of Revelation, that Christ was to return soon. I find it helpful to approach the doctrine of the "second coming" as a theological myth, describing the reality that God, the creator, is also the God of the future. Then we can examine the myth for its insight into hope and action. Thus while most believers today cannot share the sense of imminent divine intervention, I found that the theological insights of Revelation can speak to our age. I discovered in the images of Revelation powerful symbols that can express our present experience of precarious existence. I also discovered that Revelation offers the Good News of an alternative understanding of power that can renew motivation for those who have become discouraged about the possibility for positive change.

In the face of vast social problems, many who care deeply about our world have become disheartened. They seem unable to believe their action will make any difference. In response to this growing sense of impotency, I write to share the images and insights of Revelation. The images are forceful conceptions of the realities of power with which we live. We can learn much from the seven small churches John addressed in the first century of Christianity. The images he used can assist us as we struggle to understand power and the power of our faith. As those churches were able to find motivation for action in the face of the awesome, hostile power of Rome, so can their understanding of the Good News provide motivation for Christian action and ministry in our own day.

I write not as one struggling with oppression in Latin America or South Africa, but as an ordinary, middle-class Christian in the United States. This book is intended for similar people who care about our world and seek justice and peace. The stories I use are all true stories of people I have known personally. I write to counter our growing apathy and inaction. I write to affirm that in Christ no one is powerless. We must, however, discover a transformed understanding of power, and we must explore anew how faith empowers. In our age the Good News is the same Good News proclaimed to those first Christians: by the power of Christ we can conquer, and our actions can and will change our world.

This book is not a commentary on the Book of Revelation. If the reader desires a commentary, I recommend Vernard

Preface

Eller's *The Most Revealing Book of the Bible: Making Sense out of Revelation*. This commentary is very readable for both laity and clergy, and it does an excellent job of relating Revelation to the gospel of Jesus Christ. I have tried to write this book in such a way that a detailed knowledge about Revelation is un-necessary. If you, the reader, are totally unfamiliar with Revelation, you may wish to read it after finishing chapter 2 (Revelation and the Beast) of this volume.

No book is the result of one person's efforts alone; many others contribute to the work. I wish to express my thanks to the many, many people whose support made my writing pos-sible. The congregation of St. Peter's in the Valley, Louisville, Kentucky, provided sabbatical time for me away from the parish for study and research. The congregation of Trinity Church, Buffalo, New York, allowed me time off to write. Glenn Wilson and Jerry and Margaret Miller, along with many other parishioners, provided support and encouragement for this project. My associate at Trinity Church, the Rev. Susan Cox, who also proofed the manuscript, and others on the Church staff carried an extra load of work as I struggled with Revelation's beasts.

My appreciation goes also to Dr. John Koenig and Dr. Richard Corney, who guided my sabbatical studies. Mrs. Cyn-thia Shattuck, my editor, spent much time and energy chal-lenging me to restructure and rewrite portions of the text, resulting always in improved copy. Among those who read the manuscript, two people offered particularly helpful sugges-tions: Denis Woods introduced me to writings of Dean Brack-ley and Bernard Loomer, which helped clarify important concepts in this book, while Will Clarkson provided invalu-able insight and clarification. The greatest sacrifices for this book have come from my family. My wife, Jenny, and our three children have been lovingly patient and tolerant of my taking time for this work. Life in our home has provided both the corrective of reality and the support of steadfast love.

Powerlessness

Jan is in her late thirties. For fifteen years she taught art in the fourth and fifth grades in the public school system. As a conscientious teacher who cares about children, she encouraged students to share with her through art something of what was going on inside their minds. Nine and ten year old students readily express their own thoughts and feelings, their own pain and joy, through painting and other creative media. But, as anyone who has worked with large numbers of children will understand, over the years Jan became more and more aware of the large number of children who were carrying burdens of loneliness, alienation, and fear. She became more and more concerned about children who came from "good, well-to-do families" but were unwanted and knew it. These children understood the rules for their lives. As long as they behaved and did what mom and dad wanted, they were allowed freedom to do just about whatever they wanted. At the age of ten that meant watching too much television, staying out too late on weekends, and sleeping in on Sunday mornings instead of going to church.

Jan worried. She could see too many pre-teens on the road to trouble. The longer she taught, the more of "her children" she saw get involved with drugs, become sexually promiscuous, drop out of life, or cynically pursue education in order to make lots of money. Lonely children were growing up to become self-centered, self-serving, self-aggrandizing adults who would produce more lonely and alienated children. What upset Jan most was her ability to see it coming. In her students' work she could see who was lonely and who was hurting. She believed that if someone would just respond with care and love for

CHAPTER 1

those ten-year-old boys and girls, many would find healing, and some who otherwise were headed for self-destructive behavior might be saved from their dead-end course.

As a teacher Jan gave much time to her students. But time was limited. Art was not viewed by the school board (nor presumably by the electorate) as an important subject. Most of Jan's students took art only one or two days a week, and she taught in two different schools. She tried to start an art club which would meet after school, but most children—especially those with the greatest need for adult attention and support— had to catch buses when school let out or go directly to day care centers where they remained until picked up by a parent. Neither school had a staff psychologist, and the guidance officers were involved more in administration than in working with students. Jan dreamed of an afternoon program involving the physical education teacher, a school psychologist, and herself—a program that would provide more than T.V. at home or waiting in a day care center; a program that would combine fun, creative expression, a chance to talk honestly, and a supportive community; a program that would give some vulnerable children a better chance in life.

Then came the opportunity for a job with the Board of Education in the curriculum department. Jan applied and was accepted. The job offered a promotion for Jan, including a larger salary, and she hoped that from a position of greater power within the administration, she might be able to effect some changes. She hoped to see her concerns for the students addressed if not through her idea, at least in some manner. Two years later she was in my office, venting her frustration.

No one at the Board of Education, she said, cares about children! The administration makes decisions on the basis of what will gain support in the state legislature, what will keep local politicians satisfied, and what will allow particular individuals to advance in pay and position. The bureaucracy, which is supposed to make sure that property is maintained, supplies available, and books ordered and shipped, is composed of individuals who are primarily concerned about protecting their jobs. They protect their jobs by diffusing responsibility so that no one can be blamed when supplies or books are not available, and by playing politics through doing favors for superiors even when it means neglecting basic tasks. Decisions, she told me, are not made on the basis of what is best for the children, but rather on the basis of what strengthens job security and what furthers the existence and clout of the school administration. Sometimes decisions are for the good of the children, but, Jan felt, most of the time such an outcome is only incidental.

I asked her to describe the goals of public education. The goals she listed include providing a quality education for all children regardless of social, racial, or economic background, being responsive to special needs of children, encouraging constructive and productive behavior, and stimulating the desire to learn.

"Do you believe these are the goals of the school board?" I asked.

She responded that statements similar to these goals are indeed the stated goals of the board and that many people who work in administration believe that to be their task. But, she continued, there is another set of unwritten goals—personal political advancement, saving money for the city, increasing state funding, keeping one's job, working up the ladder to better-paying jobs, upholding the image of the school system, and the like. She was frustrated because she and others in the administration spent more time on the unstated goals than on the true purpose of working for education. She was angry because she had been promised an opportunity to improve the city's educational program, but, in fact, she was only given a better salary and a more prestigious position.

Jan had thought that by working hard, by encouraging creative new ideas, and by talking with those in positions of authority she could stimulate programs responsive to some of the children's needs that previously had not been met. Today she sees herself as naive: she had believed in the goals of public education. She did not understand there is another power operating in the School Board that exerts great control over the entire administration. Jan was naive to believe she could bring change and new programs by changing only human things. Her good intentions produced few results because she did not directly address the issue of power.

In October, 1975, my wife, our three children, and I drove into Valley Station, Kentucky—a large working-class suburb of Louisville—which was to be our home for the next ten years. Driving north from Fort Knox, we had passed the bars and cheap motels that are so often found near an army base only to be greeted by groups of people standing along Dixie Highway with placards and signs: "Honk If You Oppose Busing." In August, about two weeks after I accepted the call to become the Vicar of St. Peter's in the Valley, the federal court ordered busing of school students to achieve racial balance throughout the newly merged city-county school system. We were not surprised by the demonstrators, since the dissent and the violence that followed the court order were prominently carried on all the national television news programs. The demonstrations continued throughout the fall. We never felt afraid, but since we were driving a Volkswagon van—you may recall that vans were once associated with hippies—we avoided Dixie Highway at night when we traveled to and from our home or the church.

Valley Station and Pleasure Ridge Park (directly to the north) together form a large, unincorporated community of over 100,000 people. Bounded on the west by the Ohio River, Valley Station is isolated from the city of Louisville by the perimeter expressway and a large industrial area to the north, and by the L & N railroad tracks and yard on the east. In place of a central shopping or business area, the Dixie Highway strip runs eight miles north and south, lined with several small shopping centers and at least one of every fast-food restaurant known in the United States. The area grew rapidly after the Korean War as Louisville began to expand industrially. Most residents live in small, single-family homes and work in industrial jobs or low-paying service jobs. People who live in Valley Station share feelings of being neglected and even used by business, government, and social agencies. Residents of the more affluent "east end" of Louisville tend to regard the area disdainfully as working-class, redneck, and racist.

During the crisis produced by the court-ordered integration, this stereotypical, upper-class view was strongly reflected in the local and national press. Reporters seeking to know why Valley Station was so racist asked the wrong questions and interpreted the answers they received to fit their preconceptions. What I read in the newspaper was incongruent with what I was experiencing. Still, it took more than a year before I began to hear and understand what my parishioners were saying.

Slowly I learned. Now I believe that racism was not the primary force fueling the demonstrations, which on occasion became violent. Anger and resentment were the fuel, and the source of the anger and resentment was the frustration of having almost no jurisdiction over one's life. To be employed as an industrial worker means that someone else dictates when one works, when one takes a break, when one gets a vacation, and even if one works. Workers are not viewed as human beings but as means of production. Unions have improved working conditions, but unions are also corporate bureaucracies and view workers as a means of power. Monetary success or dramatic improvements in one's standard of living are the exception. Mobility, geographically or socially upward, is rare. While churches in other parts of the city experienced a membership turnover as high as 30% a year as a result of families moving in and out of town, at St. Peter's we had less than one family per year move from the area. In ten years, only one or two employees were transferred by their company. Generally the people who live in Valley Station expect life to be the same tomorrow, the next year, and ten years

later. For many the move to this suburb represented the fulfillment of their personal hopes—hopes for financial and material
improvement centered on their children. When the court
ruled that the children would be bused to schools back in the
neighborhoods the parents had moved out of, all the accumulated anger and resentment burst out, sometimes violently,
more often in peaceful demonstrations, and most often in bit-
ter conversation. The hostility against busing was primarily a
ventilation of anger at the lack of power to control their own
lives.

In the first years of the 1980's, as federal policy combined
with economic forces to accelerate the decline of heavy industry in the United States, once again we saw the impotence
of blue–collar workers to control their lives. International
Harvester closed its plant; Ford closed and then reopened a
smaller assembly line; General Electric laid off hundreds;
Staufer Chemical closed its doors; and Dupont cut back drasti-
cally. Because Louisville was not dominated by the steel or
automobile industries, generally the city did not suffer severely. But in Valley Station, where people pride themselves on
their willingness to work and their unwillingness to accept
welfare, unemployment rose to over 20% of the work force.
There was no organized expression of anger; feelings of impotence dominated us entirely; depression and despair
replaced rhetoric and demonstrations.

My ten years in Valley Station opened my eyes to a sense of
fatalism is eroding the American dream of progress, material
well-being, and upward social mobility. My twenty years as a
pastor, consulting with people who have sought to oppose injustice and to improve our society, have opened my eyes to see
that many Christians are burdened with a sense of futility
when it comes to social issues and ministry to the needy in our
society. Many voices in the church decry the apathy of church
members. I do not believe indifference or insensitivity or a
lack of faith or a lack of commitment to be the root cause of
such inactivity. The primary problem is a loss of confidence

in the belief that one's actions make a significant difference. How can we be expected to act if we believe the action will have little real effect? We are all like the blue-collar workers futilely demonstrating against busing and resigning themselves to unemployment.

As an upper-middle-class, college-educated American, I was blind to how limited our abilities are to control and improve our lives. In the professional and white–collar stratas of society we delude ourselves into thinking we are in control. A new and bigger house, a new car, recovery from an illness, a promotion, a raise in pay, an honor for work well done, and we think we have life within our grasp. We evaluate our effectiveness by how many times we have moved, by the interesting places in which we have lived, and by the amount we have traveled. We work too long and too hard and then fill any spare time with entertainments. "Busyness" masks our impotence.

Our society has made great strides in controlling disease, in developing technologies needed to make life mobile and comfortable, and in devising systems to exchange information rapidly and world-wide. But progress is a limited phenomenon. We have not learned to control the human disposition for conflict or despair, and our technological progress makes those conflicts more dangerous than ever. Beneath our veneer of confidence and *savoir faire*, we hide our fears that the world is not a safe place in which to live. When the doctor suggests we enter the hospital for tests, we hardly dare express our fear of cancer. When we read of the federal deficit, we refuse to comprehend the numbers and the suffering caused by the vast sums being spent on the military and on weapons which have the avowed purpose of being unused. When someone challenges us with the very real dangers of nuclear war, our mind numbs before the possibility of total world destruction.

Why should we seek to comprehend? Why should we concern ourselves with the arms race? or with cancer? or with the federal debt? Why not allow the mind to numb? What can we

CHAPTER 1

do? In a world where a vast majority of the people believe we should at least freeze the deployment of nuclear arms, the development, production and basing of more and more missiles continues unabated and can only be expected to spread from the earth into outer space. In a country where a strong majority favor restriction of the sale of handguns, the number of weapons sold each year increases. We fought for civil rights and economic opportunity, and today the economic gap between black and white, rich and poor, continues to increase. In 1980 Ronald Reagan campaigned for the presidency on the promise of reducing federal deficits; eight years later we had federal and trade deficits so large they would have been inconceivable in 1980. In a self-fulfilling prophecy, the belief that we cannot bring about significant change for good deflates our willingness to struggle with the issues.

As much as we would like to deny our sense of impotence, it runs through our society from top to bottom, from the young to the old. I remember conversations with my son when he was fifteen. He and some of his friends told me they do not expect to die of old age. A new assumption is entering our national life. The world and all we know will end in a fireball; we just don't know when. Should that assumption take hold, human society as we now know it will be radically changed.

While preparing my notes to write this opening chapter, I attended a concert by Joan Baez. My own thoughts were becoming a little pessimistic. Surely, I thought, one who marched with Martin Luther King, Jr. and who helped focus the opposition to the war in Vietnam would still have faith that we can change our society for the better. But we did not sing "We Shall Overcome" at that concert. The freedom songs and the old ballads were not on the program. Between songs Ms. Baez talked about her life, shared her scars, and told us that today all we could do is wait for a better time![2] Are there no more dreams? Is anyone saying, "Ask not what your country will do for you but what you can do for your country"? Have we seen so many pictures of poverty and hunger that we are

unmoved by suffering? Have optimism and hope been swal-
lowed up by despair before the impossibility of the tasks? Far
from relieving my depression, Baez did little more than con-
firm my assessment that fatalism is becoming all-pervasive.

As a parish pastor in what is frequently referred to as a
"main-line" Protestant church, week by week I seek to relate
the Good News of the Christian gospel to the lives of those
who gather to worship their Lord and to gain spiritual sus-
tenance. The psalms and hymns of the liturgy constantly
speak of God's power and might, but how do we translate the
power of God into action in our world, where we feel so overpowered? How can I, as a Christian, even speak of the power
of God if I feel forced to conform to a world that seems out of
control? Unless we begin to address the crucial issue of power
and powerlessness in our churches, we are failing in the task of
relating the faith to parishioners' lives. A few years ago excitement grew over the theology of hope. But if we don't have the
power to accomplish what God is calling us to do, then hope
that God is leading us soon becomes despair, and the theology
of hope is reduced to a dogma, unsupported by experience,
that God is in control so we need not worry. Today a popular
topic for clergy retreats and for special lay education programs
is "burn-out." Burn-out is a polite way of saying we have lost
the power. Unless the churches begin to address the issue of
power, we may soon become small pastoral counseling centers
for the despondent and the disillusioned while the world continues on its course of self-destruction.

An intriguing change is presently happening in religion.
The growth of the so-called "fundamentalist" churches is
probably the single most important phenomenon in the
United States today. The main-line denominations with their
strong financial resources, well-educated clergy, beautiful
buildings, and carefully planned programs are, at best, on a
plateau of numbers of members. In contrast the fundamentalist
churches, with emotional preaching, an intellectually indefen-
sible doctrine of the literal interpretation of Scripture, build-

ings erected with little concern for aesthetics, and a destructive moralistic and pietistic ethic are growing, dominating radio and television broadcasts, and even influencing national politics. Many main-line clergy attribute this growth to the literalistic biblical interpretation and the moralism that provide a simple faith founded on divine authority with clear directions for living. People are willing to give up thinking in our complex age, these main-liners maintain, for the assurance of salvation and eternal happiness.

I find this assessment simplistic and somewhat arrogant, and suggest a different understanding. Fundamentalist churches are growing because they promise to empower the believer. The emotional preaching powerfully moves the sympathetic listener, while their emphasis on the Holy Spirit underlines the reality of the power of God. The teaching often expresses the simple belief that if faith is strong enough, then God will heal believers of any sickness, or deliver them from any trouble. Literalism and moralism are simply the pills we must swallow to evidence the sincerity of our faith. The promise is usually explicit: if a person will only have faith and believe, then through faith one gains power over one's life. As I listen to the radio evangelists, I discover the word "power" being used over and over. One of the better known, very popular television shows is even called "The Hour of Power." The fundamentalist churches are growing, I believe, because they promise power to people who feel powerless.

We who are in the main-line denominations cannot become fundamentalists. Our commitment to reason and historical accuracy prohibit our acceptance of a literalistic interpretation of Scripture or unreasoned preaching of doctrine. But I believe the key issue of spirituality for our time is empowerment. The experience of powerlessness is almost universal in Western society. If the main-line churches are to address our society, we too must address the issue of power. We too must find a means to bring power to people who feel powerless.

Powerlessness

As part of my own search for a Christian understanding of
power, I turned to Scripture, where I discovered one of the
fundamentalists' favorite books - the Book of Revelation. Few
books of the Bible have been more neglected by Roman
Catholics and main-line Protestants than Revelation.[3] The
futile attempt to use the book to predict the end of the world
has dominated interpretation of Revelation and encouraged
reasonable people to dismiss it. Its images are alarming and
seemingly incomprehensible; its apparent delight that the
world may soon come to an end in a bloody battle is repulsive;
its message of judgment and destruction seems contradictory
to the Christian proclamation of love and forgiveness. The images of Revelation, however, are images of the destructive
capability of power. They are no more frightening than our
familiar pictures of military might and nuclear destruction, of
dictators' terrorist and oppressive regimes, or even of alcohol's
destruction of the lives of individuals and their families.
Violence, corruption, and mayhem are realities in our world.
The book of Revelation confronts these realities directly; our
dislike of Revelation may reflect our fear of looking honestly
at negative forces in our lives.

Revelation is about power. A brief look in a concordance to
compare Revelation with other biblical books is "revealing."
Revelation uses the words "power" (*dunamis*) and "authority"
(*exousia*) more than any other book in Scripture. The images
of Revelation are all images of power, conflict, oppression and
liberation. More than any other New Testament book,
Revelation is concerned with power. In symbol and image it
interprets Paul's affirmation that Christ is "the power of God"
(I Cor. 1:24).

An approach I find productive for reading Scripture is to
read the Bible as the record of the community of faith and its
response to the divine call in its particular time and place.
Those who formed the community that wrote and preserved
Scripture are particular friends of God. As we read, we become
friends with these special friends of God. In so doing we be-

come part of a community of faith broader than the local congregation and extending beyond the twentieth century. By
getting to know these special friends of God, we come to be
aware of their particular vision of who God is and how God
works in this world. We become friends with the friends of
God that we may share their vision of the Lord and thereby
grow in our own faith.[4]

Scripture is dynamic and sometimes difficult to understand
because the character of the community varies in different
situations and at different times. Some portions of Scripture
have more importance for us than other parts because we relate more closely to the community that wrote and/or
preserved that portion of the Bible. Literalism devalues Scripture by understanding it as a collection of propositions about
God and the world that the reader should learn and accept
without evaluation. Scripture is richer than a dry collection of
moralistic facts; in and through the Bible the acting, pas-
sionate person of God is experienced interacting with his
people. Literalism also devalues the humanity of the reader by
assigning him or her a narrow, passive role as a mere receiver
of information. Approaching Scripture as coming forth from
relationship and leading to relationship challenges the listener
to participate in the encounter with God through the biblical
Word.

In struggling with the issue of power, I looked for those portions of Scripture that express the feelings, beliefs, and experiences of the people of God when they too knew moments
of powerlessness. I discovered what we call apocalyptic literature (Daniel, Revelation, and other shorter passages in the
Old and New Testaments) to be just that—the expression of
the hopes and faith of the people of God in their times of
being oppressed.[5] As apocalypse views the world, it is out of
control; conditions are bad and are getting worse and worse;
the people of faith are powerless to do anything. The images of
apocalypse are images of fearsome beasts devouring the people
of God. Winged monsters looking like lions and leopards and

bears attack God's people; demon locusts ravage the earth. Clearly the community of faith which wrote and preserved apocalyptic writings had lost any ability it had to control the world around it.

The Book of Revelation, the New Testament apocalypse, gives us a description of such a faith community in the seven letters found at the beginning of this work (Rev. 1-2). Although the letters are stylized and follow a fixed structure,[6] most critics believe John, the author of Revelation, is describing actual churches, as the details that are given are congruent with our knowledge of the cities where the congregations were located.

When we examine the letters, we find churches that are small, poor, struggling to survive, suffering from discrimination by Jew and Gentile, and divided by internal squabbles. Though many commentators date Revelation during an officially authorized persecution, the letters contain no evidence of this.[7] The harassment depicted in these letters corresponds to the kinds of troubles we find in Acts and in Paul's letters— abuse by local magistrates, maltreatment by the synagogues, and pagan corruption. Instead, John's primary concern seems to be with the internal life of the congregations. They have a tendency to drift into complacency, to tolerate and even to follow false teachers, and generally to lose their commitment to Jesus and their sense of expectation for the future.

The shining stars among John's seven churches are Philadelphia and Smyrna, two uninfluential, poor, harassed congregations which, despite their weakness, hold steadfastly to their faith in Jesus. The Christians in Smyrna have been the subject of hostility from the synagogue, and John expects this antagonism to increase for a short time, resulting in some arrests. John connects the church's poverty with this persecution. The connection may result from the actual seizure of wealth or perhaps simply from the difficulty of making a living in a hostile environment. Similarly in Philadelphia the congregation, described as having little power, is also being abused by the synagogue.

To Ephesus, Pergamum, and Thyatira John writes of his concerns regarding false teaching. The names Jezebel, Balaam, and the Nicolaitans are probably symbolic. If they do apply to particular individuals or heresies, evidence is lacking that would allow us to identify them specifically. The letters indicate only that among John's concerns about tolerance of false teachings is one—echoed by Paul—about eating food that has been sacrificed to idols. John calls for purity in belief and in practice. There is danger, however, as we see in his first letter to Ephesus, when that purity becomes so rigid that the spirit of love is lost. John calls for works of love, faith, service, and patient endurance (2:19), but such works must be neither so tolerant of pagan practices that the uniqueness of the Christian life be lost nor so intolerant of pagan faiths as to become a persecutor.

Laodicea, the one prosperous church, is the only church that receives no praise. The city of Laodicea was so wealthy that following a destructive earthquake in 60 C.E. it declined the customary imperial aid to rebuild. Apparently the church's similar self-sufficiency has led to a complacent lack of commitment; it is neither "hot nor cold." Christ stands at the door and knocks, tenderly inviting this congregation to accept the pain necessary for true faith and enjoy the feast that is the reward of true commitment.

Such were the churches to which John addressed his apocalypse. Their poverty and persecution encouraged escapism and dislike of the ruling classes. Perhaps the tenuous nature of these congregations contributed to their divisions over doctrine and openness to pagan influence. We can understand why John calls them to steadfast endurance—to remember the faith they have received, to hold on to that faith tenaciously, to be alert to complacency within and paganism without, and to be fearless in witnessing to that faith when arrested or persecuted. We can also understand why John does not call for action outside the community of faith to oppose injustice in the secular community. Their size and lack of clout rendered the possibility of action for justice ineffective. What could such little, ineffective groups do in the vastness of the Roman Empire? They were simply the people of God, tossed about by the forces and powers of this world. Revelation is addressed to these powerless congregations, and it expresses their feelings, their perspective, and their faith.

Though the setting of apocalypse is a community that feels powerless before the forces of history, the vision of apocalypse is the affirmation that true power lies in the hands of God, the Lord of history. The message of apocalypse is one of hope: God is in control of history and the time of justice is at hand. Apocalypse contains a curious combination of fatalism and hope.

We find this vision of hope in the same letters which describe the seven churches as such pathetic institutions. John ends each letter with a promise "to the conqueror." Those struggling, scared, bickering Christians are expected to be victors over their persecutors and over the destructive forces in their lives. Thus John tells the followers of Jesus in Philadelphia that their faithfulness will not only protect them in the hour of trial but will also lead to the conversion of their tormentors.[8] The Christians' victory includes "power over the nations," that they may "rule them with a rod of iron," as well as the promise of reward after death (2:7, 10-11). That power is the same which Christ received from the Father (2:26-27). Given the sad state of affairs in these congregations, one wonders how John can have any hope at all, much less declare a victory.

The hope of Revelation is different from the hope proclaimed by other apocalyptic writings. Generally, apocalyptic hope looks to the future for an intervention by God to establish the kingdom. Thus in Daniel the faithful are encouraged to hold on, because the end is coming soon. Although Revelation in places reflects this understanding of

CHAPTER 1

hope, it differs from the other apocalyptic writings because the Messiah has already come.

The proclamation that Jesus was and is God's Anointed necessitated a reinterpretation of the apocalyptic themes. Not only did the Messiah come, but he was crucified! And he was raised! Traditionally apocalyptic literature associated the coming of the Messiah with the destruction of the forces of oppression and the institution of the kingdom of peace. So the message that the Messiah has come, coupled with the reality that the powers of this world continue to oppress and control, violates the usual apocalyptic understanding. That the Messiah could be crucified by a government of this world was a startling contradiction of apocalyptic belief, which held that the Messiah would speedily overturn the powers and principalities of the world. And the resurrection stood as an unanticipated new development. Revelation reinterprets the traditional apocalyptic understanding of God's intervention in history in the light of the new data—a crucified, risen Messiah. Revelation proclaims a new message: God's Messiah has come. The crucial battle between the power of God and the oppressive powers of the world has been won, and God's rule has begun.

The author of Revelation has evaluated and reinterpreted his inherited apocalyptic traditions much as Paul did with his inherited understanding of Jewish law. Just as the writings of Paul make clear that the crucifixion of the Messiah necessitates a new understanding of our relationship with God, so Revelation proclaims that the death and resurrection of the Messiah involves a new understanding of power. As in Paul grace becomes the way of relationship to God, so in Revelation faithful witness to the Lamb becomes the force that conquers the powers and principalities. By image and implication it goes on to express the ramifications of this gospel message for our understanding of reality, of time, of community, and of ministry.

John does something unique in apocalyptic writing. In the light of the death and resurrection of Jesus, rather than God's control of the future, he proclaims an accomplished victory. He does not write to encourage his people to hold on because God will soon intervene. He writes to proclaim that God in Christ has already won the crucial battle! There is a new power in the world, the power of the crucified Lord, and that power can and will overcome the power of the principalities and rulers of this world. In winning the battle Christ has empowered his followers to become victorious.

Ours is an apocalyptic age. Though we seek to deny our fears and ignore our problems, symptoms of our apocalyptic anxieties abound. In every airport bookstore, one can see it. Next to the growing number of books of fantasy, which develop familiar apocalyptic themes, one will find books on what has been termed "New Age" spirituality, a spirituality that has declared human history over and a new "galactic history" begun. The movie theater projects the symptoms of our age on screens filled with movies like *Earthquake, Apocalypse Now,* and *Friday the Thirteenth,* which provide images designed to satisfy the most ardent apocalyptic taste. We can see it in the increasing numbers of millenarian religious groups, in the profusion of sects promising salvation to the individual through a guru's secret knowledge, and in a revival of astrology. In our age, when the destruction of life on our planet through war or ecological devastation at times seems both possible and probable, we share the apocalyptic vision. We too struggle against impossible forces that can appear as unconquerable beasts.

When we consider our present-day churches, perhaps John's do not seem as different from ours as we might have first imagined. Our congregations seem weaker than in ages past, are concerned with internal issues, and have little clout in our political structures. Our churches also reflect our apocalyptic age.

CHAPTER 1

The issue we face is power. There is no reason to act unless we believe our actions can and will make a difference. Comfortable complacency seems a better alternative than pointless sacrifices. The churches will become forces for peace, for justice, and for change only if we can regain an operative understanding of the power we receive through God's love. John proclaims that Christ's victory provides a means of power to his followers. If that declaration is true, we are not powerless; we are simply unable to see the power we have, or we are afraid to act upon it. We need to translate John's thought and images into concepts more comprehensible to contemporary sensibilities. Then we need to examine the implications of this understanding for action in today's world. As persons living in a new apocalyptic age, we must recover an understanding of the power of the Lamb.

Revelation and the Beast

Revelation is about power—the oppressive nature of power, the overthrow of the oppressor, and the establishment of peace. Revelation is about two kinds of power— the power used by those who desire to control and manipulate others and the power of Christ that brings freedom and healing. The power used to control easily becomes oppressive. Appropriately, the primary symbol for such power in Revelation is "the beast," a multi-headed, conglomerate monster that overpowers everyone, forcing them to worship at its altar. The dominant symbol for the freeing and healing power of Christ is "the Lamb," who bears the scars of the crucifixion while he stands with his churches. Revelation is about the conflict between these two types of powers.

Jan's frustration with the school board resulted from a mild experience of the power of the beast. The worker who is treated as a means of production, rather than honored with the dignity due any human being, also encounters the power of the beast. The unemployed worker who is unable to find a job has begun to feel the oppression of the beast. The soldier or citizen caught in the armed conflicts between nations knows its destructive power. The message of Revelation to all who have been overcome by the power of the beast is that there is another kind of power, seen in Jesus Christ, which can confront and defeat the beast. If we are to understand John's Good News, we must first understand the power of the beast and the power of the Lamb.

The world of Jewish apocalypse is a strange and difficult world to comprehend. Most Christians avoid apocalyptic literature in general and Revelation in particular. Believing

CHAPTER 2

that Revelation inaccurately predicts the end of the world, and hearing Scripture readings describing visions of heaven, and being told of fantastic monsters and demons and angels who participate in gruesome battles, most people give up before they start. The book is confusing. The images of angels and demons come from a much earlier age and do not appear to relate to our understanding of reality. The tone is combative, vindictive and harsh. We need help in approaching the Book of Revelation if we are to understand its message about power. The following overview seeks to simplify and integrate the multiplicity of its scenes and images.

For me the place to begin is with the story that is told when one reads Revelation from beginning to end. The story begins by introducing the characters and, moving through numerous descriptions of conflict, ends with the victory of God and the establishment of a renewed creation. It is not a simple story, told in a simple way. Each scene appears to be separate. We discern the story only as we complete our reading and look back. Neither chronology nor logic provide the organizing principle for Revelation; it is what the story of a war might be like if composed of vignettes from several different soldiers and officers without a unifying chronological structure. Still, one can discern a narrative thread which moves from oppression to celebration, from vulnerability to victory.

The simplest possible outline would be divided into three sections:

> Introduction of the protagonists - chapters 1-5
> Conflict with the antagonists - chapters 6-18
> Victory and renewal of creation - chapters 19-22[9]

We will look briefly at each of these divisions.

In chapters 1 through 5 we are introduced to the leading characters in three scenes. John, who makes no claim to be the disciple John, introduces himself in the first chapter as God's servant and as a brother in tribulation and endurance. He then describes a vision he experienced of the glorified

Christ. Chapters 2 and 3 contain letters from this Christ to seven churches, letters describing their strengths and weaknesses and calling them to conquest. The fourth chapter recounts a vision of the heavenly court where God, seated upon a throne, is worshiped by four living creatures and twenty-four elders. This vision concludes in chapter 5 when the "lion of Judah," who turns out to be a wounded Lamb, comes forward to break open the seals of a mysterious scroll.

These five chapters seem more straightforward than the symbolic descriptions of conflict that follow. The scenes are clear: the first is in Patmos, the second is a collection of letters, and the third is in heaven. Those who dislike Revelation are at least comfortable with these chapters. How many sermons one has heard on the importance of being neither hot nor cold (3:16) and how many, many pictures there are of Christ standing at the door and knocking (3:20, from the letter to Laodicea)! Yet, even here we find John's characteristic kaleidoscopic imagery. The book is addressed to the seven churches in Asia (1:4).[10] There are seven spirits of God (1:4, 3:1) which are portrayed as seven torches in the heavenly court (4:5). Christ stands among seven lampstands, which are the seven churches (1:12, 2:1), holding seven stars, which are angels, in his right hand (1:16, 2:1, 3:1). Finally, the Lamb has seven horns with seven eyes, which are the "spirits of God sent out into all the earth."(5:6)

One can hardly read Revelation without wondering how much of this symbolism is intentional. I often think that John is like our contemporary country preachers or radio evangelists who begin with one text from Scripture and then, through personalized associations, develops a string of references–many of which are removed from context and changed dramatically from their original meaning. Both the apocalyptic tradition and contemporary fundamentalist preaching are rooted in the milieu of the underclasses; both search Scripture for meanings hidden from the educated establishment. In Revelation and in other apocalyptic literature, there is a clear sifting of Scripture for texts that can be combined with other texts and reused in a contemporary context to develop a point. One must wonder if the task of adding references and allusions has not sometimes become primary, while the message lies neglected. In this passage, for example, we find John using one symbol—the seven lamps—with a variety of meanings. The seven lampstands taken from Zechariah 4, symbolize Israel, the church (the new Israel), and seven particular congregations. At the same time he expresses the reality of the churches through different symbols: as lamps and as angels that are stars in Christ's hand. John's use of symbolism reflects allusive richness rather than analytical precision. With such a profusion of symbols, we must beware lest we draw unwarranted conclusions.

With that warning, how then may we understand John's kaleidoscopic development of his imagery? One characteristic stands out: John develops a symmetrical balance between heavenly and earthly symbols. The church is symbolized as an earthly reality by seven lampstands and as a heavenly reality by the seven stars, which are the angels of the churches. The vision on Patmos of Christ present among his churches is balanced by the vision of the heavenly court where the Lamb is worshiped with the One who sits upon the throne. The Spirit of God is present in heaven as seven torches, but is sent into the earth as the seven eyes of the Lamb. The letters are addressed to the seven angels, but also refer to the particular situation of each congregation. The correspondence between the heavenly and the worldly is too strong to suppose it is not intended.

We do John a disservice if we assume he naively accepts the concept of the "three-story universe." His language may be the language of earth below and heaven above, but his use of symbols indicates an intermingling of the two realities in one object or event. So the difference between earth and heaven lies in quality rather than locality. John's distinction is not cosmological, but sacramental. Within the outward and visible realities of this world, John sees inward and spiritual forces at work. The churches have both a historical, visible reality and an invisible, spiritual reality symbolized by light (lamps and stars) and the presence of the resurrected Christ. What happens to the churches depends on the interaction of historical and spiritual realities. John observes the forces operating in the present situation and through his imagery relates them to archetypal and ultimate realities. John's vision intends to disclose how transcendent power operates within the ordinary context of human existence.[11] The angels of the churches, therefore, represent the spirituality of the churches, which is at one and the same time the faith and practice of their members and God's action through the Christ who is with us. This union of the visible with the spiritual is fundamental to John's understanding of reality and pivotal for discerning the nature of power.

We come now to the second section of the book (chapters 6 through 18) in which the church—composed of the visible reality of the congregations and the spiritual reality of the Triune God—enters into a series of conflicts with the forces of evil. I doubt that anyone can trace a direct line between these chapters and Saturday morning's super-hero cartoons, but the same human impulse that leads cartoonists to develop more and more invincible, vicious, immoral, diabolical villains must have also influenced the recorders of apocalyptic visions. We know from the beginning who will win; to make the story interesting, it becomes necessary to heighten the depravity of the enemy. Revelation follows this tendency by giving us what feels like an interminable series of descriptions of destruction, plague, famine, corruption, and persecution. This is grisly reading, not recommended for the faint-hearted. However, our age, which seems mesmerized by images of concentration camps, guerrilla warfare, and nuclear holocaust, might find these portraits recognizable.

Great debates rage among interpreters over the historical background for the images used in this section. There are some clear references to Rome in the description of the "great whore, Babylon" and in what are sometimes called the "Nero ciphers" (ch. 17). Otherwise, defining any specific event, person, or government is difficult. The names of Babylon, Jerusalem, Egypt, Sodom, and Jezebel are earthly symbols, but are used to describe tyranny rather than a particular tyrant, economic idolatry rather than individual enterprises, the spirit of falsehood, but not the liar.

The lack of precise identification of people and events furthers John's purpose of disclosing how spiritual powers operate within the ordinary context of human existence. He is imaging for us the spiritual realities that underlie daily life. As in the first section, John's images of earthly powers are balanced by heavenly figures. Though his descriptions are gruesome, his work delineates the invisible forces that work through human institutions to corrupt and destroy God's creation. Again we have a sacramental depiction of the world. Behind the visible institutions of government, army, and economics lie invisible realities that seek control over human lives.

For historical reasons we might wish John had pointed a finger at particular individuals or organizations, but theologically he left the role of judge to God. John's concern in Revelation is not with a particular oppressor, but with the power of oppression.

Another difference arises among commentators concerning this middle section describing the conflict of the Lamb and his people with the powers that corrupt and destroy. Is this one story that gets retold five times? Or is it a single story running from 6:1 to 19:21 (or even to 21:6) and containing passages that look forward to what is to come and other passages that recount what has happened?[12] If we picture the structure of the story as moving upward toward the climax like stairs climbing to the top of a building, two different kinds of stairs illustrate the different theories about the structure of Revelation. If it is one continuous story, it might be visualized as a spiral staircase, which five times follows a similar cycle, but each time begins where the former flight ended. If it is a single story retold, it would be like a single set of stairs photographed from different points on the stairway. Thus the first telling focuses on the beginning (the four horsemen) and can barely see the end (one verse, 8:1). Each retelling is done from a higher level, until the last telling (17:1-20:3) focuses almost entirely on the final conflict and the victory of Christ the Word.

Those of us who do not wish to write a commentary on Revelation can easily read the story without resolving the question of whether we climb a spiral staircase or a fireman's ladder. We need only be aware that from the beginning the story anticipates the end. We should read for the imagery and not get upset by events that seem out of sequence. John is not concerned about chronology; for him the eschatological future is a present reality, though in the beginning it is difficult to see. As in the first section, John is showing us the spiritual reality behind the visible conflicts. The difference between the heavenly reality and the earthly is not one of time any more than it is one of *locus*. Whenever we experience the conflict between freedom and oppression, we experience it as part of a specific ongoing struggle and as the archetypal conflict.

Revelation began by examining symbols that portray the earthly reality and the heavenly reality of Christ and his church. It concludes with a vision of the new heaven and new earth that come to be when the first heaven and earth pass away (21:1-22:5). As we read through the story, not only does the picture of the ultimate conflict and the ultimate victory come more clearly into focus, there is also a gradual disappearance of the distinction between heaven and earth. In the beginning a distinction between the spiritual and the mundane is drawn clearly by the description of the worldly churches and the angels of these congregations. In the seventh chapter the sequence of the seven seals is interrupted with an interlude that blurs the distinction between the church of the living (7:1-8) and the community of the faithful who have died (7:9-17). That distinction is totally blurred in chapter 14

when the Lamb appears on Mount Zion with the 144,000 singing a new song before the throne. Immediately thereafter the
angels announce that Babylon has fallen (though the event
does not occur until the 18th chapter). The concluding vision
of the New Jerusalem, then, is a vision of unity defined by the
new reality that "the dwelling of God is with men. He will
dwell with them and they shall be his people, and God himself
will be with them" (21:3). The old world that was divided between good and evil, between visible and spiritual, past and
future, is now whole. Death has been destroyed, making way
for a new creation. It unites the new heaven (the spiritual
reality) with the new earth (the visible reality), the eschatological future (God dwelling with this people) with the
present reality (the victory of the Lamb), and even the Lamb's
people with the kings and rulers who formerly were agents of
the beast, but who now enter the city's gates bringing the
glories of the nations. The vision of the new Jerusalem is a
vision of the healing that comes through Christ's sacrificial
death and resurrection.

In this short sketch of Revelation's story, we see themes
that are important in John's understanding of power. First,
reality is sacramental, composed of invisible, spiritual forces
and visible, historical events and people. Power is a spiritual
reality that resides in particular persons, groups, and individuals at particular times. Second, to say that power is
"spiritual" does not imply that the consequences of the abuse
of power are unimportant. On the contrary, the numerous
descriptions of "desolation" emphasize John's serious concern
about the forces of oppression and violence and their constant
impact on all of life. And third, an important aspect of the
power of the Lamb is unity: unity between God and his
people, unity between the visible exterior and the invisible in-
terior of people and institutions, and unity among all God's
people. Inequality and division are characteristic of the rule of
the beast.

The beast is the dominant symbol for oppressive, controlling power in Revelation, although it is not actually introduced until the book is more than half over. Other symbols of oppressive evil precede the beast's entrance into the drama. The "four horsemen" appear in the vision of the seven seals; plagues, warrior locusts, and a demonic cavalry arrived at the sound of the trumpets. Yet the image of the beast is compelling; its roots in apocalyptic literature are deep, and during eight chapters of Revelation it is the dominant symbol of evil. Because of this dominant position, I will use the title "the beast" broadly as representative of the numerous portraits of overwhelming and unrestrained power found in Revelation. As we investigate the reality of oppression, we will amplify the character of the beast with insights from the other pictures of domination.

In opposition to the Divine Trinity of the One who sits on the throne, the Lamb, and the Spirit, we find here a trinity of malevolence: the dragon who comes down from heaven (12:7-12), the beast from the sea (13:1-8), and the beast from the earth (13:11-17).[13]

> Now war arose in heaven, Michael and his angels fighting against the dragon; . . . And the great dragon was thrown . . . down to the earth, and his angels were thrown down with him. And I heard a loud voice in heaven, saying, "Woe to you, O earth and sea, for the devil has come down to you in great wrath, because he knows that his time is short!" (Rev. 12:7,9-10a,12b)

The dragon who comes down from heaven, who was, and is not, and is to come from the bottomless pit (17:8), is a false imitation of God the creator who was, and is, and is to come (4:8). Readers who presume that heaven is a perfect place are often confused by Revelation's statement that war could occur there. Yet as we saw earlier, John does not view heaven either as a place or as perfect. Heaven is the spiritual reality connected with the mundane. Evil has a spiritual reality which must be fought in the spiritual realm, just as it has a visible, historical reality which must be opposed in actual time and space.

Nor should we understand Michael's fight with the dragon as a creation myth of how evil came into the world (as in *Paradise Lost*), though it is possible that such a myth is the source of the story. John is clear: Michael was able to conquer the dragon only because of Christ's sacrifice on Calvary: *"They have conquered him by the blood of the Lamb and by the word of their testimony."*(12:11) *The dragon's fall is the spiritual aftermath of the crucifixion.*[14] The crucial battle has been fought and evil has been defeated. The final victory is assured, but evil fights on madly. To live in the "end-time" means to live in the assurance that servant love overcomes evil, all the while facing evil that may appear overwhelming.

> And I saw a beast rising out of the sea, with ten horns and seven heads, with ten diadems upon its horns and a blasphemous name upon its heads. And the beast that I saw was like a leopard, its feet were like a bear's, and its mouth was like a lion's mouth. And to it the dragon gave his power and his throne and great authority. One of its heads seemed to have a mortal wound, but its mortal wound was healed, and the whole earth followed the beast with wonder. Men worshiped the dragon, for he had given his authority to the beast, and they worshiped the beast, saying, "Who is like the beast, and who can fight against it?" (Rev. 13:1-4)

Those first Christians who read John's apocalypse must certainly have thought of the Roman government when they read this description of the beast. There are enough allusions in the portrayal here and in that of Babylon in chapter 17 to encourage that association.[15] However, John seems to have more than Rome on his mind. The three animals used to describe the beast are found in the Book of Daniel, where they symbolize separate empires. The seven heads represent the sum of the heads on Daniel's four beasts, while the ten horns and the length of the beast's reign (42 months or 3 1/2 years) also occur in Daniel. In "uttering haughty and blasphemous words"

(Rev. 13:5) the beast acts like the "little horn" in Daniel (which represented Antiochus IV, who set up a statue of Zeus in the Temple and forced all Jews to worship it or be killed); its warring against the saints and conquering them is a direct quote. Thus the beast has more in common with Antiochus IV's blaspheming of the Temple in 167 B.C.E. and persecution of the Jews than with any known Roman actions in the first century.[16] John may be talking about Rome because Rome is the oppressive power of the moment, but his image calls us to associate the beast with all tyrannical governments.

The beast is the image of the spiritual oppressive reality that becomes incarnate in various ways at different times and in different places. I would agree with William Stringfellow's statement that its many heads represent the multiplicity of the powers and principalities with their many faces of evil. Evil can be found in institutions, ideologies, causes, corporations, bureaucracies, nations, armies, churches and political struc-tures. Each of these bodies has a life of its own, a life that is changing, mobile, and diverse.[17]

If in this description you find a natural affinity with the modern conglomerate corporation or the multi-headed struc-tures of government, then you are in touch with the thought-patterns of Revelation. Perhaps the aptness of John's symbolism can be seen in that we refer to the stock market as a bear or a bull. The market seems to have a power of its own that runs despite human intervention and attempts to control it. Investors are not in control; rather, they simply try to hang onto the bull and let go before the transformation into the destructive bear.

The head with the mortal wound that has healed is often associated with the tyrant Nero, who committed suicide. His death in 68 C.E. and the succeeding year of civil war might seem to have been a death blow to the beast, but with the as-cension of Vespasian, the monster came to life again. This may indeed be an historical allusion; however, a far more im-portant idea is at work here in John's development of the image of the beast. The beast is a parody, a distorted mirror image of the Lamb. The phrase "to have a mortal wound" is the same word in Greek (*esphagmenon*) used to describe the Lamb in chapter 5 as one that "had been slain"(5:6,9). Like the Lamb, the beast bears a mark of slaughter. As the Lamb is granted authority by God, so the dragon gives the beast his power, throne, and authority. The beast leads the world in worship of the dragon, as the Lamb leads the church to worship God. The beast is given dominion founded on fearful obedience ("Who can fight against it?"), while the Lamb has received a true dominion based on faithfulness and truth. Even the name "beast" (*therion*) may have been selected as a pun on the word "lamb" (*arnion*).[18] Clearly John is more concerned about the spiritual reality of evil than with the particulars of Roman rule.

His point is precise. Two spiritualities strive for a person's allegiance: the beast and the Lamb. One cannot belong to both (13:8). The importance of this choice provides the context for John's earlier call to the churches for absolute purity of faith, total fidelity to Christ, and steadfast endurance. It was not easy to choose for the Lamb.

> Then I saw another beast which rose out of the earth; it had two horns like a lamb and it spoke like a dragon. It works great signs, even making fire come down from heaven to earth in the sight of men; and by the signs which it is allowed to work in the presence of the beast, it deceives those who dwell on earth, bidding them make an image for the beast which was wounded by the sword and yet lived; and it was allowed to give breath to the image of the beast so that the image of the beast should even speak, and to cause those who will not worship the image of the beast to be slain. Also it causes all, both small and great, both rich and poor, both free and slave, to be marked on the right hand or the forehead, so that no one can buy or sell unless he has the mark. (Rev. 13:11,13-17a)

The third member of the malevolent trinity rises out of the earth. Elsewhere called the "false prophet," it is like the first beast in having horns that imitate the Lamb (also see Dan. 8), but it speaks like the dragon. Through great signs and wonders it functions as "the deceiver of the whole world," manipulating all who dwell on the earth into worship of the beast.

Much has been written about the mark of the beast, which is identified as the number 666. This number may be a cypher for the name Nero, but scholars are far from unanimous in accepting this explanation. The simplest explanation for the mark is given in our text: "No one can buy or sell unless he has the mark." The term "to be marked" (*charagma*) is the technical term for the imperial stamp on commercial documents and for the impress of the emperor's head on the coinage.[19] We know from the gospel records and other sources that for the devout Jew the use of a coin with Caesar's image on it was a burning political issue. Clearly part of the beast's dominion lies in control of the economic sphere. From the first image of evil, the vision of the four horsemen, to the destruction of Babylon, we find economics imaged as a weapon used by the enemies of God. The third horseman on his black horse (6:5) carries the scales of an economic system gone awry, bringing starvation and enslavement. Babylon is rich with material wealth—purple and scarlet cloth, gold, jewels, and pearls—but is drunk on the blood of the saints (17:6). The villains of Revelation include the merchants along with nations and kings. Unjust political structures are not the only expression of the spiritual reality of oppression; economic injustice ranks high among the abuses experienced by the beast's victims.

The mark of the beast is a sign of allegiance.[20] The beast regulates all commerce by requiring obedience from all who wish to buy or sell. No one is allowed to enter the economic arena—which indeed is filled with false images and deceit—without making a sign of allegiance to the state, which regulates and controls the economy. Using the Roman coins for commerce and trade constantly remindered the first–century Jew (and presumably the Jewish Christian) not of *Pax Romana*, but of Roman occupation. In the two Jewish revolts against Rome (66-70 and 132-135 C.E.), among the first actions of the rebels was the minting of coins and weights. The beast controls people and demands allegiance through economic power.

I warned the reader that the world of apocalypse is a strange world. We must realize that John's readers were familiar with such images from sermons and other apocalyptic tracts. We find the images puzzling and curious; they would more likely respond emotionally. For us to be able to respond to this powerful, all-encompassing picture of dominating control with more than curiosity, we must recognize contemporary powers that contain the dynamics of John's images. The next chapter seeks to provide a picture of "powers" from the modern point of view.

The Power of Power

A<small>S</small> I walked into the store, I noticed a distraught mother pulling her son behind her through the front door. The little boy was about three years old and less than cooperative. I have no idea why the boy did not want to go in the store, nor do I know why the mother was upset. But I remember thinking, she's going to regret treating her son like that.

In the large discount house I did not see the mother and child while I shopped for some supplies I needed, but at the checkout I saw them again, in the next aisle. She was still in a hurry; he grabbed some candy from a shelf. "I want this!"

"You know you can't have that candy," came the mother's firm reply. "It will ruin your dinner and rot your teeth. Give it to me."

The boy began to cry. People in the next aisle looked to see what was happening. The mother was embarrassed. She grabbed his hand. "Give me that candy!"

"I want it! I want it!"

Extremely annoyed, she took the candy from him. Had it not been for the people watching, I suspect she might have slapped him. He grabbed another from the box: "I want it!" Tears were running down his face. Instinctively he knew that in this store, especially in the checkout line, his mother would not physically overpower him as she might if they were alone. He knew she was in a hurry and he was not. He selected his battleground well. She was humiliated by his bad behavior. Perhaps she thought, I didn't raise him to behave like this. She was humiliated by his persistence; she could see he was going to get his way, but she's supposed to be in charge.

"I don't know what's gotten into you. You are usually such a sweet child. It'll spoil your dinner." Then to the cashier, "Add in the candy bar." She took his arm and dragged him from the store. It was clear who had won.

The arena of power is not restricted to the corporate board room or the chambers of government. Power operates in every human relationship. It is a part of life, beginning with the first cry at birth. Wherever two or three are gathered together, there are differences of power among them. It exists whether or not we seek it or even acknowledge its existence.

Power depends on many factors: how much we want something, how competent we are to achieve it, how much others seek to hinder us, how persistent we are, what our power base is, and the setting of the struggle. Doubtless there are many other personal, psychological, and sociological factors that enter into every power struggle.

Power, says Max Weber, "is the probability that one actor within a social relationship will be in a position to carry out his own will despite resistance."[21] Certainty is not possible when one seeks to exert power within a relationship. The probability of success is determined by the relationship between the parties, by the motives, desires, and resources of the one who would wield power, and by the level of resistance in the recipient, be it an individual or a group. Briefly stated, power is the ability to exert enough control on the people around us to achieve a goal we believe to be important.

Power between people depends upon inequalities among them; in turn, it encourages greater disparity. Inequality between persons and groups is part of the givenness of life. We differ in skills, energy, and family heritage; in intelligence, emotional sensitivity, and creativity; in our capacity to influence and control our environment. The idealist might wish for a world where such differences did not exist, but when we consider the rest of the animal kingdom, we find inequality is part of the given there, too. With animals, such differences are important as a means of ordering the social structures that enable the species to survive. Inequality is part of creation; we presume it is good. Inequalities may be used to affirm each person's unique characteristics and to order our social structures. Or they may be used by the strong to restrict those who are weaker, taking from them basic requirements of human life and damaging them physically and psychologically. Inequality is inevitable. The abuse of power turns inequality into injustice.

We think of the powerful person as someone who is in control, who gives commands, and is able to enforce obedience, someone who can effect change and produce desired results. Power lies in the scientific and technological knowledge which has led to the conquest of many diseases, to our increased mobility, to our elevated standard of living, and to the development of marvelous tools for instant, world-wide communication. Power is exercised through economic and political structures, or through one's persuasive capabilities to convince others to follow. Power is at times exercised by physical force or the fear of it. Be it through knowledge, economic strength, force of personality, official position, or toughness, power is a means of getting what one wants. In a family, a business, a school, a church board of governors, a union, between schools or churches, between nations—the whole society is an interplay of clashing forces that sometimes balance and at other times dominate or submit. From athlete to corporate executive, from panhandler to union negotiator, everyone knows the exhilarating experience of achieving a goal. We also know what it is to be powerless, unable to accomplish our goals or to resist another's imposing on our lives.[22]

This common understanding of power is essentially linear. It flows from positions of greater power and affects those with less power. It is unilateral as opposed to mutual; we view the powerful person or group as one able to advance its own purposes while being minimally influenced by others or the environment. The role of the recipient is largely overlooked.

The more powerful the person or group, the less its own purposes are influenced or resisted by others or the environment.
The powerful person achieves the goal whether or not those
affected by the action desire the same end.

This linear understanding of power as the ability to control
and influence the other leads logically and in actual practice
to an understanding of human life as competitive. Any gain in
power by one person is experienced as a loss in power by
others. When Bill Jones retires as chairman of the board, he
relinquishes power; Mary Smith, who succeeds him, gains
power; Tom Brown, who also wanted the position, fails. If
Sarah French and James English work together on the same research project, but he publishes first and gets credit for discovering the new enzyme, then his stature, clout, job security,
and income are likely to rise, while hers will not. (Unless, of
course, he is exposed and their fortunes reverse.) The competition for supremacy takes place at all levels, from the petty
bluffs of one-upmanship to the arms race between nations.
The world of power is sometimes called a "zero-sum game."
One wins and the other loses, producing a total balance of
zero. Though we might enter into mutual relationships with
some few others, the competitive nature of linear power means
we must always be on guard lest a neighbor's gain take away
some of our power. Even in personal, intimate relationships we
find ourselves anxious that we get our share and wary of becoming dependent.

In the West, our view of power as linear combines with our
individualistic and competitive understanding of life. This understanding of human social relations has been dominant in
historical interpretation, in political and economic theory, in
ethical and theological systems, in military thought, in relations between the sexes, and in the ordering of social life.[23]
We see human community in terms of a hierarchy of power.
At the top of the ladder are those who wield great power, and
at the bottom are the powerless. Actually within the human
community there are many ladders—economic, political,

military, physical prowess, knowledge. And there are different kinds of ladders. On some we compete as individuals; on others, as groups; on still others, as nations. The goal within this structure is to be "upwardly mobile"—to have a better standard of living than one's parents, to work for a better and stronger company, to be first among nations. Because there are only a few persons at the top of each of these ladders and many at the bottom, we might more accurately visualize the ladder as a pyramid.[24] Our social structure, then, is perceived as a complex system of such pyramids, which together form a giant pyramid with a few very powerful people at the top. This pyramid of power, which I will call "the way of the world," provides an image compatible with contemporary ways of seeing the world.

The pyramid is primarily a structure of unequally distributed power. The uneven allotment of material wealth is the result and outward sign of the apportioning of power. This pyramid is distinct from the hierarchical structure of organizations. Any organization larger than a discussion group will have a hierarchical structure. It may be autocratic, authoritarian, controlling. Or its members may honor and support one another's freedom and dignity, share power and decision-making, listen carefully, and encourage participation. Or the structure may fall between these two extremes. Being hierarchical does not automatically mean power is concentrated in the top officers, though in hierarchical structures there is a strong tendency to invest greater power in the upper levels of authority. When John says we must choose between the spirit of the beast and the spirit of the Lamb, he is being realistic, not moralistic. One cannot give freedom and authority to others in the group and still maintain total control.

We are encouraged to base our sense of self-identity and self-worth on the relative strength of our linear power. The more power we have, the higher we are on the ladder and the more important we believe ourselves to be; the less power, the lower on the ladder and the less important. This evaluation is not simply subjective. Our position on the ladder is rewarded by the world with possessions, titles, positions of authority, and honors, which in turn function as further enhancements of our power.[25]

The year is 1989. You are driving into Chicago on Ohio Avenue. At a traffic light you peer out of the window. Your gaze is drawn upward, over the roof of a small coffee shop to the large black-and-white image affixed to the side of a building. There, stretching upward for six stories, is Michael Jordan, basketball's latest superstar. What is the monetary value of being able to put a ball through a hoop better than anyone else? About $10 million a year. Last year Jordan signed an eight-year contract with the Chicago Bulls for $25 million, but that is only the beginning. The major portion of his income comes from endorsements. For example: Nike recently gave him a new seven-year package valued at more than $19 million. For Nike, that's a bargain; in one year they sold $110 million in Air Jordan shoes and apparel. He has a three-year, $1.5 million deal with Coca Cola; a three-year, $750,000 contract with McDonalds, and the same with Chevrolet; a five-year, $1.2 million package with Wilson; and various other "paltry" arrangements with smaller companies in the $100,000 range. What was the worth of Jordan's last-second shot to upset Cleveland in the first round of the playoffs? Or of his last-second shot that beat Detroit in the Eastern Conference finals? Seen on national T.V. with a large audience, those shots could be worth $1 million each.

The world of athletics forms a relatively simple pyramid. Those few at the top are rewarded with enormous salaries, honored in halls of fame, featured in magazine and newspaper articles, and sought as guests on every T.V. talk show. The importance of such a superstar player is recognized because his performance can make or break a team—on the playing field and in the box office. In 1987, when Jordan joined Wilt Chamberlain as the only other man to score 3,000 points in a season, the Chicago Bulls were responsible for one-third of the

league's attendance increase. In 1985 retail sales of NBA
products totaled about $80 million; two years later the figure
was over $300 million, and Jordan was responsible for much of
this increase.[26]

The seduction of athletes into basing their identity and
sense of self–worth on performance in the sport is confirmed
by the small number of superstars who, after retirement in
their thirties, make any significant contribution outside of the
sports field. A large number of athletes squander their educational and financial opportunities and end up in virtual poverty.

Like most systems, ours is driven by both a carrot and a
stick. If the rewards of a fancy car, a big house, a prestigious
neighborhood, a good job in an internationally known company, nice clothes, trips around the world, gold credit cards,
and a large bank account are not enough to entice one toward
upward striving, if the promise of personal security, a good
self-image, and honor in the community are not seen as goals
worthy of great effort, then fear will drive us to seek a higher
rung on the ladder. The human condition is one of insecurity.
Bad things happen to all sorts of people, hard workers as well
as slackers. Fear of a reduction in status and self-worth, fear of
illness, fear of financial hardship after retirement, fear of
failure, dislike of being looked down upon, fear of death, fear
of a turn-around that would result in economic difficulties or
physical hardship—all of these fears and more drive us to work
hard to accumulate wealth, power, and self-sufficiency.

Of course, the goal of self-sufficiency is a delusion. The very
system designed to relieve fear actually produces fear to keep
the system going. The more power we have, the more we fear
losing it; the higher we climb on the ladder, the greater is the
danger of tumbling down. Striving for financial security has
the curious effect of leading not to security but to more striving. Striving to succeed produces the competition that keeps
us driving ahead with all our energy until we collapse.

The other factor that keeps people working to be upwardly mobile is wants. I am constantly amazed at the capacity of the human species to want just a little more than income will provide. Encouraged by advertisements, conversations with friends, and the fun of having something new, our wants increase slightly faster than our ability to purchase. A popular slogan has been running the poster and bumper sticker circuit lately, "The one who dies with the most toys wins." I took that to be a cynical comment on the absurdity of working night and day to accumulate but I know people who accept it as their philosophy of life.

Power is commonly understood as our ability to influence our surroundings enough to climb the ladder and to protect the position already achieved. The higher one gets, the more power is needed to protect the position and to move still higher. Our desire for power to provide for our ever-increasing wants tends to become addictive. Power, we think, provides security and self-sufficiency; the loss of power means we are not as important as before. The truth of this maxim is seen in the self-perpetuating tendency of power: we seldom relinquish it voluntarily. We loosen our grip and make concessions only when we are forced to do so by some competitor who has acquired sufficient power to bring us to the negotiating table, as the women's movement and the conflicts between labor and management illustrate. Given the expansive character of human fear and wants, this desire for power may become insatiable.[27] Power is capable of taking over our lives. Many will become its willing subjects.

One of the spectacles of the late 1980s has been the sight of some of the nation's wealthiest citizens risking everything in reckless illegal ventures. Ivan Boesky, a Wall Street arbitrageur worth an estimated $200 million, went to jail for insider trading. Martin Siegel, a young, millionaire takeover specialist, was convicted of receiving briefcases full of cash from Boesky at secret rendezvous in exchange for confidential information about Siegel's clients. Leona and Harry Helmsley, heads of a real-estate empire valued at $5 billion, were tried on income tax evasion. The sons of billionaire oilman H. L. Hunt—Bunker, Herbert and Lamar Hunt—were found guilty of conspiring to corner the world silver market. Why did these people feel compelled to push beyond the bounds of ethical and legal practices to pursue gains that by any rational standard were superfluous? Was it the desire to be number one, the need to be special? What drives such a person? An addiction, a pathological fear, or some mindless need to achieve?[28] The reasons must vary with each person, but fifteen-hour work days and incessant striving are symptoms of all those who have triumphed in the ways of the world and lost their freedom in the process.

The way of the world is not without compassion, but even compassion is of a linear kind. Since human communities are seen as cooperative societies composed of independent, self-reliant members, it follows that the entire community will be stronger if the less fortunate members—the handicapped, non-productive, and disadvantaged—are beneficiaries of charity from the more fortunate. Such charity is viewed as practical and effective (and therefore important) when it enables the less fortunate to approximate more nearly the self-sufficiency of those higher up the ladder, provided of course that their self-sufficiency does not cost too much and does not threaten the status or power of those above. The linear character of such *noblesse oblige* denies any mutual interdependence or any common understanding of personal worth.

Most social reforms attempt to provide some access to the ladder for those at the bottom of the pyramid, but the character of power insures that such reform, while it may help some, will not change the lot of the majority. Compassionate charity is possible because wealth can be shared without disturbing relationships within the pyramid. Wealth depends on the relationship between people and things: mine can increase without necessarily reducing yours. But power is based on the relation of people to people; consequently any increase in my power necessitates a decrease in the power of those above me in the pyramid.[29] The inequalities of power are preserved by the powerful and instinctively used to amass wealth and greater power. Despite reform and social service programs, the divisions in life between people, classes, and nations become wider and deeper. The rich get richer, and the poor, poorer. The strong become stronger, and the weak become weaker, at least until a harvest is reaped, as our contemporary revolutions involving blacks, women, and underdeveloped nations illustrate.

Obviously the poor suffer not only materially, but also developmentally and psychologically. Societies in which a few at the top dominate the growing numbers at the bottom are destructive to human life and dignity. Large numbers of oppressed poor represent a drag on the economic health of a society as well as a threat to stability. Those societies which allow movement from positions of low status to positions of greater security and power benefit by the contributions of more people to the economic whole; movements for reform that allow upward mobility are good not only for the poor, but for the entire system.

Less clear is the observation that those in positions of power are also in bondage and suffer psychologically, if not physically. The Ivan Boeskys of this world are not the only ones hurt by the system. We see the symptoms of captivity in the modern prevalence of the diseases of stress. A husband and wife both work to provide the "best" for their children. They end up away from home three to five nights a week. When they are home, they are so tense that the house is filled with bickering. On other evenings they are so tired they just watch T.V. We can see an alienation that threatens to destroy what it means to be human. Those who are captured by the need for power become insensitive to others, neither listening to them nor supporting their abilities and freedom. Too often the survival of the fittest in human society means the rule of the least humane.

The Power of Power

The strong and the weak are both caught in the same system. We see ourselves as individuals in competition. Striving for security, we exercise power within a system that promises security and comfort but only covers up that existential anxiety with possessions, titles, honors, and toys. While the pyramid has its origins in the self-centered hearts of individuals, it preserves and encourages egoism by rewarding selfish and self-seeking behavior. Because of their vulnerability, the weak seek security through coveting the power of the strong; the strong use their power to preserve their position. No one is in control; all strive for a security that cannot be found in this world.[30] This system is controlled only by the invisible, spiritual reality that makes use of our fears, wants, and shaky identities.

In other parts of the New Testament, the spiritual reality behind the way of the world is referred to as "the prince of this world." In the Book of Revelation it is depicted as a beast. As we seek to relate this model of power to John's image of the beast, we need to review briefly two important New Testament concepts: its understanding of principalities and powers, and its understanding of the fall.

We have already seen that John combines symbols of spiritual forces with images of earthly institutions as a way of describing a single reality. John's confluence of spiritual and mundane is not unique to Revelation, but reflects a basic New Testament understanding that reality is composed of outward and visible manifestations and of inward and spiritual realities. In the New Testament, powers and principalities are understood as both spiritual and visible.

Ours is a scientific and materialistic age. When we read about angels and demons, we assume that ancients used these spiritual beings to personify illnesses and describe events that have natural and psychological causes. Therefore we tend to reject as superstitious the New Testament language about heavenly powers. John's treatment of "heavenly" realities in Revelation should have challenged our assumption that we understand the ancient point of view. Their views of powers and principalities were not as simple as we might presume, and we can learn from their insights.

Throughout the New Testament all powers, principalities, and institutions are viewed as having both an inner aspect—the spirituality of the institution—and an outer aspect—the tangible, visible expressions of power in the organization itself.[31] None of these "spiritual" realities has an existence independent of its material counterpart, for both the inner and outer aspects come into existence together and cease to exist together. In our modern view of the world, we must see this inner spiritual force not as some separate, heavenly entity, but as an invisible aspect of the material and tangible manifestations of power. The spirit of a state or organization is an invisible reality that exists as an integral part of the organization.

The spirit of an organization is more than a personification of certain aspects of the institution; the spirit has a strong power to influence the individuals who are members of the group. In other words, terms like "mob spirit" or "team spirit" describe realities that come into existence when a "mob" or "team" forms and causes people to act in ways they never believed themselves capable of acting.

In this way the "spirit of America" is more than a slogan; it is a reality that affects the lives of all who live in the United States. That spirit is composed of the unseen dreams and values and mores of the people past and present who live in this land; it is embodied in our institutions and in certain symbols like the Statue of Liberty, and articulated in statements such as "Give me your tired, your poor, your huddled masses," or "We hold these truths to be self-evident, that all men are created equal." These and other phrases affect us in ways they could never affect someone who never lived in the United States. They express the spirit of the country we are part of, and that spirit has power over us. We may rebel against the values expressed by the spirit of America, but that rebellion, far from denying its existence, acknowledges that power's hold upon us.

Our modern tendency to ignore the spirituality of an organization leads us to underestimate the power of this invisible guiding force.[32] Although created and staffed by human beings, decisions in institutions are not made so much by people as for them, out of the logic of institutional life itself. Why is a superb salesman promoted to be a sales manager when he has not been trained in management, shows no natural ability for it, and will probably not perform at his best? The logic of the business dictates the promotion. Why are excellent parish pastors "elevated" to judicatory, administrative positions? Again, organizations reward excellence with advancement up the ladder, whether or not such advancement makes sense for the individual.

Because the institution usually antedates and outlasts its employees, it develops and imposes a set of traditions, expectations, beliefs and values on everyone in its employ. Usually unspoken, unacknowledged, and even unconscious, this invisible network of influences constrains behavior far more rigidly than any printed set of rules could ever do. Why do lawyers tend to wear suits? Why do people apologize when they swear in front of clergy? Why is success equated with a move to the suburbs? The spirits of institutions and the spirit of our society govern dress, social class, life-expectation, even choice of marriage partner. The result of ignoring the spiritual reality that lies within the organization is slavery to the unseen power or chronic, nonproductive conflict with it.

Modern American Christians, perhaps in reaction to the Puritan version of Calvinism, have over-simplified the biblical understanding of the fall. The fall includes far more than the idea that people are self-centered and need to become more altruistic. Scripture presumes that all of creation is infected by the fall, including the spiritual realities of the powers and principalities. The results of this corruption for both individuals and corporate realities is threefold: a loss of identity

CHAPTER 3

as servants of God, idolatry, which expresses itself in worship of and allegiance to powers other than the love of God, and self-centered arrogance that seeks to make oneself a god.

The powers and principalities as part of God's creation exist to serve a role in his plan for our world. Paul's admonition in his letter to the Romans that Christians should be subject to governing authorities represents this understanding of the place of the state in God's plan (Rom. 13:1-7). All authority comes from God and those in authority are "ministers of God."[33]

Unfortunately, the fact that powers were created to serve a place in God's plan does not guarantee that they will so serve. We must temper the picture of the state given in Romans 13 with the picture of the beast in Revelation 13. The powers, like human beings, are part of a fallen creation, tainted with sin and in need of redemption.

Again we might consider the spirit of America. As a nation we often desire to be number one, not one among equals. In our pride, at times we impose our will on other countries by military or economic force instead of seeking a common good through negotiation, dialogue and respectful nurturing. To achieve our own goals of security and material prosperity, we form alliances with all sorts of foreign governments, including oppressive dictatorships. The spirit of America, like all fallen spiritual realities, has a shadow side.

American Pietism—both in its social gospel and in its evangelical forms—has understood the fall largely in terms of individual sinfulness and placed little emphasis on the fallen estate of the rest of creation. In evangelical religion, personal salvation is stressed; in the social gospel, the preacher seeks to convince people to get involved in outreach. Presumably society will be transformed when enough individuals have been converted to change the social structures. Such an understanding of redemption implicitly assumes that people control institutions, powers, and principalities, while ignoring the reality that groups exert control over their members. To seek change in American policies by converting individuals while ignoring the corporate spirit is an exercise in futility, as is illustrated by the large numbers of individuals who, though religious and moral, are blind to their company's economic enslavement of low-skilled workers or to the militarization of the U.S. economy or to the ecological destructiveness of a consumer economy. Electing Christians to Congress will not necessarily make Congress Christian.

The distinction between racial prejudice and racism illustrates the fallen character of both individuals and institutions. Racial prejudice is the unfair and ungrounded prejudgment by an individual of others on the basis of race. The prejudice may be affirmative—all blacks are good athletes—or negative—black people are lazy—but in either case it is based on inadequate information and reflects an individual's sinful judgment. Racism, on the other hand, is a social force, deeply embedded in the heart of our society. Racism is the systematic subjugation and control of one racial group by another. Racism and individual prejudice are related, but they are also distinct. A person may have very little racial prejudice and yet support racism by supporting an institution that has a pattern of systematically excluding African Americans from full opportunity and full participation. Racism acts as a spiritual force within our social structure even when the people causing it have no intention of acting from prejudice and are unaware of doing so.

In Revelation John images the spiritual realities that become incarnate in various times, ways, and places, including our own. The beast is an image of dominion that has become demonic. Dominion is essential to social relations, but it soon becomes demonic when it ceases to be a way of ordering society and becomes a way of dominating people. This demonic spirit can appear in any structure, organization, institution, corporation, bureaucracy, army, nation, church or cause.

CHAPTER 3

The pyramid is one image of the structures of power. Structure is not evil; authority and a clear chain of responsibility are essential for an organization to function. Hierarchical power is not inherently oppressive. In crisis organizations like the police force or a medical emergency unit, mobilization requires strong linear power. Power and authority are essential to prevent society from breaking down into chaos and anarchy.

In its fallen state the pyramid of power becomes "beastly." By rewarding those at the top, institutions in their fallen state discourage sharing and encourage the taking of power. In an unholy alliance, our arrogance, idolatry, and loss of identity combine with a principality's seductive promise of dominion, glory, security, and worth to produce an incarnation of the beast. Without intentional choice or clear consideration, we ally ourselves with the beast. It is easy for us to be seduced.

A friend of mine manages a hosiery mill in Tennessee. A small, independent mill, it has grown over the past few years thanks largely to the superior quality of its product. For several years, one of its major customers, a large retailer, increased its order. Some at the mill welcomed this increase; the future for the hosiery mill seemed secure. Others were concerned about the growing dependence on one customer. To preserve the mill's independence, efforts were made to add new customers. The efforts were well-timed, because the next year, this large customer suggested that the mill lighten the weight of its socks. In other words, now that the brand name was established, the customer suggested using less yarn and therefore make a sock of lower quality for the same brand name they had been selling. Both the mill and the customer would have increased their profit margins. The mill refused to make the same sock at a lower quality, though it meant risking the loss of the customer. The customer did not leave, and quality is still a major attraction of the mill's products.

This is the way of the world. Steady business, a secure future, and higher profits were promised to the mill, but the cost was the mill's independence. The powers of this world want our allegiance. They tell us to seek happiness and security; they promise to satisfy our needs; then, without any conscious decision on our part, we discover we have lost our freedom. Contemporary middle-class Christians who reside high in the pyramid view the system as benign, the provider of order and prosperity. We encourage the poor to get a good education and to work harder. We fail to see the barriers caused by the inequitable distribution of power. We have difficulty comprehending the hostility of workers toward those who manage them. We do not understand why people lose faith in government. But we may not be seeing clearly.

The poor, harassed congregations of Revelation resided at what was the bottom of the pyramid of power in their day. They did not have the power to insure the basic need for personal safety. From their defenseless position they viewed those above them with hostility. We can understand why the synagogue that participated in harassing them was disliked (2:9, 3:9), and why the businesses that demanded a day's wage for a day's ration of food (6:6) were seen as the enemy. We can understand why the government that plagued them with prison, threats and beatings (2:2-3, 2:10, 2:13) instead of providing economic justice and physical safety was viewed as a monster. The image of the beast is what the pyramid of power looks like when one is on the bottom, unable to climb further up.

In its fallen state, power becomes beastly. Promising us a sense of self-worth based on our status and wealth, prodding us with a vision of material comfort and financial security, deluding us through advertising to devote our energies toward getting a fancy car or a larger house, inviting us to deny our anxious fears by working for "success," the beast seduces us into giving it allegiance. We surrender conscience and become blind, willing servants of a power that restricts human development, transforms ineradicable inequalities into life-denying injustices, and threatens to destroy our world.

CHAPTER 3

One of Revelation's favorite words for describing the action of the beast is "blasphemy." The beast takes the divine trinitarian form and even mimics the sacrificial wound of Christ. It bears written upon its heads a "blasphemous name," and its mouth utters "haughty and blasphemous words"(13:1, 5-6). We can define blasphemy as refusing to accept our status as servants and stewards, but claiming instead autonomy from God and domination over people and nature. The role of the third member of this blasphemous trinity, the deceiver of humanity, is to delude human beings into thinking and acting as if their moral worth were determined by their commitment to the survival, growth, and vanity of an organization. This is idolatry, the essential meaning of the beast's demand for worship.[34]

The story of Jan and the school board is an excellent example. Created to assist in the task of educating children, the organization inevitably takes on a life of its own and turns from servant to master, rewarding those whose actions further the strength and growth of the school board. At its worst, the organization (or principality) may move from master of human lives to oppressor. The reader may wonder at what seems to be an exaggeration: a school board can become inefficient, but surely it will not become an oppressor! The racial segregation of southern schools in this country up until the early 60's, as well as the continuing existence of practices so discriminatory as to be oppressive, provide evidence that this is no exaggeration.

Part of the powerlessness we feel as we seek social change results from trying to change structures without recognizing or acknowledging the power of the spirit of the organization. We must understand better the spirituality of institutions; we can begin by acknowledging the power of power to control and consume human life.

"Who is like the beast; who can fight against it?"

The Impotence of Power

When you drive into Buffalo, New York on the thruway from the south, just as you spot the office towers of center city, to the east of the thruway beyond the empty land left by old, abandoned railroad yards you can also see a large expanse of park-like land. In the middle of this grassy area stand eight high-rise apartment buildings—clearly a public housing project. When I first noticed these apartments, I thought how wise the political powers in Buffalo were to surround dense dwelling with green parks. Later I drove by to have a closer look. The buildings, less than thirty years old, were abandoned, their windows broken, and the park was a field of weeds.

In the 1950's urban renewal came to Buffalo. Amid the hopes of downtown renewal, improved housing, and new opportunities, fifteen blocks of land were cleared in the Ellicott district. Developers did not rush in simply because of the availability of land. Promised housing programs did not materialize. Then, finally, in 1958 work began on a new high-rise complex. Over five hundred new, quality apartments opened in 1959 to replace the thousand or more units that had been torn down. Twenty-three years later, in 1982, the buildings were closed. The official reason was that high-rise apartments were not conducive to family living. Gangs had developed; harassment and violence were common in the buildings. They were closed to be remodeled. Factors other than gangs may have influenced the decision. In housing projects funded by federal assistance, the aid covered 100% of the cost not covered by rents, but the Ellicott Mall apartments were underwritten by the state with a limited amount of subsidy per unit. Closing these apartments produced a large savings for the Buffalo Municipal Housing Authority. Today, seven years later, Ellicott Mall remains closed. It stands as a silent monument to government inefficiency.

The story is repeated in city after city. Studies suggest that urban renewal, highway building, and other municipal development programs have destroyed three dwellings for every one unit built by federal and state housing programs. Is it naive to think government housing programs should increase the quantity and quality of low-income housing?

I began looking at other government institutions. We now understand that our jails and prisons do more to train people in crime than to rehabilitate them. Recent concern about about the high rate of student drop-out and the poor quality of education produced by our schools raises questions about what is happening to public education. Could it be that we now have housing agencies that are producing homelessness, correctional systems that are producing criminals, and educational institutions that are producing ignorance?

A 1985 study of social services in New York City determined that approximately $7,000 per capita of private and public money is specifically allocated to the low-income population. A family of four would theoretically be eligible for $28,000, which would place them in the moderate income bracket. However, the study showed that only 37% of the money reaches the clients. Nearly two-thirds is consumed by those who service the poor.[35]

Are our social service institutions turning against us? The criminal justice system, housing programs, and educational institutions exist to serve society. Why are they failing? More regulation does not seem to be providing a solution. How can we control these programs? What is to be done?

> The Lamb opened one of the seven seals, and I heard one of the four living creatures say, as with a voice of thunder, "Come!" And I saw, and behold, a white horse, and its

rider had a bow; and a crown was given to him, and he went out conquering and to conquer.

When he opened the second seal, I heard the second living creature say, "Come!" And out came another horse, bright red; its rider was permitted to take peace from the earth, so that men should slay one another; and he was given a great sword.

When he opened the third seal, I heard the third living creature say, "Come!" And I saw, and behold, a black horse, and its rider had a balance in his hand; and I heard what seemed to be a voice in the midst of the four living creatures saying, "A quart of wheat for a denarius, and three quarts of barley for a denarius, but do not harm oil and wine!"

When he opened the fourth seal, I heard the voice of the fourth living creature say, "Come!" And I saw, and behold, a pale horse, and its rider's name was Death, and Hades followed him; and they were given power over a fourth of the earth, to kill with sword and with famine and with pestilence and by wild beasts of the earth. (Rev. 6:1-8)

The vision of the four horsemen of the apocalypse, John's first image of evil, presents a dynamic picture of the movement of evil from good intentions to death and destruction. The image begins with the truly handsome figure of the conqueror with crown and bow on the white horse. This figure is so beautifully drawn that a few commentators have even identified him as Christ![36] As we have seen in the descriptions of the malevolent trinity, evil loves to wear the mask of divinity. Is it not true that, like the cowboy in a white hat and on a white horse, we almost always enter into conflict for righteous reasons? We fight to oppose aggression, to oppose communism, to defeat tyranny and bring freedom, to make the world safe for democracy, to end war. The key word here is "conquer." The power of the beast begins with our good motives, but it perverts our motives with the assumption that we should impose our righteous understandings on others. We,

CHAPTER 4

knowing what is best, should take control of the situation and establish the right. The beast tempts us to do the right thing in the wrong way, seeking to control rather than to free.

The second seal reveals the second stage of domination. Once a power accepts controlling and enforcing obedience as the primary means of exercising its authority, then the blood-red horse with its sword-wielding rider will take peace from the earth. Even wars that are fought for righteous reasons bring destructive results.

The third rider on his black horse carries the scales of an economic system gone awry, bringing famine, starvation, and economic enslavement. The last rider is Death and Hades: the ultimate power to control and the final consequence of being seduced into battle.

Although this image derives from nations' going to war as an image of the spirituality of oppression, it shows us two important aspects of that power. First, just as the beast is described as a parody of the Lamb, so evil often appears as a counterfeit good. We do not see the destruction present in going out to conquer any more than we see the burden present in the way of the world, the pyramid of power. The delusion that we are doing what is right is one of the primary deceptions of evil.

One difficulty with the image of the beast as a portrait of evil is its repulsive appearance. No one would want to follow such a gruesome monster. Part of John's purpose was to paint evil with pictures so repugnant that those who are tempted to follow its ways would turn back. John's churches have been tempted by false teachers. Pergamum and Thyatira have been led astray. Ephesus and Laodicea have lost their original commitment. And he calls on Sardis to repent. If they could see evil for what it truly is, then they would not be tempted.

But John knows evil does not appear so hideous in the beginning. The first view of evil is often benign, attractive, desirable, and exciting. He refers to both the serpent and the false prophet as the "deceiver of mankind." No one knowingly

The Impotence of Power

would get caught in the clutches of the beast. We are deceived and seduced into following its way. Then we discover that we have taken a wrong path, that our world is out of control, and we do not like what is happening.

Evil is able to take good motives and positive actions and twist them. A more prestigious job at a higher salary is attractive, especially when, as with Jan, it comes with the promise that she might become more effective in her vocation. Without realizing what has happened, one may become imprisoned by a good job and be unwilling to raise strong objections to the inefficiencies or even injustices one observes. Similarly, in the church we easily justify major efforts for growth and expansion of the institution in order to minister, yet never get around to doing the ministry. Without being aware that it has happened, a minister can become imprisoned by the need for acceptance by the congregation and avoid all controversial issues. In the beginning governments are enthusiastic about helping the poor, but later our programs may become targets for political patronage and graft.

John portrays another aspect of evil: it does not remain benign, exciting, and attractive. If allowed to run its course, it becomes hideous, repulsive, and violent to the point of self-destruction. In Revelation the destructive quality of evil is projected in large pictures; less clear is the idea that evil becomes self-destructive.[37] After the beast is introduced, John's description concludes with the proverb, "If anyone slays by the sword, with the sword must he be slain" (13:10). Babylon, the "destroyer of the whole earth," destroys the world she depends on for her glory. Thus John claims that the beast, the spirit Babylon rides upon, turns and destroys the city (17:16f). In our experience the number of dictators who fall to revolution confirms this self-destructive character of evil. Oppressive actions carry within themselves the seeds of self-destruction.

The ultimate power for domination is violence and the threat of violence. When any power or principality understands its role to be the controller of people, it will enforce that role with the threat of violence, and if necessary, will use physical force and death. Although war and revolution best illustrate this ultimate dependence on force and its ultimate destructive outcome, as an image of the spirituality of dominion we may apply this idea to other areas of human life as well. One of John's themes is the role of economics in oppression. Though the analogy goes beyond the text, I do not believe we violate John's thought-pattern if we apply the four horsemen to the world of business.

A business is started and enters the market place, providing jobs, producing and selling a product, and contributing both to the health of the economic system and to human welfare and comfort. But it is a competitive, "dog-eat-dog" world, and the business must survive. To make a profit, it must conquer part of the market. One need not watch many ads on television to recognize that gaining part of the market depends as much on manipulation of the consumer with sex, patriotism, and dreams of status as it does on the quality of the product. Although it begins with the commendable goals of economic and human welfare, a business soon discovers it must fight to gain a market. Beneath the first seal is a rider on a white horse.

If the business gains enough control, then the second horseman may appear. The goal of providing a needed product backed by the guarantee of the business is replaced by the desire to be number one and to beat all competitors. The quarterly profit statement becomes more important than worker satisfaction and long-range decision-making. Company growth increases pressure to preserve the company at all costs. Opposing injustice is difficult enough in a small group; in a large corporation, shaking the foundations is unacceptable. The larger the organization, the stronger is the temptation to deny problems and ignore the needs of the individual. If the consumer does not naturally need the product, the company finds a way to create the need with market strategies and manipulative advertising. The corporation seeks enough control of the market to exert leverage and to prevent competition. The nineteenth-century "robber barons" stand as symbols of free enterprise becoming destructive. But of equal concern should be the efforts of businesses to avoid restriction of unhealthy products like cigarettes, to prevent legislation requiring pollution control, and to encourage workaholism among employees.

The corporation that is able to establish market leverage must act to preserve that leverage with all its power or it will not remain strong. Kickbacks, corruption of government officials, $185 coffee pots on Air Force jets are just a few of the outward signs that the third horseman still rides and still brings chaos and abuse to an economic system.

Following the resignation in 1988 of James Webb as Secretary of the Navy because of his objection to Congressional cuts of the Navy budget, former secretary John Lehman was interviewed on "All Things Considered," on National Public Radio.[38] In describing the complexity of managing budget cuts, he stated that our country's military expenditures equal the combined expenditures of the thirty largest Fortune 500 corporations. Our Defense Department is far and away the largest single economic entity in the entire world. The growth of what President Eisenhower termed in his famous farewell address "the military-industrial complex" has continued unabated. Today the single largest business in the world is focused around the power of the fourth horseman, death.

The single most important symbol in Revelation for the incarnation of the beast is the "whore of Babylon." Babylon, of course, symbolized Rome for the first-century reader, but the seven heads and ten horns reflect the beast more clearly than they reflect the imperial city of Rome. Babylon is the embodiment of the beast in the world of political and economic power, be it Babylon, Thebes, Tyre or Sidon, Sodom or Rome, or in our day, New York, London, Moscow, or Tokyo.

> And I saw a woman sitting on a scarlet beast which was
> full of blasphemous names, and it had seven heads and
> ten horns. The woman was arrayed in purple and scarlet,

> and bedecked with gold and jewels and pearls, holding in
> her hand a golden cup full of abominations and impurities
> of her fornication; and on her forehead was written a
> name of mystery: "Babylon the great, mother of harlots
> and of earth's abominations." And I saw the woman,
> drunk with the blood of the saints and the blood of the
> martyrs of Jesus. (Rev. 17:3b-6a)

Babylon is beautiful and rich, dazzling to look upon,
covered with precious jewels and golden jewelry. Her beauty is
so amazing that even John "marveled greatly" and had to be
corrected by his angelic guide (17:6f). But Babylon's glitter is
seductive; she is full of deceit and obscenity. Her relationships
are impure. Kings and merchants, princes and men of wealth,
shippers and all the great men of the earth grow fat and rich
on her lavish wealth, but they make war upon the Lamb and
the Lamb's people.

In this image and in John's concluding image of the New
Jerusalem, we see more clearly than in any other book of the
New Testament the urban setting of the early Christian
church. John's Christians were not shepherds and farmers.
They were workers in the textile industries of Laodicea and
Thyatira. They provided services for the merchants and
traders in Sardis, Ephesus, and Smyrna. Perhaps some were
slaves laboring in the bronze and copper guilds of Thyatira.
Others may have worked as money changers in the banks of
Laodicea, or on the docks of the ports of Ephesus and Smyrna.
Some may even have worked in the halls of government in the
provincial capital of Ephesus. They knew the glitter and excitement of the city. From their position at the bottom of the
economic and social pyramid, they also knew its abominations. They knew how phony the glitter could be, and how
real the hardships. The image of Babylon, the great whore,
drunk on the blood of the saints, expressed and still expresses
the view of those who are victimized by urban life.

The worst word John could conceive—"fornication"—he
uses to describe the economic and political practices that

bring wealth and prosperity to many in the city. Because of the Old Testament opposition to fertility cults, the term "fornication" carried for John and his readers connotations of idolatry as well as sexual immorality. The Temple of Artemis at Ephesus was one of the seven wonders of the ancient world. Each city had its temple, and temple festivities provided diversion and relief for the citizens. Civic life and pagan observances were intertwined; it is, then, no wonder that pagan influence was such a problem for John's congregations. In the context of its basic Old Testament use, "fornication" should be contrasted with the Jewish understanding of God's love as steadfast (*hesed*), a covenant love which has endured through the ages.

The essential character of relationships described as "fornication" is the lack of commitment. Fornication is a temporary relationship contracted to satisfy one's wants and needs; when these are satisfied, there is no longer any need for the relationship. Fornication is a relationship of mutual use of the other for personal desire. It combines the immorality of using others to satisfy personal need and the idolatry of using a god to pursue personal gain.

We understand human society as based on a mass of contracts, written and unwritten, entered into by individuals who seek to meet their own needs.[39] John's concern does not seem to be that some grow wealthy while others grow poor; rather, he indicts the whole system of contracts and alliances that make for economic prosperity, political order, and even peace. Can this system be deserving of John's denunciation? What is so wrong about making a living?

To purchase a home, for example, I enter into a relationship with a home owner (or builder), a bank, a local and a state government through contracts. In return for shelter for myself and my family, I will provide fees and payments of interest and principal. Obviously, all business and government depends on contractual agreements to function. Just as power is an inevitable part of human life, just as there is nothing wrong in principle with institutions and principalities, so contractual arrangements are a necessary part of living in this world. We should see contracts and contractual relationships as part of creation and therefore, good.

But what happens if I am injured in an automobile accident and am unable to work? My wife's income cannot cover family and housing expenses. Generally those with whom the contractual arrangements were made will allow us time to sell the house and develop new economic arrangements for living. There are times, however, when financial conditions make restructuring difficult, and financial institutions, by their nature, place business and profit ahead of human compassion. No manager will survive who continually sacrifices profit because of customers' particular situations and needs, even though the bank remains sound and solvent. Banks are established to make a profit. In the world of business, the goal of the business—to make a profit—is more important than the needs of any individual. It matters not if he or she is customer, client, manager, or director: the individual human being will be sacrificed for the goals of the "bottom line."

The point is not that banks are bad or that profits are sinful or that some other economic system would be better. The point is that institutions subtly and slowly begin to serve institutional goals rather than the people whom they were created to serve. They move from servant to master. Their appetite for growth seems insatiable. In the Third World debt crisis, in the large number of foreclosures against midwestern farmers in the mid-1980s, and in the Savings and Loan "bailout" of 1989 we see symptoms of the later and more destructive stage.

Pressure for such movement exists in all such organizations, in all economic and political systems. Human participation in the movement toward dominion is fornication with seductive Babylon. With fear and promises, organizations ensnare people into service. The combination of human greed and institutional growth continues unabated. We regulate our institu-

The Impotence of Power

tions; we regulate our regulators. Seeking to control the institutions or the people seems ineffective. We seem caught in a perpetual cycle: abuse leads to destruction, which leads to revolution or reform, which leads to new abuse. Will this cycle end only after we have destroyed life on this planet?

As I have sought to understand the spiritual aspects of organizations, one trait emerges as the single most important characteristic of organizations infected by the beast: the need to control. The ability to control and determine results is at the heart of our understanding of power. Our technological achievements attest to our ability to control, and our lives are more comfortable and more interesting as a result. But with regard to people and to politics, the power to control does not work well.

Joe and Barbara have been married for three and a half years. They have one child, about a year old. They called and came in to see me because their marriage seemed to be coming apart. They said that they believed in marriage, that they did not want a divorce, that they thought a loving and stable home with both parents was important for children. They both loved their child, but they were having more and more difficulty coping with each other. Joe and Barbara had not married young, both were in their twenties and finished with their education when they married. I was surprised that they were having problems.

As we talked, I became more surprised and more confused. The list of their complaints about each other was long, but from my perspective, not terribly serious. There was no physical or emotional abuse; no alcoholism; no adultery; nothing that would lead one to abandon dreams and values and goals in life. He didn't carry out the garbage. She was always thinking up more jobs for him to do. He took too much time measuring and planning before he would finally get a repair accomplished. She didn't want to have his friends over for dinner. He hid the amount of his income from her. She didn't save enough money. They tried setting up rules and schedules,

CHAPTER 4

but that approach added even more tension. When the rules were followed, they were followed grudgingly. When they were broken, complaints were amplified. They fought a lot, especially over money. But why were they talking about divorce? These problems did not seem insurmountable.

As we continued to work on forgiveness and communication skills, one day I asked them to read the marriage vows to each other. "I, Joe, take you, Barbara, to be my wife, to have and to hold from this day forward, for better for worse, for richer for poorer, in sickness and in health, to love and to cherish, until we are parted by death."

There was a long pause. "I don't think I ever realized what those words meant," said Joe.

"Does that mean you want to get out of this marriage?" I asked.

"No," Joe replied slowly, "it means I don't really know what kind of relationship I've gotten into."

That statement started us on a new investigation. If better-worse, richer-poorer, sickness-health were not the terms Joe had actually intended when he got married, what were the terms that dictated his true expectations for marriage and thus formed the basis for their relationship? What we found out I have since discovered to be true for many, many marriages. Joe and Barbara said the traditional words, but implicitly they ignored what they were saying and instead made a covenant that went something like this: I, Joe, take you, Barbara, to be my wife, to love and to cherish as long as my needs are being met, as long as the irritations are less than the benefits, and as long as you do not impose your personal problems upon me.

After three years of making demands on one another (in agreement with the implicit vows) and trying to fulfill the other's expectations, they were tired and resentful and a very unhappy couple. They chose to try to begin again with this new idea of marriage based on forgiveness and commitment, but it is not proving to be easy.

The Impotence of Power

I suggest that Joe and Barbara's concept of marriage is more typical in the United States than what Christians believe marriage should be. I think that many couples who marry in this country today do so without understanding the implications of what they are doing and saying. I believe they marry in order to have their own needs satisfied, and they do not expect to have to deal with any real problems on the part of their spouse. And when the irritations become more numerous than the satisfactions and benefits, they sue for divorce. Certainly this is not true of all couples who marry, but it is true of many, and it explains the high divorce rate and the high level of unhappiness within marriage. If making demands and living up to demands is central within a relationship, there is no way to avoid resentment, guilt, anger, and growing pettiness and unhappiness.

Joe and Barbara's marriage was not a marriage as the church understands it, but a relationship of mutual use of one another for personal satisfaction. This was not their intention; it was the result of their implicit contract. So when the marriage became unsatisfying, it seemed appropriate to them to terminate the contract through divorce. How did their understanding and action stray so far from what they themselves wanted and, when given a choice, chose to pursue? The power of the beast! The spirituality of our culture.

Joe and Barbara were seduced by the idea that one lives and works in the pursuit of happiness. We all recognize that being happy is more enjoyable than being miserable. But to move from that recognition to setting up happiness as a goal of life is a major shift that many make without considering the ramifications. Joe and Barbara just wanted to be happy. They were in love and believed that getting married would ensure their joy. The beast seduced them, leading them to think that their marriage contract meant having their personal needs met and not being upset by the other's problems. Under this contract marriage became a series of expectations, demands, and disappointments. Slowly and subtly their happiness was eroded by their desire to control each other. In many marriages, the conflicts progress to violence and abuse. The attempts to control the relationship are the fuel for its destruction.

If society is based on self-serving individuals entering into contracts and organizations as competitors for space and the limited resources necessary for advancement, then individuals must always be on their guard. In such a society, whatever communities of love and trust emerge from these conditions must necessarily be fragile, contingent, and derivative. In a contractual community the individuals "do not feel for each other, they do not live for each other, they do not find their essential nature fulfilled only in communion with each other."[40] Intuitively John sees that the whole system of contractual relationships must be indicted as "fornication" because it allows the beast to destroy community. There is no community of love and trust in Babylon.

Within personal relationships, the power to control is incapable of creating a healthy affiliation. While attempts to manipulate and control people may bring quick satisfaction, in the long run they destroy the relationship. When a husband, a wife, a parent, or a friend exerts pressure to control, the other is left with a choice: submit or rebel. Constant submission destroys; it creates instead a robot that is little more than the mirror of the neurotic other. Constant resistance, on the other hand, may lead to arguments and threats which at times may escalate to physical as well as verbal and emotional violence. Yet the desire for control is addictive; each setback increases it. A cycle of manipulation, deceit, and domination takes charge of the relationship. We become imprisoned within our need for power and our fear of trusting even the one we love. Normal, rational human beings may become possessive, distrustful, and even violent. In other cases families become noncommunicative, existing in joint living arrangements organized by hundreds of spoken and unspoken rules.

When I want something, I honor my wife by simply asking and explaining what I want and why. She is then free to respond to my request positively or negatively. A negative response is not a rejection of me personally, and a positive response is a gift of love that strengthens our relationship. But if I seek my way by force or manipulation, there is no way she can give me a gift. The very act of seeking control in a relationship damages intimacy.

Similarly, when an institution assumes its task is to control people, it begins a process which, if unchecked, will lead to its becoming an oppressor. The glories of the church have almost always been those times when it was small and helpless. When it has been able to exert control over society, and assumed it should manage the world, its oppressive tendencies have showed themselves inevitably in witch hunts, inquisitions, and suppression of knowledge. Beneath the desire to control lies the premise that the good of the institution is more important than the individual people who are its members. To place institutional glory above human integrity is the blasphemy for which the beast is known.

The controlling institution is not healthy, and it continues to get more infected. The only solution it can see to its problem is to try to get a better set of rules or to control more closely the actions of its members. The sick corporation will place power in the hands of a few managers, will provide the least possible amount of information about the health of the business, will use the retirement and benefit structure to control employees, will respond to crises with new sets of rules, and will stress the need for loyalty to the company. The sickness of such a company can be seen in the low morale of the employees, who become resentful, lethargic, and nonproductive. Profit-making organizations that get this sick are likely to go out of business, but government agencies and nonprofit service organizations can remain ill for years and years.

The seduction of control is the counterfeit offer of a quick solution, but life in this world is not easily controlled. Plans often go astray. We seek control, but control produces resistance. We enter into contractual relationships out of fear of what can go wrong and in the attempt to control the future. Behind the contractual relationship lies fear of the world and fear of the other person. The power to control, be it people or nations, is based on coercion of one sort or another: on the threat of violence, the tearing down of the other's self-esteem, and ultimately on inflicting suffering and death. With people the power to control is not power to create, but only to restrict and destroy.

The need to control has an addictive quality about it that explains the tendency of the beast to move from servant, to dominator, to oppressor. Without restraints like the economic forces of the market place to force change or destroy the institution, the only solution we seem to have is to try to control the institution. Controlling a contractual community changes the true situation only slightly. Who will control the controllers? What will prevent the controllers from also becoming infected? Trying to control institutions and governments with linear power simply adds another layer of power on top of the existing pyramid. Our multileveled bureaucracies and complexes of state and federal regulations are the results of attempting to control the powers and principalities with further controls. The arms race stands as the most important symbol of the impotence of technological power to control itself.

No wonder we feel powerless. Seeking simple security and comfort, we have become entangled in a confused web of contractual relationships in our intimate life, in the life of our local community, and in our national and international relations. On the one hand, the web is so extensive that to change even one small relationship seems impossible. The powers seem helpless to reform themselves or to change the system, while we are afraid to let go of the security our relationships offer.

We need a different way. We need a different understanding of power, and we need some different assumptions about human relationships. In the image of the Lamb, John promises us an understanding of power that is strong enough to confront the beast, yet brings unity and healing. In the image of the New Jerusalem, he pictures the transformation of human relationships.

The Lamb

Imagine that you are a Jew of the first century, C.E., living in Philadelphia, a city founded two hundred years before as a center for the spread of Greek culture. Born ten years after the great earthquake of 17 C.E. that destroyed the city, you were raised in a family dominated by two concerns: the preservation of the Jewish faith in a proselytizing foreign culture, and the anxiety that another quake might bring death and ruin. Though several days' journey from Judea, you too have sought to preserve the memory and the dream of the independent Jewish state, a dream that had died sixty years before your birth. Your children bear the names of the heroes of the Jewish revolt—Judas, Simeon, John, and Esther. Chanukkah, the feast celebrating the rededication of the Jerusalem Temple and the freedom of the Jews from Antiochus, is indeed an annual high point, bringing light to the dark winter months.

But life is dull and filled with hard work. In the synagogue the writings of Daniel, Ezekiel, the Apocalypse of Ezra, and the Testaments of the Twelve Patriarchs speak to the drudgery and anxiety of life in Philadelphia and to the dream for a restored Jewish state. To the devout Jew, the Roman rulers seem like the beasts of Daniel and Esdras. Descriptions of earthquakes in Ezekiel and Esdras (they remind you of the stories of the great quake before your birth) are vivid reminders that God will soon intervene and gather his faithful multitude. When you sing the Psalms of Solomon, how you long for the Messiah of the house of David to come, cleanse Jerusalem, and destroy the sinful. Some day, you tell yourself, the Lion of Judah will come and with the breath of his mouth consume the persecutors of Israel.[41] But until that day you will have to keep on working just to feed the family and hope no misfortune will come upon you.

Or imagine that you are a God-fearing Gentile of Philadelphia, attracted to the synagogue by the morality of the Jews who work in your city. Their theology of one God makes sense, while their purity of life reflects the best ideals from Greek philosophy put into practice. But most important, while the Greeks and Romans seem to believe the world will stay the same forever, the Jews look forward to a time when those who abuse others will themselves be judged. You have been to Ephesus and seen the wealth of the Temple of Artemis. You have been to Pergamum and seen the ostentatious luxury of the rulers, to Sardis and seen the prosperity of the merchants and traders. And though you work hard on your small farm, the income from the wool is never enough to buy even an extra cloak. The words and hymns from the synagogue speak to you. You look forward to a time when the tables will be turned, and the righteous will know comfort, and the taskmasters will suffer the hardships to which they have put their slaves.

Then one day a traveler comes to the synagogue proclaiming that the age of fulfillment—the "latter days" foretold by the prophet—have dawned. In accordance with the Scriptures, Jesus of Nazareth, who had lived with, taught, and healed the common people, had been put to death by the rulers and was raised by God to reign as his Messiah. Now he is the head of a new Israel which includes both Jews and Greeks, slaves and free, men and women. The sign of this Christ's glory is the presence of the Holy Spirit in the community of the faithful. And he will soon return in consummation of this new messianic age. The traveler calls on all the people present to repent of their sins, to believe in Jesus, and to be baptized in his name.[42] You and many of your friends believe. This is the news you have been waiting for. You are baptized. You continue to meet at the synagogue and to study the Scriptures, but on the first day of the week you gather to break bread together, to remember the death and resurrection of Jesus, and to keep the faith alive that he will soon return, bringing his kingdom.

But the return does not take place soon. The missionary Paul and other teachers came to the area preaching this same Good News. The hard times and hard work continue, although more and more people come to believe in Jesus. The Jews who do not believe take over the synagogue and drive out the believers. Some Christians in neighboring cities are killed because of their faith. There are hard feelings. How long will it be before the Lord comes as judge and avenges the blood of those martyrs? What can we do, what should we do, in the time of waiting? There are so many questions that need answers. Despite the waiting and the hardship, the Spirit is alive in the church. The community of faith provides help for those who were hurt during hard times; when patience grows short, the community provides the support to endure. But what is the meaning of the waiting? How does a crucified Messiah save?

If you can imagine what it might have been like to be a member of that early body of believers, then with the eyes of imagination read, as though for the first time, John's words about the Lamb:

> I saw a strong angel proclaiming with a loud voice, "Who is worthy to open the scroll and break its seals?" And no one in heaven or on earth or under the earth was able to open the scroll or to look into it, and I wept. . . . Then one of the elders said to me, "Weep not; lo, the Lion of the tribe of Judah, the Root of David, has conquered, so he can open the scroll and its seven seals."

> And between the throne and the four living creatures and among the elders, I saw a Lamb standing, as though it had been slain, with seven horns and with seven eyes, which are the seven spirits of God sent out into all the earth; and he went and took the scroll from the right hand of him who was seated on the throne.

> And when he has taken the scroll, the four living
> creatures and the twenty-four elders fell down before the
> Lamb, each holding a harp, and with golden bowls full of
> incense, which are the prayers of the saints; and they sang
> a new song, saying, "Worthy art thou to take the scroll
> and to open its seals, for thou wast slain and by thy blood
> didst ransom men for God from every tribe and tongue
> and people and nation, and hast made them a kingdom
> and priests to our God, and they shall reign on earth."
> (Rev. 5:2-10)[43]

This passage is the climax of John's vision of heavenly worship found in the fourth and fifth chapters of Revelation. The imagery derives from Isaiah 6, Ezekiel 1, and Daniel 7, but the setting and liturgy likely reflect the worship of the early church in Asia.[44] It is not fanciful to see here an idealized meeting place for the assembly of the church, with the bishop seated upon his throne (*cathedra*), the elders seated on either side, and the deacons (the seven spirits) standing before the throne, with the holy table (cf. 6:9), and with the scriptural scroll in its place. The liturgical order follows the pattern of the regular Jewish morning worship, which began with the praise of God as Creator and then moved to a celebration of the Torah, the law, followed by thanksgiving for God's redemption at the Red Sea. Beginning with the praise of God as Creator (cf. 4:11), this passage in Revelation speaks of the scroll before concluding with the thanksgiving that the Lamb has ransomed for God people from every tribe, language, race, and nationality.

The first-century Christian would have been familiar with the imagery, the setting, and the thought sequence here portrayed. Perhaps in Christian worship thanksgiving for God's redemption through Jesus had replaced the Jewish thanksgiving for deliverance from Egypt. The early Christian believer in Asia would have been prepared to hear praise of God, followed by thanksgiving for the Scriptures which point to Christ's triumph, the victory of the Lion of Judah. But the figure of the Lamb must have come as a surprising image.[45]

CHAPTER 5

John's development and his choice of words would indicate that he intended to startle his readers.

In the languages of the Mediterranean (including Greek and Hebrew) there are many words for sheep and lambs. John uses a special word for the Lamb throughout Revelation, *arnion*, a word used only one other time in the rest of the New Testament.[46] *Arnion* is a diminutive form of the more common word for lamb, *arnos*, found in the New Testament only in Luke in the phrase, "as lambs among wolves"(Lk. 10:3).[47] The biblical use of these words in the Greek Old Testament indicate that the animal depicted is a young lamb, while the diminutive form emphasizes youth and vulnerability. The Lion of the tribe of Judah, which was to destroy the enemy, turns out to be a little, young lamb standing on the hillside, defenseless against man or beast. That he bears the marks of slaughter not only identifies him with the Crucified One but also underscores his meekness, helplessness, and vulnerability. John has carefully chosen an image that conveys unprotected and perilous existence.

The phrase "thou wast slain" (*esphages*, Rev. 5:6,9) certainly refers to the crucifixion. However, the word is more commonly used in relation to a violent slaughter by a weapon like a sword, and not to a legal execution. It is an appropriate word to describe the slaughter of the Paschal lamb at Passover, and John has used it in a liturgical setting where Jews would have anticipated reference to the deliverance from Egypt. This connection of the crucifixion with the Exodus is confirmed by other Exodus metaphors found throughout Revelation.[48] Salvation in the Exodus was a victorious deliverance from the power of Egypt and the overthrowing of the forces of Pharaoh in the Red Sea. Despite his evident vulnerability, the Lamb has ransomed his followers from captivity to make them a kingdom and priests (Ex. 19:6, "kingdom of priests") to reign on earth. They have been delivered to establish a new realm and a new community on earth where God is acknowledged as king.

And so our first-century Christian begins to put together a great puzzle. He has discovered through Christ's endurance on the cross that he is free from guilt and sin, that he is a spiritual heir of Abraham and an inheritor of eternal life. He experiences the risen Christ, and discovers himself a new creature. He has become part of a new community that gathers regularly for worship and mutual support. All of this has happened because Jesus Christ loves us and frees us by his blood (1:5f). Jesus is "the faithful witness, the first born of the dead, and the ruler of the kings on earth." Now the Christian sees: *This is a new kind of exodus, deliverance from bondage to the world and from fear of rulers and merchants into a new community of caring. Christ's love and faithfulness have not only freed us, but are making us into a new nation.*

Just as Egypt fought against the followers of Moses, so too the powers of this world are antagonistic to this new nation of followers of Jesus. We have done nothing to them, but they hate us. They hate us because we no longer believe we are inferior to them. They hate us because we do not participate in their superstitious worship of Roma and the other gods. They hate us because we are different, and because we believe the world can be better. We are freed from the old bondage that told us we would always be servants and they would always be masters.

With this hint of insight, our first-century Christian reads on. The story that began with the glorified Christ and seven little churches ends with all of creation being made new. He has always assumed that Rome and all the officials and merchants and aristocrats were the important people, but John says the future will be shaped by the Lamb and his followers. He thinks about John's opening vision of the son of man, who stands in glory in heaven and holds the seven stars in his right hand (1:12-20). *John said those stars were seven churches, including the church in Philadelphia. Is John saying that the church in Philadelphia, perhaps the poorest of churches in the least important city of Asia, is as important as the stars of heaven? The story of Philadelphia and all the other little churches, he thinks, is part of a*

CHAPTER 5

great and universal mission being directed by God from his throne. What happens to these churches and what they do is part of what God is doing through Jesus Christ to destroy evil and to renew creation.

John called Antipas, who died for his faith in Pergamum, a "faithful witness." Did John mean that his death was somehow like Christ's death, that it will make a difference in the world? Sometimes the discouragement and the frustration, not to mention the discrimination against us, make our efforts seem pointless. Did Jesus feel powerless like us when he faced Pilate? Is that what John means by calling him a lamb? John says that we in Philadelphia have kept the "word of patient endurance," and that our patience will bring even the Jews who do not believe back into the church. When we are faithful, even when it is difficult or costly, we are like lambs, too. If the Lamb is leading a new exodus and establishing a new nation, then when we are like the Lamb, we are a part of this new exodus. Just as I discovered life through the suffering of Jesus, so others will discover life through our faithful witness, and they, too, will be free.

John has depicted the powers of this world as beasts, devouring people and destroying creation. To oppose them like a lion is to be like them, violent and fearful. True opposition would be a different kind of action, as different as a lamb is from a lion. Just as truth destroys the lie, just as honesty destroys deceit, so the acceptance of unjust suffering shows the unjust powers in their true light. People will know we need a better world. Suffering for others is the way to freedom, for self and for the others. The beast's way can only control and enslave. The Lamb is unprotected and vulnerable, but it is not weak. It takes a lot of strength to bear suffering. It is much easier to fight back. The Lamb must be strong, strong enough to suffer for others.

Looking at the whole story, the first-century Christian realizes that the true shapers of the future are not the powerful who give orders and inflict punishment; the true leaders are the followers of the Lamb who, by suffering as Christ suffered, align themselves with his way and his kingdom.

John develops this thesis of the conquest of the Lamb by developing the images of the Lamb and the beast through a series of parallel contrasts, which show us more clearly the character of the Lamb and the nature of his power.[49]

Both the beast and the Lamb have horns, indicating power and dominion. The seven horns of the Lamb are covered with eyes, the spirit of truth that sees injustice and deceit and oppression for what they are. The beast's horns are covered with crowns, flaunting its dominion. The Lamb's kingdom stands in opposition to the kingdoms of this world, which blaspheme God by seeking dominion over people. Founded on truth, his kingdom is less easily overturned than a kingdom founded on deceit. Seeing the world as it truly is, including the evil which one cannot change, frees, liberates, and heals the Lamb's people.

As we have already seen, the beast imitates the sacrificial wound of the Lamb with his own healed mortal wound, a wound it uses to attract a following. The Lamb received his wound in the lonely task of ransoming his people from captivity. Pseudo-suffering is only another form of manipulation. If found out, the manipulator may well be despised. True sacrifice, when recognised, leads to a sincere response of thanksgiving and commitment.

The beast is a symbol of brutal force; the Lamb is a symbol of unprotected vulnerability. The beast coerces through fear and might, but the Lamb has no such power. The followers of the Lamb are not manipulated, cajoled, or constrained to follow; they freely choose the Lamb as their leader. By his love and sacrifice, the Lamb transforms the heart and inspires devotion. Love compels the followers of the Lamb, not force.

The beast controls people by fear and death; the Lamb liberates people from bondage and heals people and brings life. The beast uses people for the glory of the principality, and in the process they get hurt. The beast kills people and drinks their blood, but the purpose of the Lamb is to free people from destructive enslavement, even at the cost of its own life.

CHAPTER 5

Through his own blood the Lamb liberates his people and raises them to new life. Those who follow the beast receive short-term gain but spiritual death, while those who follow the Lamb know eternal life now and will live with the Lamb forever.

The beast has a sword that is used to take peace from the earth; the Lamb has a sword that issues from his mouth, the Word of God, which destroys the power of deceit and falsehood. No wonder the beast rages in anger and makes war on the saints; truth, the revelation of God, and the witness of the Lamb and his followers bring the beast's true nature into the light where all may see. In response to the beast's rage, the Lamb and his people sing a new song, even in the midst of persecution, celebrating the victory that will be theirs.

The beast numbers people, and only they can participate in buying and selling; the Lamb gives his name to his followers and invites them to his wedding feast.

For the beast, people do not matter; all that matters is how they serve it. Despite the austere style of John's apocalypse, there is a personal quality in the relationships between the Lamb and his followers. They deal in names, not numbers. The Lamb is a shepherd who leads his people to living water, while the beast punishes by exclusion from the marketplace those who do not give it allegiance.

The beast seduces people into following him with deceptive images and half-truths; the Lamb is called "faithful and true," and in his people's mouths no lie can be found. Trickery persuades people to follow the beast, but followers of the Lamb see the world as it truly is. When people see that they have sold their freedom for petty gain, they will turn against the beast.

The beast's city is the whore, Babylon, glamorous and wealthy, but sterile, controlling, and a destroyer of human life. The relationships between the beast and Babylon and its people are self-aggrandizing, temporary fornications that foster only individual welfare and security. The Lamb's city is the new

Jerusalem, brilliantly and radiantly beautiful, a new creation, bringing healing and bearing fruit. Jerusalem is the bride of the Lamb; their relationship is the covenant relationship of marriage. Commitment and steadfastness characterize God's relationships with his people. The relationship does not serve the purpose of self-aggrandizement, but serves the deeper need of personal growth, altruistic love, and service of others. The quick and easy way is always tempting, but prudence as well as truth dictates following the way of personal integrity and the honoring of others.

The beast utters blasphemies, claiming allegiance and worship for itself; the Lamb and his people worship God, the One who sits on the throne. The priority system is reversed. For the beast everything, even God, is a means toward an end such as national pride, economic prosperity, or social stability. For the Lamb and his people, the only end is God and the freedom of those God created and loves; any goal that would enslave cannot be tolerated. Worship of God keeps priorities straight.

While the figure of the Lamb attracts us, it hardly seems possible for the innocent and vulnerable Lamb to conquer the vicious and deceitful beast. Any fight between these two could hardly be fair; it would be a slaughter. Indeed, that is John's message. Six times John builds the scene toward the great and final battle, and each time the beast is destroyed without a struggle.[50] At the climactic moment, the beast rolls over and dies. Here is a typical example: "I saw the beast and the kings of the earth with their armies gathered to make war against him who sits upon the horse [the Word of God] and against his army. And the beast was captured, and with it the false prophet who in its presence had worked the signs by which he deceived those who had received the mark of the beast and those who worshiped its image" (19:19-20). No matter how carefully one looks for a true fight between good and evil in Revelation—a fight in which there is some question as to the outcome—no such conflict is to be found. Why? Because the key battle has already been fought. In the death and resurrec-

CHAPTER 5

tion of Jesus, evil has been decisively defeated. Satan has been "conquered by the blood of the Lamb and by the word of their testimony" (12:11). The outcome awaiting the beast and its people is defeat and destruction. The Lamb, however, will reign in a new, redeemed creation. The way of control and coercion ultimately leads to death, while worship, steadfastness, honesty, community, and freedom lead to life.

The way of the Lamb is not only the better way, John proclaims, it is the way that will be victorious. John presumes the Lamb's victory by addressing the church members as "conquerors" and by refering to Jesus as "the ruler of kings on earth" (1:5.).[51] Power based on deceit, propaganda, and seduction will lose in a confrontation with truth, honesty, and faithfulness. People who seek their own self-interest first will rebel when they see they are being tricked and manipulated and are dying spiritually. In the long run, one who invites followers to a feast, who offers freedom, and who treats people with dignity will have greater power then one who threatens and enslaves.

The first unequivocable statement that the Lamb has won the major battle and will be victorious is found in the passage about the Lamb's being worthy to open the scroll (5:5). One could easily assume the scroll is the Jewish scriptures that have been fulfilled, and thereby made clear, by Christ. On the other hand, in apocalyptic writing the scroll is the record of what is to come. But John does not tell us, as the traditional apocalypse does, what is written in the scroll. He seems to be combining several images to indicate that the scroll is God's redemptive plan, foreshadowed in the Old Testament and moving into the future, of how he will reassert his sovereignty over the sinful world.[52] The Lamb provides the key to understanding God's plan, the key to understanding life. The Lamb through his death and resurrection enables God's plan to unfold. The Lamb is worthy to open the scroll because, like a lion, he has "conquered" (5:5). By his sacrifice he has freed us from our sins (1:5), ransomed us from the beast (5:9), and established a new kingdom on earth.

We can see that the way of the Lamb is more desirable than rule by the beast. We can hope that all people might be converted and follow this honest, just, and moral way of life. Knowing God is the ultimate power, we can also see that if Jesus is God's Messiah, then the power of the Lamb must be greater than that of the powers and principalities of this world. But when I am confronted by the power of the nations, when I consider the strength of our corporate structures, when I read about the power of a mob, when I feel my own wants, fears, and lethargy take control of my actions, then I must wonder if John's Good News is realistic. How did Jesus of Nazareth "conquer" the powers and principalities? Can we see the power of the Lamb operative and effective in history and in our lives?

The Victory of the Lamb

They answered, "He deserves death." Then they spat in his face, and struck him, saying, "Prophesy to us, you Christ! Who is it that struck you?"

The soldiers stripped him and put a scarlet robe upon him, and plaiting a crown of thorns they put it on his head, and put a reed in his right hand. And kneeling before him they mocked him, saying, "Hail, King of the Jews!"

Two robbers were crucified with him, one on the right and one on the left. And those who passed by derided him, saying, "You who would destroy the temple and build it in three days, save yourself! If you are the Son of God, come down from the cross...and we will believe."

About the ninth hour Jesus cried with a loud voice, *"Eli, Eli, lama sabachthani?"* that is, "My God, my God, why hast thou forsaken me?"

How difficult it is to view the pathos of the cross and think in one's heart and mind, "Now that's power!" The cross is not our picture of power, nor our picture of the conquering hero, nor even a picture of competence. Jesus does not appear to be in control, but rather under the control of harsh and unjust rulers. Far from being in command, Jesus is dependent on others' judgments if he is to be relieved of suffering. Unable to prevent cruelty, he is vulnerable to whatever tortures or degradations the soldiers wish to inflict upon him. The cross is an image of powerlessness and vulnerability, of suffering and impotence, of defeat and despair. We can understand how Jesus became associated with the lamb in Isaiah's prophecy, for indeed he is "like a lamb that is led to the slaughter" (Is. 53:7). But how can we understand Jesus as "the power of God"? Indeed that is a stumbling-block and a folly (I Cor. 1:23-24). It is one thing to articulate the differences between the way of the Lamb and the way of the beast; it is quite another truly to understand that the power of the Lamb is the greater.

In images and in narrative, Revelation proclaims that the crucified and risen Lord has overcome the power of the principalities and rulers of this world. Images, however, do not describe or explain how Jesus is victorious over those powers, nor how his victory empowers us. Some translation is required to move from John's affirmation of the victory of the Lamb to an understanding of how Jesus' death and resurrection confounds the powers of this world as well as saves the individual.

The world is hard on those who do not have the power to compete for their share of its limited goods and services. We know this to be true in our modern social structures. The person born into a single-parent, welfare-supported family rarely gets the education needed for a good job, often does not develop the habits needed to carry responsibility well, and seldom has the self-security or the emotional support needed to keep trying in the face of failure after failure. Our society bases class divisions largely on economic wealth. As a result we have more movement from bottom to top than most social structures in human history. In the first century, where birth, citizenship, and nationality as well as economic clout determined one's social status, the system was more rigid, and the poor were even less able to compete. Life at the bottom of the social pyramid was, is, and always will be, hard: "The poor you will have with you always."

But if the way of the world is painful to the poor, it is also destructive to those in positions of power and status. Loneliness, insensitivity to the condition of others, over-work, manipulation of others to hold onto one's position, constant evaluation of others on the basis of what they can do for

CHAPTER 6

you—all these add up to a person who has lost the best qualities of life. The way of the world is cruel to those at the bottom of the pyramid and poisonous to those caught in its upper levels.

Jesus proposed a different way. "When he had washed their feet, and taken his garments, and resumed his place, he said to them, 'Do you know what I have done to you? You call me Teacher and Lord; and you are right, for so I am. If I then, your Lord and Teacher, have washed your feet, you also ought to wash one another's feet. For I have given you an example, that you also should do as I have done to you. Truly, truly, I say to you, a servant is not greater than his master; nor is he who is sent greater than he who sent him'" (John 13:12-16).

The world teaches:	Jesus taught a different way:

Blessed are the rich
  for they shall rule the world.
	Blessed are the poor
	  for theirs is the kingdom of
	  heaven.

Blessed are the calm and col-
lected,
  for little can touch them.
	Blessed are those who mourn,
	  for they shall be comforted.

Blessed are the aggressive,
  for they shall be promoted.
	Blessed are the meek,
	  for they shall inherit the
	  earth.

Blessed are those with finesse,
  for in avoiding controversy
  they shall come out ahead.
	Blessed are those who hunger
	and thirst for righteousness,
	  for they shall be satisfied.

Blessed are the cool and callous,
  for they shall emerge untroubled.
	Blessed are the merciful,
	  for they shall obtain mercy.

Blessed are the manipulators, for they shall achieve power.	

Blessed are the patriots
  for they shall make the country
  strong.
	Blessed are the pure in heart,
	  for they shall see God.

The Victory of the Lamb

Blessed are the nice,
for all will speak well of them.

Blessed are the peacemakers,
for they shall be called son
of God.

Blessed are those who are
persecuted
for righteousness' sake, for
theirs is the kingdom of
heaven.[53]

And the world, threatened by Jesus' teaching and by his freedom from the power of the social order, identified him as the enemy.

> The chief priests and the Pharisees gathered the council, and said, "What are we to do? For this man performs many signs. If we let him go on thus, every one will believe in him, and the Romans will come and destroy both our holy place and our nation." But one of them, Caiaphas, who was high priest that year, said to them, "You know nothing at all; you do not understand that it is expedient for you that one man should die for the people, and that the whole nation should not perish." (John 11:47-50)

The moment of confrontation between the Son of man and the beastly forces of dominion was not Armageddon, nor some major battle, nor a first-century Super Bowl. The beast avoids visibility—secret meetings, a night-time arrest, a closed and hurried trial. The moment of confrontation occurred when Jesus—a small-town carpenter's son, meek, poor, hungry, thirsty, and persecuted—stood before Pilate—a small-time politician in an unimportant province of the Roman Empire, rich, cool, patriotic, and anxious for order in the land. We should not allow the clandestine and hasty prosecution of Jesus to convince us that the crucifixion was a tragic mistake. The powers of the world recognized a true enemy, one who would turn their world upside down, and they mobilized their ultimate weapon, the power of death, to remove the threat.

CHAPTER 6

Jesus stood before Pilate, defenseless and vulnerable, while Pilate decided his fate—the Lamb before the beast. It appears to us that Pilate was in control and Jesus was defeated and powerless. But was Jesus really defenseless? Was Pilate really in control? When we are able to see that Jesus, not Pilate, won in this contest, then we have begun to see the spiritual realities celebrated in heaven.

First we look to see which man was truly vulnerable. The one controlled by fear was Pilate, not Jesus. Pilate feared what would happen if he disobeyed the crowd. He feared a riot or any civil unrest in Jerusalem, especially when there were so many pilgrims in the city. He feared what his superiors in Rome might think should there be any trouble (John 19:12). Pilate was a politician whose position depended on keeping the peace and keeping his superiors happy. Even more, he feared facing the fact of his vulnerability. He thought of himself as powerful, able to kill one and spare another: "Do you not know that I have power to release you, and power to crucify you?" He was not able to face the fact that he was not free enough to release an innocent man: "You have no power over me unless it had been given you from above" (John 19:10-11). Vulnerable to pressure, fearful of truth, a slave to political manipulation, Pilate knowingly condemned an innocent man to death.

In contrast, Jesus was free from fear's control. In Gethsemane he had faced fear and resolved to do God's will, though it meant confronting the authorities and facing death. He did not have—and did not seek—political power: "If my kingdom were of this world, my disciples would fight" (John 18:36). Having no desire to maintain political power, he was not susceptible to political pressure.[54] Jesus accepted the reality of his position, a position he could have avoided only by denying his call to teach and heal. In this stance of acceptance he was neither defensive nor aggressive. His strength is impressive before the shaking Pilate, who thought he had the power.

So Pilate operated out of fear while Jesus stood secure. Still it appears that Pilate was the one in control. Was not he the one who made the life and death decision? It would seem so, yet who really made the decision?

All four gospels record Pilate's assessment that Jesus was innocent. He then tried to get the crowd to change its mind about demanding Jesus' death. First he argued with them, "I find no evil in this man." Then he had Jesus beaten and mocked in a purple robe and crowned with thorns, thinking that this abuse might satisfy the crowd. Finally he succumbed to the crowd, against his own judgment, for fear of unrest and a bad report to Caesar. Clearly Pilate was not in control because he was so vulnerable to the control of others. Pilate had no power because he feared the loss of power.

On the other hand, Jesus could have escaped. He saw what was coming. He could have gone back to Galilee, quit teaching, become a carpenter again, and died of old age. If in fear he had pleaded to Pilate for mercy, he might have gotten away. But he refused to play by the world's rules. By word and deed he had called for a righteousness greater than that of the Pharisees and for a vision of human relationships more universal than the *Pax Romana*. Jesus' acceptance of his death told them (and us) in the most complete way that survival at the cost of one's humanity is not survival. Jesus had power; he saw more clearly than anyone else what was happening; he knew he need only be true to his faith and he would be invincible. He knew that servant love, sacrificial giving, and loving one's enemy would show the cruelty of power. In the end, when its nature was revealed, he would be victor.

All of this is fine in theory, but in the end, did not Pilate really win? After all, Pilate went home to dinner and Jesus suffered a humiliating and painful death.

It does appear to us that Jesus was the loser. How hard it is to see the realities of heaven! The contest is not to determine who will live longer, Jesus or Pilate. The contest is between the way of Jesus and the way of the world. In this confronta-

CHAPTER 6

tion the way of the world is revealed as the destructive beast it can be; the way of Jesus, as redemptive. To see Pilate as victor is to be imprisoned by the desire for worldly comfort and power. To see Jesus as victor is to be free.

Today millions of people worship God because in and through this sacrifice of Jesus they discovered the God whose name and nature is love. Individual lives, families, businesses, governments have been changed because of this one man and his life. "At the name of Jesus, every knee shall bow,...and every tongue confess that Jesus Christ is Lord, to the glory of God the Father" (Phil. 2:10-11). At the name of Pilate, people either remember the coward who could have saved Jesus, or else think of nothing at all. Pilate, the ruler, was imprisoned by his power; Jesus, bound and powerless, was free. Jesus is the first-fruits of an authentic, restored humanity because for the first time we have one who is not a slave to any power. Surely we must recognize that the way of Jesus won, still wins, and will overcome the way of the world.

This proclamation that Jesus has defeated the oppressive powers of this world is not restricted to Revelation, but is found throughout the New Testament. In our day this theme has been somewhat neglected, the result of an over-emphasis on individual salvation and the tendency of twentieth-century interpreters of Scripture to demythologize references to demons, angels, powers and principalities. In the eighth chapter of Romans, Paul is not delivering a funeral sermon, but affirming the victory of Jesus and the empowerment of the followers of the Lamb: "In all these things we are more than conquerors through him who loved us. For I am sure that neither death, nor life, nor angels, nor principalities, nor things present, nor things to come, nor powers, nor height, nor depth, nor anything else in all creation, will be able to separate us from the love of God in Christ Jesus our Lord" (Rom. 8:37-39). The war is not over, but the crucial battle has been fought. The Crucified has won the essential victory (Eph. 1:20-23). In the cross, God "disarmed the principalities and powers and made a public example of them, triumphing over them"(Col. 2:15).[55] Now is Christ "the head of all rule and authority," and in him "you have come to fulness of life"(Col. 2:10).[56]

The beast has been disarmed by the defusing of its ultimate weapon, death. Though the beast tends to control through seduction and blasphemous authority, as we have seen, the ultimate foundation of its ability to control is violence and death. Significantly, Jesus' raising of Lazarus from the dead was the action that led to the plot by the religious authorities to put him to death (John 11:17-44, 45-53). In the resurrection, God not only affirms the messiahship of Jesus, but also overcomes the power of death. Without arguing about the details of exactly what happened on the first Easter morning, if nothing happened, then the beast retains the power of death.

The resurrection does not remove all risk. One still must accept its truth on faith. Nor does Jesus' resurrection logically prove there will be life after death for all his followers. Personal resurrection is also a matter of faith. The Lamb's people continue to face the death of the body (what Revelation calls "the first death"), and it remains frightening and painful. The final destruction of death is the last battle; it will signal the final defeat of the beast and will inaugurate the new creation (Rev. 20:14; 21:1; also I Cor. 15:24-26). But if there were no hope of life beyond the grave, then the cost of living with integrity would go up a lot. The resurrection is crucial for affirming that Jesus is Lord and has disarmed the powers that rule by threat of death. Through the resurrection we know that nothing—not powers, not principalities, not death—can separate us from the love of God that we know in Christ Jesus.

The image of the Lamb is primarily an image of the crucified Messiah. That the Lamb is worshiped in heaven (ch. 5) and appears on earth with his followers (ch. 14) broadens the symbol to include the resurrection. However, the primary way John develops the theme of the conquest of death is through the special place he grants the martyrs and those

CHAPTER 6

who have died in their faith. The martyrs are safely kept under the heavenly altar until the restoration of creation (6:9-11). Those who have died in their faith are before the throne of God, where they no longer hunger or thirst, and God wipes all tears from their eyes (7:13-17). The martyrs will be raised first and will rule with Christ for a thousand years (20:1-6). John's message includes what was already an accepted apocalyptic theme of life after death for the righteous, with particular honors for those who give their lives for their faith.

There is a mirror side of death that the beast also uses to control us, the human desire to find immortality. Deep within each of us is the desire to be remembered forever. If we could only be a Caesar and have great monuments built to immortalize us; if we could build a Rockefeller Center in our name. If we could only be the president of a great corporation, then perhaps our name might be associated with the corporate identity like Ford or Edsel; after all, corporations do not die. Then we would be remembered. Using our desire for immortality, the beast encourages us to believe that by climbing to the top of the pyramid we become one of the great "immortals."

To affirm that a lonely, abandoned, carpenter's son—who was arrested with little resistance, convicted, and crucified—is God's Messiah destroys this mirror side of death's rule. True greatness lies not in being head of a giant corporation and getting the world to serve you, but in loving service to others. True greatness lies in the ability to care for others to the point of self-sacrifice. The declaration that Jesus of Nazareth is the Messiah turns the world's values upside down. To believe in Jesus is to affirm that sacrificial, servant love is the only way for true life and true greatness. To know that Jesus is Lord is to reject the power of death, to reject coercion by the fear of death, and to reject the attraction of a false immortality.

Jesus did more than simply disarm the principalities and powers. Through the crucifixion, God "made a public example of them" by his triumph (Col. 2:15). The crucifixion reveals the seductive and blasphemous nature of the powers. The people who killed Jesus were not heinous, vicious, plotting, or crafty dregs of humanity. The religious leaders desired to preserve religious institutions and their own prestige. Pilate was a small-time politician. The soldiers were just doing their job. The disciples were just afraid. The crowd was composed of ordinary people, frustrated and upset with life, venting their anger on Jesus.

These religious and political systems were possibly the best of the ancient world. The ethical monotheism of Judaism was the purest and most sophisticated of ancient religions, and the Roman Empire brought peace to the world and was renowned for its superb system of law. But the seductive spirit of the beast convinces leaders that they, like gods, are due worship and obedience as providers of the public good. It convinces the people to grant allegiance to those who would pervert justice and use the power of death for peace. The powers try to hide their fallen nature; they seek to present themselves as good, as servants of humanity and of God. In killing God's Messiah, the blasphemy is unveiled, the illusion unmasked, and the truth revealed: the powers are not acting as God's instruments, but as his adversaries (I Cor. 2:8). The crucifixion forever shows the true blasphemous character of their demands for allegiance.

The crucifixion also reveals the oppressive and destructive character of such power. By surrendering any attempt to control the situation through manipulation or coercion, by accepting undeserved suffering at the hands of the authorities, and by practicing the love for enemies that he taught, Jesus shows how demonic the beast's actions can be. There is no justification or rationalization for the abuse that Jesus suffered. "Now is the judgment of this world, now shall the ruler of this world be cast out; and I, when I am lifted up from the earth, will draw all men to myself" (John 12:31; also 16:11, 33). The prince of this world is judged because the quality of his action is clear. We see, we are repulsed, and we are drawn to follow Jesus.

Finally, we must remember that for the beast to be unable to control is for it to be defeated. The blasphemous character of the powers and principalities is their desire to force all to serve them by working for the institution's growth, image, and prosperity. When the beast is unable to force someone to serve its purposes, it is defeated. The confrontation with Christ was clearly no contest. He was not a slave to any power or institution or custom. Nor would he allow himself to be made a slave, even to save his own life. Jesus took the worst that could be handed out—false accusations, torture, spite, public ridicule, and finally the death penalty. But he returned love, even from the cross, "Father, forgive them....Woman, behold your son; behold your mother....This day you will be with me in paradise." There is no greater love than to suffer and to give one's life for others. The beast was unable to destroy or stop that love, and it was that love which triumphed. The cross remains to this day as the symbol of the supreme act of love, consciously and willingly accepted by an innocent man. No act of love this deep, this strong, this pure, this giving, can ever be seen as a defeat. The ruler was more controlled than controlling; the power was revealed as malevolent and impotent. The Lamb faced the beast and conquered. The victim is the victor.

Wherever the cross of Christ is truly preached, those who hear come to know that God has "delivered us from the dominion of darkness and transferred us to the kingdom of his Son" (Col. 1:13, also Eph. 2:1-3). In winning the battle, Christ equipped his followers to complete the victorious struggle: "We are not contending against flesh and blood, but against the principalities, against the powers, against the world rulers of this present darkness, against the spiritual hosts of wickedness in the heavenly places. Therefore take the whole armor of God, that you may be able to withstand in the evil day, and having done all, to stand" (Eph.6:11-13).

The Victory of the Lamb

Christ makes us free. To accept Jesus as Lord is to be freed from the power of death. In the cross this work is accomplished. The battle is won. The beast is disarmed, unmasked, unable to control the Lamb and his people. Thanks be to God who gives us the victory through our Lord Jesus Christ!

Lamb Power

The figure of the Lamb and the victory of Jesus on the cross present us with images of a different kind of power. We seek, from our twentieth-century world view, to understand how this other kind of power functions. One of the difficulties we have in thinking about power in terms other than linear is our lack of a label or phrase that might be used to encapsulate this concept. In the 60's we heard about "Black power" and "student power." More recently in the 80's the press popularized "people power" in the nonviolent revolutions in the Philippines, in Poland, and in Haiti. I would suggest that the image of the Lamb in Revelation presents us with a wonderfully appropriate slogan for the power known in and through Jesus Christ—Lamb power.

Lamb power is characterized by vulnerability rather than self-protection, by acceptance rather than control, by honesty and truth rather than propaganda and deceit, and by steadfastness rather than grappling after the quick solution. Allowing the person of Jesus to inform the image of the Lamb, we can say that such power is the capacity to endure even great suffering for the sake of others. We misunderstand, however, if we see this characterization as weakness and passivity. Great strength is required to stand firmly against evil or to love enough to suffer for another. The Lamb's power may seem passive, but it gets results. The consequences of the customary use of linear power are bondage, increased fear, and, at times, violence. The long-term result of exercising the power of the Lamb is healing, freedom, new life, community, and unity. The Lamb leads its people in an exodus toward freedom.

I had the good fortune to be taught this lesson by my wife, before we were married and before I ever read Revelation or thought about the Lamb. As a result of her teaching, today we have a good marriage and I have a fine guitar that I play rather poorly.

My wife's name is Jenny. We met at church camp. Few romances are more intense or more quickly forgotten than camp romances. However, we dated off and on while I was in college and in seminary. Since I was in college about a thousand miles from where she attended school and since our homes were about five hundred miles apart, the romance was more off than on.

When I graduated from seminary in New York, I returned to Tennessee and was assigned, much to my surprise, to Jenny's home church. I was twenty-five years old, ordained, beginning work, and ready to be serious about marriage and family. Jenny came home that summer, and we soon picked up where we had left off. Only she was not so sure about me. By Thanksgiving, I knew what I wanted, so I asked her to marry me. She said, "No," and returned to school five hundred miles away. At Christmas I asked her again. This time she said, "No. I've applied to be an airline stewardess and been accepted. I go to flight school in March."

That was not what I had hoped to hear. But there was only one thing I could do. I had to say, and mean it, "If that is what you want, then I want that for you. I will do all I can to sup-port you in this decision." I still consider that one of the more difficult actions I have ever taken. Both her parents and my parents had been married on December 26, so we made a ten-tative agreement that if things worked out and we decided to get married, then we would be wed on our parents' anniver-saries the following Christmas.

Frankly, with Jenny getting ready to leave for flight school in a couple of months, that vague promise did not seem very hopeful. I decided, however, to stick by my desire for our mar-riage and my commitment to her freedom. But I needed something to do while she flew around the country and I waited. So I decided to learn to play the guitar. I knew something about guitars, as my brother played one very well. I spent several weeks visiting every pawn shop in Memphis looking for a good one at an inexpensive price, and I found an excellent Gibson for $125. We dated regularly in December, January and February. I did not say another word about getting married. I even toned down speaking of my feelings, as I knew she felt pressure from me. Just over a week before she was scheduled to leave for Atlanta, in February one night she turned to me and said, "I don't think I want to be a stewardess after all." We were married May 11, and I now have a very good Gibson guitar that I play poorly and no regrets.

I did not understand then, but that was Lamb power: loving, accepting and supporting the other's freedom, giving without demanding results. I tend to be an achiever, a doer, and frequently a dominator. Jenny by the grace of God refused to be dominated, and I, also by the grace of God, was able to love freely. That established the foundation of our relationship: we are independent people who cannot and must not try to control each other. When that forms the basis of our relationship, our marriage works well. I seek first to support Jenny in her life, and she offers support to me in mine. God was using this relationship to train me not to be the domineering, overbearing, male chauvinist that I tend to be—a lesson I fear I must often relearn.

How different this is from the way of the beast, in which the individual seeks to arrange the world to meet his or her needs. Had we followed the world's way, each would have tried to get the other to do his or her bidding. Using whatever control, influence, or powers of persuasion I had, I would have worked to get her to marry me. And she, seeking to protect her independence, would have resisted as strongly as possible. My victory would have been her loss, or, conversely, her victory would have been my loss. The way of the beast sets up a hierarchy of winners and losers, a "zero-sum" game.

Lamb Power

The way of the lamb is entirely different. When instead of seeking power over the other, one surrenders control and enters a mutual relationship where the outcome is unknown, there are two winners. Jenny would not be dominated and thereby deny her God-created value as a human being. But in the way she refused, she left me a choice. My acceptance of her desires, even though it meant the likely defeat of my hopes and aims, opened for her a new situation and a new choice. The result for us was a new relationship and new life. We both won.

Even if Jenny had left to fly and had not returned to marry, I would still have become a less dominating and manipulative person. If I had continued to demand and push, Jenny would have been personally stronger as a result of leaving. Clearly I prefer the way the story ended. But if there had been a different ending, we each would have grown in so far as we followed the way of the Lamb. The way of the Lamb is a "plus-sum" game. Lamb power leads to healing, growth, greater maturity, and new life.

The distinction between these two ways is an important distinction at all ages. I remember a rather minor incident told in a group of mothers and fathers who were meeting to become more effective parents. One mother's young son loved to walk right beside the lawn mower when his father was cutting the grass, so that the grass would shoot out on his bare feet. Both parents felt this was dangerous because of the possibility of rocks or other debris being thrown out by the mower and striking their son. But no matter how much they explained or how severely they punished their son, whenever Dad got the mower out, here came the boy, bare feet in the discharge of the mower.

In the group a new approach was suggested. The next Saturday morning before Dad began to mow, Mom took her son aside. "Bill, I know you enjoy walking beside the mower when Dad is mowing. The grass feels funny on your feet, doesn't it?"

"Yes."

CHAPTER 7

"And I know you enjoy being outside with Dad, too."

"Yes."

"Do you sometimes pretend that you are big, like Dad, and that you are really mowing the yard?"

"No, I just like to walk in the grass the mower is throwing out."

"It tickles your feet, doesn't it. It makes them feel good."

"And the cut grass tickles the bottoms of my feet. It makes me want to run and jump."

"It is fun, isn't it. But you know it is also dangerous, don't you?"

"Oh, Mom!"

"Well, we just want you to know that we care about you and don't want you to get hurt."

The boy left and went to his room for a few minutes. Just as Dad was getting the mower out, he came back into the kitchen. "Mom, the mower can be very dangerous, can't it? I mean, it can throw rocks or hit coke cans and throw that out with the grass, can't it? And if someone was walking beside the mower, the can would cut his foot, wouldn't it?"

"Yes, Bill. Mowers are dangerous."

"I really like to walk beside the mower, but I think today I'll sit on the porch and watch Dad."

And that was the end of the boy's desire to walk beside the mower. They never had to lecture or discipline him over that again. As long as he saw himself in competition with his parents, and as long as he saw them as persons seeking to impose their will on him, he fought back by refusing to obey. Once he knew he was understood, and once he was allowed to make a decision for himself, then he made a good decision and followed it. A win-lose situation became a win-win interchange.

The parent's temptation, of course, is to try mutual relationship as a more clever means of imposing his or her will on the child. But when we do try such manipulation, children do seem to perceive our intentions and refuse to cooperate. A parent must carefully weigh the level of danger before granting a child freedom to decide. Because the dangers become great in the teenage years, when the parent's ability to control is very limited, I believe our task as parents is to move as quickly as possible from imposing our will on our children toward encouraging responsible decision-making.

Within all our relationships we constantly must choose between the way of the Lamb and the way of the beast. Why we choose the way of the beast is one of those mysteries we label (if not explain) with the doctrine of the fall. The temptation is to achieve an easy, quick solution. Shouting does gain immediate attention. Forcefully imposing our will does get us what we want in the short run. Bribing and making bargains does accomplish our goals quickly and more easily than trusting the other person to use good judgment. But in the long run, dominating a relationship can only destroy the very relationship we desire.

Another story, which sums up very well these thoughts about intimate relationships, comes from the Jewish tradition of story-telling, a tradition that brings much insight to faith. A distraught father came into the rabbi's study and without taking time to make his usual polite greeting, or even to take a seat, began right away. "Rabbi, you've got to help me with my son, my eldest! He is giving up all the Jewish ways; he may soon leave our faith. He eats nonkosher food when he is away from home. He is dating a non-Jewish girl. He drinks like a Gentile, and he shows no respect for his parents or for any of our traditions. I feel I am going to lose my son unless I can do something soon to stop him. Please help me! What can I do?"

The rabbi was quiet for a moment, and then looking up at the concerned parent, said, "Love him more than ever."

This story is not saying that where there are real problems—like emotional dysfunction or drug or alcohol abuse—nothing should be done but the same old way of loving. Quite the contrary. When we love more than ever and there are true problems, we will seek help. This story is telling us that techniques and knowledge will not—alone—solve our human problems. In our relationships with our children, with our wives or husbands, with our friends and associates, and even with our enemies, the basic force that will bring healing and creative new possibilities is loving and caring. Even without knowledge and proper techniques, loving and caring brings healing; with them, dramatic changes are possible. But without the loving and caring, all the knowledge and all the help and all the techniques will never break through estrangement. To love and care means to let go of some old ways, old angers, old images, and to be vulnerable, seeking first the others' welfare and fulfillment, crying, risking, and venturing into the future.

Basically, Lamb power is the power of vulnerable but strong love to change the world. Where there is rigidity and hostility, vulnerable loving has power to bring freedom and openness. Where there is violence, it turns the other cheek. Where there is loneliness and despair, it cries and hugs and shares the sorrow. In all things, large and small, personal and political, the power of vulnerable love can bring healing and possibilities for new life. But we must let go of the desire to control. The healing and new life may come in ways we neither foresee nor desire. The exercise of such power involves a kind of death; we must surrender the urge to manipulate the outcome. Resurrection is not an unusual miracle; it is the way that the power of Christ works.

In our personal lives most of us have learned that listening to people is more powerful than yelling at them. We have learned that encouraging people to develop their own point of view is more productive than trying to get them always to agree with us. We see that rules do not bring closeness in a relationship, but trust may. In intimate relationships we have learned that patience, trust, and caring are more effective in the long run than manipulation, rules, and coercion. But we do not think of these actions as powerful; instead they seem like the abandonment of power and the submission of oneself to the mercy of another.

Because the act of giving oneself in selfless loving does make us feel powerless and vulnerable, we fail to recognize the dramatic difference between the power of the Lamb and powerlessness. Powerlessness is the experience of those who are defeated in their efforts to exert linear power and are unable to see any way other than resignation. Whether the struggle be a father with a teenage son, or a street person seeking food and shelter, or a political activist desiring a reduction in military expenditures, powerlessness is the experience of being unable to achieve a goal and finally giving up, a defeated person. Lamb power involves surrender, but surrender is entirely different from resignation. Resignation means ceasing to struggle because one is defeated. Resignation involves quitting and leads to despair, defeated by another's strength.

Surrender, on the other hand, is a positive act. It involves turning one's life and will over to God, giving oneself into the hands of another. Surrender involves abandoning the strategic use of force to achieve one's goals. It is based on acceptance of reality and the recognition that giving is the alternative that will lead to peace and wholeness. Surrendering, even to the cross, leads to change and new life. Sometimes resignation and surrender look alike, but the difference between them is the difference between death and life.

Fred is a salesman and a member of AA. He has been sober for about three years. The way he found sobriety began with three basic steps: 1) He admitted he was powerless over alcohol—that his life had become unmanageable. 2) He came to believe that a power greater than himself could restore him to sanity. 3) He made a decision to turn his will and his life over to the care of God as he understood him. The reader who is familiar with the twelve steps of AA recognizes these first three steps. Together they provide a brief but complete definition of what it means to surrender oneself in the battle against the destructive consequences of alcohol. Such a surrender is not resignation, and Fred's actions can help us understand this important difference.

Before Fred surrendered his life to his Higher Power, he spent most of his energy bouncing back and forth between two sets of behaviors. One set was governed by the desire to control; the other, by the feelings of defeat and resignation.

Probably most of his energy was spent in attempts to control his drinking and the behavior of the rest of the world. Above all else, Fred wished he could drink the way other folks do: to have one or two drinks, be relaxed, and enjoy an evening with friends. But though he promised himself to have no more than three, he always drank many more and frequently caused a scene. Once upon a time, people thought he was the life of the party; slowly they became embarrassed by his actions. So Fred stopped going to parties where people only had one or two drinks.

Fred needed to maintain his supply of alcohol and to have it available whenever he needed it. He feared waking up in the middle of the night and being unable to get back to sleep; he feared waking up in the morning feeling shaky and unable to function. He feared meeting strangers and having to talk with them without the lubricant of a little whiskey. As Fred perceived the world, alcohol was an important tool in his employment as a salesman. Drink promised him self-confidence, social ease, and admiration. For Fred alcohol was the universal medicine that enabled him to sleep, to calm the morning anxieties, and to reduce business and social stress. So he had bottles hidden away wherever he might need them.

Fred's desire to set up his own world where life seemed more manageable had two major obstacles: other people, and his fear that he might be an alcoholic. He learned to attack both of these problems with a unified strategy. He drank too much, he believed, not because he was addicted to alcohol but because his wife, his boss, and all the other people he had to deal with were always getting on his nerves. Learning to blame others for his failures greatly assisted Fred as he sought to deny that drinking was causing his problems. Should his boss criticize a report, Fred rationalized that he was being given too much work for the amount of time allowed. If his wife suggested that he could do better with a little less to drink, he responded that he would drink less if she would complain less. Fighting, anger, hostility, and constant resentment became normal components of most of Fred's relationships.

As Fred sought to control his drinking to conform to the world and to control the world to allow his drinking, Fred's wife sought to control Fred. She begged him to stop drinking. He would promise to stop and sometimes refrain for weeks, even months, but each promise ended with another drinking bout. She hunted for his hidden bottles, and when she found them, dumped the contents down the sink. Since she also had a job and since Fred always needed money, she had to be careful to keep her money from getting into his hands. But somehow Fred was able to get her credit card number, write a check on her account, or even take money from her purse. Slowly any joy or mutual support within their relationship was replaced by suspicion, criticism, and fighting.

The need to control explained only part of Fred's actions; the rest of his life was driven by resignation, depression and despair. Fred meant to keep his promises. He was a good man and a sincere person. He intended to refrain from getting drunk. And when each promise ended with failure, Fred felt guilt and defeat. Though he would never admit it, he knew he was in trouble. He knew he was hurting his wife, his child, his job performance, and his future. But he was unwilling to give up alcohol entirely and unable to stop drinking after the first one. He thought about suicide; he began to collect guns. But he was also fearful of death. Finally he resigned himself to doing nothing. He gave up, assuming that he would become a bum on the city streets and eventually die there.

His wife too felt the despair and defeat of living in a world out of control. She felt guilty, half-believing that she was the cause of Fred's unhappiness and his drinking. She felt inadequate because she was unable to do anything to control him or to change the situation. She was fearful about what their constant arguments were doing to their son, and afraid that some day Fred's temper would get the better of him and he would become violent. One night when he was home alone, he took one of his guns and shot holes in the living room wall. She left. Later she got a divorce, unable to tolerate the situation any longer. In her resignation she carried with her the fear, the anger, the hatred, the guilt and the despair that alcohol had brought to their lives. Perhaps that is part of the reason their son chose to live with his alcoholic father.

Alcoholism is an illness, a physical addiction. The only way Fred knew to combat his affliction was to try to control it. Promises, blame, arguments, days of sobriety, hiding, and lying resulted from his efforts. Slowly all his values and desires dissolved into his addiction. Slowly, ever so slowly, Fred, his wife, and his son all became enslaved by this cunning, baffling, and powerful disease.

The attempt to control the disease by individual will power is the spirituality of the beast. Nearly everyone encouraged Fred to control or to stop his drinking, but his attempts at control led mostly to failure and defeat with the accompanying feelings of guilt, anger, and despair. Because he could not accept that he was a failure but would not deny the spirituality of the beast, which looks down on alcoholics as weak, his only alternative was denial. Denial of truth (the primary function of the false prophet) became the touchstone in Fred's thinking and feeling and acting. Unable to control his drinking, Fred manipulated the world to provide a system of excuses for his drinking. As long as he sought to control the illness through the spirituality of the beast, he remained its victim.[57] The way of controlling was for Fred a way of death. Had there been no surrender to a greater power which could restore sanity, Fred would have died physically as well as emotionally and spiritually.

After his wife left, Fred found another woman to take her place. They had dated for about six months when she suggested forcefully that he get help with his drinking problem. She had been attending Al-Anon and counseled him to go to an AA meeting. Finally, very reluctantly, he went. There he heard the news of a different way. There he heard someone who had experienced what he was experiencing, who had failed as he had, who knew his anger and his guilt. But this person was happy, without alcohol, and he was looking forward to a bright future. There he learned that the way to a new life was not control, but surrender. Fred is still an alcoholic. But through the love of a friend, the acceptance of a caring community, and his own surrender of the desire to be in control, Fred has found a new and healing way to live with his illness.

If the common understanding of power involves setting goals and controlling events, then the understanding of power that frees from bondage and brings new life begins with accepting reality as it is, not as we would have it, and surrendering even the desire to control. This is a totally different understanding of power. It begins with a different kind of faith: faith that though our world is indeed unmanageable, there is a God who can bring us sanity and new life. Turning one's will and life over to God is a totally different kind of action from seeking to manage the world and the people in it. The results of this kind of faith and action can be seen in the healing of a life that was once broken. Just as the desire to control leads one on a journey toward self-destruction, so the act of acceptance and surrender also marks the beginning of a journey that involves self-examination, confession, humility, and the forgiveness and restoration of relationships wherever possible (AA Steps 4-11). Finally it results in a life of service and support of others (AA Step 12).

Acceptance of reality and surrender of life and will may seem passive, but they are positive steps that change lives. Acceptance is often experienced not as resignation, but as a kind of waking up. New possibilities open when one recognizes that life is unmanageable and stops trying to control everything and everybody. Turning one's life over to God, far from being passive, is an act of freedom, an act of opening up whereby one lets go of self-concern and begins to live each day as God directs. Surrender represents the change of allegiance from the way of the world to the will of God. Acceptance and surrender, waking up and opening up, express the power of the Lamb. The difference between resignation and surrender may seem subtle and slight when one is seeking to maintain control, but the difference is the difference between death and life.

It is one thing to affirm the power of servant love in personal relationships, and even in the struggle to overcome addiction, but can these lessons be applied to our business and political lives? Acceptance and surrender would appear to keep a person out of the process of social change. Does the concept of Lamb power really provide any help in facing racial oppression or political despotism?

I have focused on the personal aspects of this power of vulnerability because, as I stated in the preface, I am not a Central American peasant struggling to survive under the rule of a cruel dictator. I believe there is great danger in assuming that we know the right way for people living in such situations. Still, the question is important. If the Lamb cannot overcome the beast of a Hitler, a Somoza, or a Marcos, then we have succeeded only in establishing a new kind of escapism. Instead of heaven in the sky when we die, we would now escape into a dream of personal growth toward wholeness and peace, a personal salvation that watches the world crumble and the beast devour its victims.

Three pictures of resistance to oppressive powers quickly come to my mind: black demonstrators in Birmingham, Alabama turned back by water hoses, police dogs, and club-carrying police while Police Commissioner Conner watched; rows of nuns kneeling in the streets of Manila saying their rosaries as the tanks of Ferdinand Marcos rolled toward them; Gandhi's passive resistance campaign at the Dandi salt works in which follower after follower went to the gate, was beaten, and returned again to the gate to be beaten again. I had studied the life of Gandhi and read much of his writing, but that scene in the movie was for me a first realization that "turning the other cheek" was active, not passive—an act of power, not submission.

The nonviolent refusal to comply with evil is not cowardly surrender, Dr. Martin Luther King, Jr. wrote in 1958. Turning the other cheek and loving your enemy represent "a courageous confrontation of evil by the power of love, in the faith that it is better to be the recipient of violence than the inflicter of it, since the latter only multiplies the existence of violence and bitterness in the universe, while the former may develop a sense of shame in the opponent and bring about a transformation and change."[58]

Finding himself the spokesman of a movement he did not begin, sent to jail more than a dozen times, his brother's house and the motel where he stayed bombed in the night, King preached these words during the demonstrations aimed at integrating the stores in Birmingham in 1963, seven years after the bus boycott:

> We must say to our white brothers all over the South who try to keep us down: We will match your capacity to inflict suffering with our capacity to endure suffering. We will meet your physical force with soul force. Do to us what you will, and we will not hate you. And yet we cannot in all good conscience obey your evil laws, because noncooperation with evil is as much a moral obligation as is cooperation with good. Do to us what you will and we will still love you. Threaten our children and we will still love you....Say that we're too low, that we're too degraded, yet we will still love you. Bomb our homes and go by our churches early in the morning and bomb them if you please, and we will still love you. We will wear you down by our capacity to suffer. One day we shall win freedom, but not only for ourselves. We will so appeal

> to your heart and your conscience that we will win you in
> the process, and our victory will be a double victory.[59]

Under the leadership of Dr. King, the civil rights movement held onto its commitment to nonviolence. Firmly rooted in biblical faith, King's message focused on noncompliance with evil, on honoring the dignity of every human being—black and white, friend and enemy—and on acting out of freedom even though equal rights were denied by law. Other groups in the movement were not so grounded in the faith or in nonviolence. They saw demonstrations only as a means to certain ends; when they seemed ineffective in achieving the goals, then violence became the means.

No government in our age has more fully epitomized the spirit of oppressive and aggressive domination, of racism, cruelty and injustice, than that of Hitler's Third Reich. What happened in those countries where the beast of the swastika was opposed in ways other than violence? There are no examples of civil disobedience available to us. In Norway and Denmark, however, the leadership refused to be ruled by fear, and the effectiveness of their resistance is remarkable. The story of Denmark's opposition to Hitler offers some important insights.[60]

Denmark's army was almost nonexistent when Hitler turned and attacked this neutral country in 1940. Denmark was occupied in a matter of hours without military resistance. Then the conquerors began the process of taking over the local government, using fear and prejudice to make it serve the invader's purposes. But one man refused to cower in fear, and his example gave courage to the nation. Daily King Christian, the seventy-year-old ruler of Denmark, mounted his horse and rode through the streets to greet his people who filled the streets to see their beloved king. On one occasion he took down the German flag and replaced it with that of Denmark, an action clearly prohibited by the laws of the occupying forces. Fear would not rule in Denmark as long as Christian remained king.

In 1942, the German government ordered all Jews in Denmark to wear the star of David. The order was issued on a Friday. That night as the Jews gathered for their regular Sabbath observance, King Christian joined them in the synagogue. His stand was supported by the Lutheran bishop and clergy. The Jews were not to be isolated in Denmark. Given courage by one man's refusal to give in to fear, the people of Denmark refused to join in Europe's insane prejudice against the descendents of Abraham.

Denmark did not overthrow German rule through underground or nonviolent resistance. But in September, 1943, an anti-Nazi German shipping clerk learned of a German plan to round up all the Jews on the night of October 1. He informed the Danish leaders. When the raid came, 472 Jews were taken. All others were in hiding in Protestant churches, in Catholic cloisters, in homes of friends and strangers, in hotels and on farms. Subsequently these Jews were transported to the coast and smuggled across the straits of Ore Sound to neutral Sweden. The action of a very few people who faced fear with calmness and integrity prevented the rule of fear and saved the lives of over 7,500 human beings.

The power that Germany exercised in occupied countries was a result of the amount of control they were able to exert *and* the amount of power the occupied people believed they had. When the Danish leaders refused to cower before the invader's might, though the opposition seemed symbolic, they reduced the amount of power the occupiers had to the amount of control they were actually able to exert. Responding to power with fear gives victory to the oppressor. Such power always depends on fear.

The Good News proclaims that in the perfect love of God known through Christ, fear is cast out. We need fear no one, no power, no principality, nothing in heaven above or earth beneath, for nothing can separate us from God's love known

CHAPTER 7

in Christ Jesus. Dwelling in this perfect and fearless love, recognizing the true character of the spiritual realities in this world, we are free to stand firm against evil. Even our smallest actions, if done fearlessly, will add to the defeat of fear and the disarming of the oppressor. Every act matters. Fearful compliance empowers the beast; courageous action disarms it.

I believe nonviolent resistance is the basic and fundamental tool for opposing injustice. History teaches us that the suffering, death, and destruction resulting from armed revolution is always far greater than that resulting from civil disobedience.[61] When violence is used, even in opposition to brutal despotism, it becomes very difficult to prevent the spirit of oppression from gaining dominion.

The key to understanding the way of the Lamb, however, is not violence versus nonviolence, but vulnerability as opposed to coercion. Violence does not automatically make a group coercive, nor does nonviolence guarantee against it. While it is harder to impose one's will through passive resistance, it is certainly possible. Tears can be as manipulative as anger. Passive aggression is still aggression. Thus Gandhi distinguished between the "nonviolence of the weak," which seeks to destroy the opposition, and the "nonviolence of the strong" (satyagraha), which seeks the opponents' good by freeing them from vicious actions. The key word is "liberation." The beast seeks to control; the Lamb aims to free.

We miss the point if we think of the cross as a kind of creative and surprising strategy for getting one's way. Jesus accepted the cross not as a strategy, but as the only way to be faithful to the vision of a kingdom based on the servant love of God. The cross represents the abandonment of strategies to control the course of history.[62] The forsakenness of the cross is found precisely in the sacrifice of effectiveness to faithfulness. Suffering is not, within the Christian understanding, a tool to make people come around to our view point. The cross is not simply another way to win.

Lamb Power

Exercising the power of the Lamb means accepting the cross, abandoning coercion for faithfulness to servant love. If we are to follow the Lamb, we cannot remain safe and secure in the upper levels of the social pyramid, commanding justice but unwilling to risk suffering with and for others as a result of our stance. Vulnerability—the primary characteristic of Lamb power—includes by definition the possibility of suffering.

One of the fallacies of the U.S. social welfare system is the assumption that we can solve the problems of poverty and nonproductivity without a significant level of taxation and without a level of personal involvement that may become painful. When those who run the welfare agencies assume they can help without personal pain or material discomfort, they fill out forms. Their only vested interest is in having enough poor or elderly clients to keep them employed. When those who run the welfare programs get involved with their clients, then they hurt because of the despair of their friends; they give their own money to help; they get taken; they know frustration; they often burn out. Their primary concern becomes changing this society to allow greater dignity and opportunity, better health care and housing, more security and greater freedom for those on the bottom of the economic ladder. In their pain, frustration, and identification with the poor, they are aligned with the ultimate triumph of the Lamb. Do-gooders who assume we can effect change and bring peace without painful involvement are untrustworthy.

How unlike the common understanding of power is the power of the Lamb. To risk losing the one you love, to allow a child to make a decision about his own safety, to love a rebellious teenager, to admit defeat and go to an AA meeting, to put one's life on the line in opposition to injustice—these actions do not fit the popular picture of power. Nor do we experience them as powerful. It would be nice if vulnerable, sacrificial love *felt* more like power, or if the victory of the Lamb were so clear that living by this reality would not involve the risk of faith. Much evidence supports John's proclamation that the Lamb has defeated, is defeating, and will defeat the beast. Historically we know that a small group of faithful Christians faced lions, gladiators, and systematic persecution with valor, transforming the Roman Empire and through it the entire western world.[63] We see in our personal lives, in the lives of others, and in our society that the way of the Lamb brings power to transform and heal. Ultimately, however, the assurance that the Lamb is victorious does not depend on the gathering of evidence, but on whether the Christ is indeed the risen Lord. If Jesus is Lord, then he is the wisdom and the power of God. To accept Jesus as Lord is to proclaim that the power of the Crucified, the power of servant love, is the power of God, the strongest power in the universe. The meaning of history will be determined by the cross and not the sword, by the power to suffer for others and not by the power to inflict suffering on others.

In the first half of this book, I have described two ways of life. The way of the beast promises us control, comfort, wealth and security, but leads to conflict, loneliness, anxiety, destructive violence, and death. The way of the Lamb centers on vulnerable identification with the servant love of God and the suffering of all humanity. It leads through resurrection to growth, unity within oneself, community with others, new possibilities, peace, and life. Our common understandings of the world and of power are defined by the way of the beast. Even though we seek the goal of life as defined by the Lamb, we often use coercion and control—tools of the beast—and end up captives of fear, anger, and death. To exercise the power of the Lamb we must develop a new ability to see the world differently, a different set of goals, and a different motivation for our actions.

To See with New Eyes

The letters to the seven churches at the beginning of Revelation indicate that John understood what real churches are like, for these churches are not outstanding examples of love, commitment, and strength, but distinct, believable communities. The letters reveal the smallness, the weakness, the squabbling, and the complacency of these congregations. Ephesus has lost its initial enthusiasm and love. Smyrna is poor. Pergamum and Thyatira tolerate worldly teaching and immorality. In Sardis the faith has all but died. Philadelphia has little power. And Laodicea is so rich and prosperous it has become lukewarm about the faith.

We would expect John to write to small, harassed, divided congregations with a message encouraging them to hold on until Jesus returns and rewards them for their faith. But John surprises his readers. The conclusion of each letter promises that the churches are the conquerers if they "have ears to hear what the Spirit says." Once again John confounds us. Not only has the weakling Lamb defeated the ferocious beast, but John also tells us that the locus of power for the Lamb lies in congregations like these seven pitiful examples in Asia Minor.

Just as we do not naturally and immediately think of Jesus of Nazareth when we think of power, neither do we readily think of the local church as a locus of power. We do not normally look around the congregation of the church we attend on Sunday morning and say to ourselves with conviction, "Here is the power! Here is the community that will change the world. Here lies the force, the ability, the energy, and the might that God is using to restore a damaged creation." More typically, we might look at those who have gathered for wor-

CHAPTER 8

ship and think, "I wonder if the Joneses will get a divorce. Ms. Brown looks like she is having a difficult time handling her children alone. Why don't we have more men in church? Why don't we have more people committed to worshiping every Sunday? I hope I remembered to lock the door when I left the house." We may be aware that a particularly powerful business leader or politician who belongs to the church and attends frequently is away. Other VIPs belong but never attend. If we think at all about the power of the local congregation, we might think how much more powerful we could be if everyone were truly committed and active.

In proposing a lamb as a symbol of power and the local church as a means for conquest, Revelation challenges us to stretch not only our conception of power, but also our understanding of how power is exercised. To hear, understand, and act on John's message, we need to question our ordinary view of the world, to reevaluate our assumptions about power, and to develop some new images to interpret our perception. We must reconceive reality.

John's apocalyptic medium reinforces his message and assists in the task of reconceiving reality. Through the way he uses images, as well as through the structure of Revelation, John seeks to enable a transformation of the mind so that we may hear what the Spirit says to the churches and begin to exercise the power of Christ.

> I John, your brother, who share with you in Jesus the tribulation and the kingdom and the patient endurance...was in the Spirit on the Lord's day, and I heard behind me a loud voice like a trumpet saying, "Write what you see in a book and send it to the seven churches."

> Then I turned to see the voice that was speaking to me, and on turning I saw seven golden lampstands, and in the midst of the lampstands one like a son of man, clothed with a long robe and with a golden girdle round his breast...in his right hand he held seven stars, from his mouth issued a sharp two-edged sword, and his face was

like the sun shining in full strength. (Rev. 1:9a, 10, 11a,
12-13, 16)

From the first chapter to the final vision of the new
Jerusalem, Revelation is composed of a series of images cascad-
ing across the page, some dramatically, some briefly, creating a
collage of imaginative perception. The rational faculties cannot comprehend the kaleidoscope of passions and sounds. The
imagery is designed more to affect the emotions than to communicate a clear message to the intellect.

Revelation does not describe a rational world; it depicts a
dream world.[64] Where else save in dreams does the opening of
a scroll become so important that one would weep bitterly
when no one worthy to open it can be found? How can a
slaughtered lamb live, much less stand? We can intellectualize.
We can remind ourselves that the Lamb is a symbol of Christ
who died and was raised. Clearly that is true, but as a concept
it is lifeless and abstract. We need to suspend the analytical to
allow the intuitive, artistic, and feeling portions of our thinking to respond. In the dream world, one might discover the
living and the dead as one. In the dream world one might encounter a lion that on closer inspection turns out to be a lamb.
In dreams logical and physical consistency are suspended as
the mind contemplates a deeper vitality that transforms and
informs reality. Such is the world of Revelation. John, indeed,
makes clear that he is writing in the world of ecstatic vision—
the world of dreams. He was "in the Spirit."

But to anyone who has studied apocalyptic literature, it is
equally clear that the world of Revelation is not the world of
John's personal, subjective inspiration. The symbols, view-
point, and style are those of apocalyptic literature in general.
Many of the images are the stock images of apocalypse,
derived from the Old Testament, other Jewish apocalypses,
and the myths of Eastern, Greek, and Roman cultures. The
assumption about history and the coming kingdom seems to be
the standard assumption of Jewish apocalypse: As times get

worse, the time for the kingdom to arrive is getting closer. The structure of the book is meticulously designed, reflecting a love of the sacred number of seven.[65] Carefully spaced throughout the work are hymns and songs suitable for use in the liturgy of the Christian community.[66]

Revelation is not a purely subjective writing, nor is it an analytical, philosophical book. Rather, Revelation is a carefully composed literary work aimed at the emotional, intuitive, artistic side of human thinking.[67] Revelation is a work of art, a kind of poetry of images. One comes to understand art not through the intellect, but by loving the colors or the movement or the texture. Similarly the way to begin to understand Revelation is to allow the collage of images to engage the imagination. That the author's apparent expectation of the imminent return of Christ (possibly by the end of the first century) was incorrect does not disfigure the entire work any more than Paul's similar expectation destroys his theological insights. The images remain: of power and vulnerability, of corruption and beauty, of defeat and victory, of justice, hope, peace, and community. One can still feel the impact of these images when reading the work devotionally, allowing the words to bypass the intellect and relate directly to the heart and the emotions. Thousands of worshipers feel the joy of Christ's victory when in church they sing one of the many great hymns based on Revelation or canticles like "The Song of the Lamb" or "The Song of the Redeemed."

But art is not pure emotion. Beneath the forms and figures there is a structure and an intention that places the feelings in context, bringing new insight or a particular vision of life. To establish the context for understanding John's work, we turn now to those hints and clues that he gives us.

The most obvious hint is his identification of some of his symbols. The seven stars and lamps are the seven churches, the Lamb is Jesus Christ, the bowls of incense are the prayers of the people (5:8), the whore of Babylon is Rome, eating the scroll is the experience of receiving God's Word which compels prophecy (ch.10), and the rider on the white horse (Rev. 19:11, not 6:1) is Christ. In the symbols he identifies, John indicates that he is not writing about other-worldly things. He is writing about ordinary Christian congregations, about the government, and about receiving the Good News of Christ. Through this use of symbols and images to describe ordinary things, he invites us to see the mundane in new ways. The little, luke-warm, struggling congregation where we worship each Sunday, is it not truly a star in heaven? Could it be that the glittering, prosperous city with its bright lights and beautiful people is a vicious, seductive junkie growing fat off the labor of the poor?

The structure of the book also helps set the context for understanding this work. There are probably as many diagrams of the structure of Revelation as there are commentaries. No pattern is so clear that all can agree on John's form; instead, several different patterns are interwoven, producing a fascinating mosaic of forms and disguising the author's basic structure. Though most commentators have differing ideas about John's structure, two characteristics are identified by all. First, John recapitulates his story. Either he retells it several times, or he describes what is coming before he gets there and then looks back toward the beginning as he approaches the end.[68] Through this use of recapitulation, the author again seems to be asking us to look at reality one way and then again another way. He tells us to use one set of symbols to stretch our understanding, and then another set to cast a little different light on the subject.

The other agreed-upon structural characteristic is the author's tendency to interrupt the narrative with a kind of interlude. In the narrative of the seven seals, the action stops for a glimpse at the thousands of thousands of God's faithful servants on earth and in heaven (ch. 7). The narrative of the seven trumpets is interrupted by the eating of the scroll and the account of the two witnesses (10:1-11:13). Other interruptions are short exhortations or reminders (e.g., 14:12f). These interludes in the narrative serve to pull the reader back, away from involvement with warrior locusts and demonic cavalry, and to the task of applying these images to the concrete world. The author reminds us that he is talking about worshiping Christians struggling under oppressors. Don't get so involved in the images, he seems to say, that you forget the basic task, which is re-imaging reality.

Another clue the author gives is the context of his visions. "It was on the Lord's Day," the first day of the week, the day of Christian worship. The songs and hymns of worship carefully spread through the work support this setting. Over and over, the action is divided by scenes of worship—at times the worship is on earth and at times in heaven.[69] The climax of the book comes with the wedding feast of the Lamb, where those who have been faithful receive the "water of life." The day, the words, and the images together set the scene. The "real world" for the Book of Revelation is the world of liturgy, eucharist, and baptism, the world of the church as worshiping community.[70]

The clue that ties all this together is the way the author develops and uses his symbols. The Lion of Judah, the Messiah, is the slaughtered Lamb. The symbol of power and might is transformed into one of vulnerability and weakness. Conversely, the corrupt powers of this world are at times first presented as symbols of beauty and honor. The first of the "four horsemen" rides a white horse and wears a crown, going forth to conquer (6:2). Only later do we see the famine, destruction, and death that comes from conquest. When the trinitarian beast first appears (ch. 13), it is worshiped as an awesome power and is able to work miraculous signs. Only later (16:13) is it clear that what issues from its mouth are foul spirits like frogs. The harlot Babylon is described as "arrayed in purple and scarlet, and bedecked with gold and jewels and pearls, holding in her hand a golden cup" (17:4). But the cup is filled with abominations, and she is drunk on the blood of the saints.

To See with New Eyes

As John's symbols develop, they often reverse their first impression. This reversal reflects a reversal in the way of seeing the world. The Messiah we would expect to be the strong deliverer was unprotected and submitted himself to a shameful death. The powers of this world, which we hope to be glorious and beautiful and powerful, often turn out to be controlling, deceitful, manipulative, and destructive.

The message of Revelation centers on this reversal. In the world Christians are shunned, arrested, killed, beaten, and thrown into prison. But in the heavenly court where the true spiritual realities are seen clearly, there is rejoicing because Satan has been conquered "by the blood of the Lamb and by the word of their testimony, for they loved not their lives even unto death" (Rev. 12:11; also see 5:5, 5:9f, 11:15, 14:8, 15:2, 17:14). In the letters to the seven churches (chapters 2–3), those who can hear what the Spirit says know themselves to be conquerors even though they may appear weak, poor or oppressed. Jesus stands before Pilate, who in frustration says, "Will you not speak to me? Do you not know that I have power to release you, and power to crucify you?" (John 19:10) But the heavenly hosts bow down before the Lamb, saying, "Worthy is the Lamb who was slain, to receive power and wealth and wisdom and might and honor and glory and blessing!" (5:12)

The Good News according to Revelation is that reality is not as it appears to be. Through faith, personal reflection, and historical perspective, we can discern the possibility that the way of the Lamb is stronger and better than the way of the beast, but from day to day we do not exercise the intellectual distance that allows us to see it in terms of the truths of heaven. In daily life it appears that those who are discriminated against lose, that the poor are powerless, that lambs get eaten by wolves. Dictators too frequently seem to be the ones in power. Aggressive competition, the world teaches us, is the way to climb the ladder of success. Only now and then does the Christ-like person appear to be the victor. The average Christian simply does not appear as a heroic conqueror, but as an ordinary person trying to do what is right and exert a little influence on a small segment of society. To perceive the Good News we must learn to see the world in a new way.

John's purpose in Revelation is not to convince us to hold on, because Jesus is going to return soon; it is to enable us to see the world in light of the victory on Calvary. The medium of apocalypse supports the message. Through the imagery, through the structure, through the liturgy of hymn, lament, and song, Revelation forms a kind of therapy aimed at the creative and emotional side of our perception and designed to change our way of seeing things.[71] The "dream world" has a truth that changes our understanding of the "real" world. The mythical truth that Christ reigns can then become the basis for our perception of the world. With new eyes to see and with new ears to hear, we know that no matter how things look, the true power that will be victorious is the power of vulnerable, suffering, servant love. The first step toward empowerment with the power of the Lamb is learning to see things differently so that in our day-to-day living we can begin to see reality as it is, not as it appears.

The setting for Revelation is not the persecuted community as much as it is the worshiping community. And John implies something very special about the worshiping community. When we examine the liturgical material in relation to the narrative, we discover that the kingdom is realized in the hymns before it arrives in the narrative. The new song in the vision of the Lamb describes the believers as having been made a kingdom of priests to rule on earth (5:10). Later the worshipers in heaven declare that "the kingdom of the world has become the kingdom" of God and his Christ (11:15). In the act of worshiping, the Christian experiences the kingdom of God.[72] In the community centered in devotion to the One who sits upon the throne and to the Lamb, the worshiper experiences what it is like "when the dwelling of God is with

men. God will dwell with them, and they shall be his people"
(21:3).

In John's time and in our own day, worship is central in experiencing the kingdom and in empowering the people. As the
worshiper sees the majesty of God, the desire to be in charge
and take control is consumed by the vision of true greatness.
Before the One who is glorious, the paltry glories for which
people strive are seen in their true light. As worshipers gather
to break bread together, to share the cup of salvation, and to
sing the song of victory to the Lamb, they come to know their
true worth—each person is worth dying for. Each person is unconditionally loved and accepted by God, who gave his son for
our sake. Every person is of ultimate worth and importance on
the basis of their humanity alone. Before the throne of grace
no one can be valued simply in terms of where they stand on a
ladder of status or power. The ladder is exposed as a fraud. The
worshiper understands the unity of every person with every
other. Perhaps this sense of unity is underscored by John's self-
identification simply as "a servant of God" (1:1) and "a
brother" in the tribulation and the kingdom (1:9). The worshiping community is centered around God and focused on
relationships.

As John sees the churches he addresses in this apocalypse,
their virtues are their toil, their patient endurance, their love,
their steadfastness and faithfulness, their service, and even
their poverty. These characteristics which make them appear
humble and vulnerable are in fact attributes the Lamb uses to
empower its people to defeat the beast. The community with
little wealth, prestige, or political power is not susceptible to
manipulation based on its fear of the loss of clout. The community that honors poverty and endurance will not be taken
in by glittering wealth, while one valuing faithfulness and service is not likely to be seduced by promises of self-aggrandizement. Worshipers who have discovered that their true worth
lies in following the Lamb will not seek it through lording
over others. The community that has experienced eternal life

CHAPTER 8

will not be controlled by fear of death. The community centered in worship of God will not give allegiance to the idolatrous claims of the beast.

Within the worshiping fellowship the Christian discovers a taste of the kingdom, a true experience of community that transforms lives and turns the world upside down through the servant love of Christ. Through the liturgy, which may well have included the reading of apocalyptic prophecy like Revelation, the first-century believers' lives were decisively changed. No longer suffering helplessly at the hands of persecutors and detractors, they were empowered for the future. They came to comprehend that their faithful witness, their acceptance of suffering, would bring salvation and judgment to the world just as Jesus' suffering resulted in the overthrow of evil.[73]

A renewed perception is where we begin our search to understand the power of the Lamb. The need to change one's perception of the world is as necessary today as it was in the first century, and the role of worship is as central now as it was then.

When we look at the world, the mind is not a passive recipient of data. We do not perceive reality simply as it is. Rather the mind actively shapes the data it receives on the basis of certain presuppositions and interests. Recently I was driving a group of teenagers to a retreat. A sixteen-year-old who had just gotten a driver's permit sat in the front seat next to me and pointed out all the Mercedes, BMWs, and Saabs. To me all cars look pretty much alike, but a teenager who is concerned about status and about automobiles notices the differences. Perceptions are filtered through our personal interests and our presuppositions about life. Knowledge comes from the dialogue between the reality perceived and the mind's preconceptions. The knowledge and beliefs that emerge from this dialogue then form the preconceptions which filter our perception.[74] At the level of personal values, this process becomes even more complex and more deeply involved in our relationships and our history.

As long as most of our lives are formed by and through the contractual communities of the beast, the way of the world will also form the basis for our perception of reality. This perspective, which is largely unconscious, is the framework our mind uses to organize the reality it perceives. When our society encourages the idea that we are individuals in competition for a limited supply of goods and services, then we tend to see ourselves in competition with others and work hard at "getting ahead." We tend to perceive others as a potential threat to our position and prosperity. If most of the groups and organizations to which we belong understand that the way to solve problems is through controlling and managing all the factors involved, including the people, then we become so accustomed to this way of problem-solving that we become blind to any other approach.

For example, although antagonism between labor and management seems to be damaging American's ability to compete internationally, neither labor nor management seem able to consider alternative ways of cooperation. Recently the "Japanese model" has presented itself as a more effective way to run a business, but reform by both labor and management seems slow. The problem is not only the inertia of changing unions and management systems; the problem is also the inability of leadership to perceive alternative approaches. We are likely to greet any alternative with the conviction that such a method may work elsewhere, but not in our case.

Our society tells us our value lies in our productivity. Believing we understand the world, we do not raise questions about our value until retirement or some other crisis forces us to reconsider. We are blind to the alternative revealed by the crucified Messiah because we do not look to Christ as the incarnation of power. Among the most important powers of the beast are illusion, propaganda, and the economic system.

Our blindness, of course, does not result solely from the subterfuge of the culture, but from the alliance of our fallen nature with that of the powers and principalities. The beast promises self-esteem to those who compete successfully, economic security and material comfort to all who give it allegiance. Failing to comprehend love as the creative power of the universe is easier than perceiving that through love we always have power to bring new possibilities for healing. As long as we believe we are powerless and therefore not responsible, we may opt for comfortable complacency. How easily we ask the rhetorical question, "What can one person do?" and shrug our shoulder: "Nothing." Sacrificing personal comfort and security for others is something we usually prefer to avoid. We are blind to this alternative view of power not only because we are used to another kind of power, but also because believing ourselves to be helpless requires less effort.

Finally, part of our blindness results from the true difficulty of discerning, even when we conscientiously seek to understand, how to bring love effectively and powerfully into desperate situations. The victorious character of servant love is not blatantly obvious; the application of such love requires great wisdom and discernment. We must work hard if we are to have eyes to see and ears to hear what the Spirit says. Creativity, imagination, hard work, and careful study are required if we are to exercise Lamb power in this world. We have only begun when we stop shrugging our shoulders and start asking, How can the power of the Lamb be applied here?

The first step for appropriating the power of Christ in our lives is to learn to see the world differently. Our blindness is deeply ingrained, the result of the world's training in combination with our desire for comfort and reward, our laziness, and our fear. To see reality truly as it is requires conversion. Revelation points to the worshiping community as the place for developing this new style of perception. The church as gathered believers—singing hymns, breaking bread, and sharing in fellowship—is the place where God restores our sight.

Within the worshiping fellowship the Christian is to be healed of blindness and empowered for action.

Though the church as an institution is infected by the beast, by her very nature the Christian church is always out of step with this world. Even in the most prosperous churches, when the story is told of how true greatness was nailed to the cross by pious religion and good government, a tension arises between our view of the Christ and our view of the world. In most churches that tension is felt strongly; there is a deep realization that somehow our worship of the Lamb is ill at ease with our life in the world.

The church is a different kind of community from the communities of the world. Anyone is welcome to attend, and even in the most homogeneous of congregations the diversity is greater than in most groups in our society. At the altar in a church in Youngstown, New York, near Niagara Falls, the chief counsel for Occidental Chemical Company, which is blamed for much of the pollution at Love Canal and other toxic waste sites, kneels beside the chairman of an environmental group that has demonstrated at Occidental plants. The founder of an environmental advocacy group serves on the church board with a vice president of Union Carbide. That is a setting with possibility for growth and change.

The worshiping community does not have the capability to manage society, which is why we do not view the church as a locus of power. Though church leaders constantly seek ways of enforcing authority, only in its worst moments has the church been able to control its members. Instead it gathers to sing and pray and hear the stories of God's acting in human lives. To the world and to those who seek to change society, the church must seem somewhat irrelevant. But if John is correct, the worshiping community is the environment where we may gain the capacity to see unseen realities. In a society that is stagnating with bureaucratic controls, building prisons as a means of stopping crime, and burdening the future with enormous debt to build weapons it must never use, the group that

CHAPTER 8

spends two hours every week to gather, to share concerns, to seek to know the divine nature of reality, to share a simple meal of bread and wine, and to sing a few hymns can provide the foundation for a different way of changing our world.

At its best, within the worshiping fellowship the Christian experiences a recentering that begins to mend the brokenness that is part of our natural, fallen state. As we surrender our lives and wills to God, there is a loss of egoism, a destruction of the core of self-concern. Discovering a community of mutual support where a person not only survives but thrives through serving others, we no longer feel threatened and alone. Secure in the knowledge that nothing can separate us from the love of God in Christ Jesus, though still afraid, we are no longer controlled by fear of the loss of possessions, position, or even life. We remember the story of Jesus and rediscover our identity as children of God, as people who are worth dying for. True worship breaks the cycle: we no longer have to compensate for feelings of inadequacy by competing, or seek to reduce fear by increasing control. True worship results in transformed people who act out of genuine concern for others and for the will of God. To bow down in worship before the One who sits upon the throne and the Lamb is to become a new creation through the redeemed community. As our worship gives us a vision of God, the victory of Christ begins to inform our seeing, and we begin to perceive the weakness of the beast and the power of the Lamb. We begin to see the world as it is, not as it appears to be.

Coming Out Of Babylon

After this I saw another angel coming down from heaven,
having great authority; and the earth was made bright
with his splendor. And he called out with a mighty voice,

"Fallen, fallen is Babylon the great!
It has become a dwelling place of demons,
a haunt of every foul spirit, . . .
For all nations have drunk the wine of her impure
passion,
and the kings of the earth have committed fornication
with her,
and the merchants of the earth have grown rich with the
wealth of her wantonness."

Then I heard another voice from heaven saying,

"Come out of her, my people,
lest you take part in her sins,
lest you share in her plagues."(Rev. 18:1-2c,3-4)

Throughout Revelation John portrays two communities. There is the community of the followers of the
Lamb, who worship God, are members of the churches, will be
invited to the supper of the Lamb, and are part of the new
creation toward which world history is moving. And there are
those who have given their allegiance to the beast and live in
garish Babylon, prosper through economic and political deal-
ings, and will bring the destruction of the old order. Both are
spiritual realities known and incarnated as the struggling congregations of Asia Minor and the oppressive government of
Rome.
　　Babylon is the outward and visible manifestation of the
spirituality of dominion, personified in the beast. Babylon is

the high office where rulers and merchants compete for power and worldly glory. Her garb portrays wealth, luxury, and sophistication, which she uses to seduce people into the self-serving and temporary relationships of fornication. Pleasure, sensuality, and self-aggrandizement are among her major attractions. For her, people are commodities, like gold or cattle; they are means of wealth for merchants and rulers. Babylon seduces people into serving the beast. More than a city or a state, Babylon is the culture that beckons one to seek first one's own comfort, security, and prestige.

As the exiles were called out of the historical Babylon and as the Hebrew slaves were led out of Egypt by Moses, so John calls upon the followers of the Lamb to come out of the domain of the beast. As Revelation understands redemption, it is not primarily a matter of saving individual souls by converting them to believe in God. Redemption is liberation from bondage under the beast's domination and leads to a new order of rulers and priests who are free from the rule of death.[75] Christ by his death and resurrection leads us on a new exodus out of slavery, out of the oppressive city of Babylon. Jesus is a new Moses. Those who have "conquered the beast and its image and the number of its name, stand beside the sea...and sing the song of Moses, the servant of God, and the song of the Lamb" (15:2-4).[76]

In this understanding, Revelation stands in the mainstream of the New Testament.

> The Spirit of the Lord is upon me,
> because he has anointed me to preach
> good news to the poor.
> He has sent me to proclaim release to
> the captives
> and recovering of sight to the blind,
> to set at liberty those who are oppressed. (Lk. 4:18)

Jesus, in defining his ministry in his first sermon in Nazareth, embraced the vocation of bringing vision to those who could not see and liberation to those who were bound.

Jesus' teaching, his table fellowship with drunkards and sinners, and his confrontation with the religious and political rulers of his time illuminate the destructive realities of this world. Jesus died on the cross to bring freedom, not to help people accept their imprisonment. The Gospel offers liberation from the powers that enslave. But the Good News does not force a person to accept freedom; like those who responded to the first Moses, one must choose to leave the security of Egypt to be free. In Revelation John gives us images that can help us apply that liberation to our own lives and our own communities.

In many churches salvation too often seems to be understood largely in individual and pastoral terms. Faith becomes primarily a means of relieving guilt, resolving problems of personal identity, and coping with grief in the face of death. Prayer and meditation may be used as techniques to help individuals avoid the medical consequences of too much stress. Such an approach is not untrue to our faith, but it is out of balance. In practice it may result in clergy helping prosperous parishioners feel good about personal losses and problems while doing nothing to challenge unjust structures of society. Such an imbalance merely acts to reinforce the status quo.

The scriptural understanding of salvation includes spiritual healing and affirms that God's love extends beyond death, but it also includes deliverance from bondage as a central theme. The result of being in right relationship with God, of having guilt relieved and brokenness healed, is restored vision to see our bondage and power to be freed from our enslavement. In responding to the growing sense of powerlessness among the faithful, we must recapture the understanding of salvation as liberation.

Repeatedly Revelation makes clear that a person cannot be a follower of both the Lamb and the beast. One bears either the mark of the beast or the name of the Lamb. The desire to live in prosperous Babylon even while we desire to be good Christian folk leads us to compromise our faith to the point

CHAPTER 9

that we become blind and impotent. To gain the power to bring change, we must be free from the domination of the beast. Lamb power can free us; it will make us conquerors. But we must come out of Babylon.

What does it mean to "come out of Babylon"? The complex system of ladders which make up relationships in the pyramid of power all have one thing in common: to climb a ladder places one in competition with others. Whatever the desired goal—be it becoming president of a company, joining a country club, or gaining a promotion at work—some who pursue the goal will win, some will lose and never again compete, and some, by remaining in a competitive position even though they did not win this time, will draw. The only options in competition are win, lose, or tie. To come out of Babylon means to let go of that need to compete. To discover the kingdom of God, one must find a new way of relating to others.

Bob and Jennifer had been married eight years. They had three children; the oldest was six years old. With the birth of their second child, the stress on their relationship had increased. Individually they came and talked with me. Each said the same thing: We are not happy, we get along all right, but we don't talk much any more and we don't enjoy each other. Their marriage was becoming a noncommunicative, joint rooming arrangement, and they wanted something more.

After several meetings I became aware that they very skillfully handled their disagreements so neither one would win. Bob and Jennifer clearly loved each other. They were intelligent and caring human beings. Out of their kindness for one another and out of their desire for a good marriage, they had developed the skill of ending all of their arguments in a draw. Bob was an excellent athlete. Perhaps his skill in competition helped him instinctively know that intimacy would be destroyed by winning arguments.

I remember the conflict that helped us find the key to what was wrong. Bob wanted to go to the football game Saturday afternoon but knew that Jennifer wanted him to "be home with the family." She suspected that he was planning to go to the game and leave her at home, again, with the children. He would leave for the game before lunch and not get back until dinner time. Then some of his friends would come over, and they would rehash every play that evening. The ground work was laid for a win-lose conflict.

On Thursday afternoon, Bob came home early. "How about a movie tonight?" Jennifer was dying to get out of the house. "Wonderful!" she said. "I'll get a sitter."

As they were going out the door, Bob said, "By the way, I would like to go to the game Saturday afternoon. Jim has an extra ticket."

Jennifer stopped. The movie was a bribe. But she wanted to go out. And she wanted to have a nice evening, not a fight. To object and argue would ruin the evening. "Sure, why not." Bob won.

But on Friday, Jennifer was angry. She had been set up, bribed, at a time when she could not respond honestly. She phoned Bob at work to ask him to pick up some diapers on his way home. Then she exploded: How could he set her up like that? He knew she wanted him home Saturday. The kids were going to grow up without knowing their father. Why didn't he just send his check home and stay at Jim's house all the time! Then he could watch all the sports he wanted.

On the phone at work, Bob could not respond. He said they'd talk when he got home. When he got home, he said he wouldn't go to the game. Jennifer won.

But when he tried to phone Jim, no one was home. He remembered Jim was out of town and would not be back until just before the game. He sat, watching television, brooding. Finally, Jennifer told him it would be better for him to go to the game than to sit around the house moping all day. Bob said, "Thanks." He had won after all.

Saturday morning came. Instinctively Bob knew he had won, and that his victory would cost him. "Jennifer, why don't

CHAPTER 9

I take care of the kids this morning. It will give me time to be with them and will give you a chance to get out of the house." She had not planned to go shopping. There was not time to go shopping. She did not particularly want to go shopping. But she needed to pick up a few things, so she said, "Thanks," and went shopping because his offer was a peace offering. In accepting it she knew they had tied.

But it was a tie, not a resolution. Her permission for his going to the game was not a gift, nor was his willingness to care for the children. Both ended the matter with feelings of resentment. The emotions were set for the next round.

Such was the pattern of their arguments. The conflict would continue until they were able to end it in a tie. I stand in awe of Bob and Jennifer. Within a destructive system of win-lose competition, they had developed a way to keep things from getting out of hand. Given more time, perhaps they would have learned to repress their desire for emotional intimacy and have developed sets of rules and compromises to prevent arguments. Then they would have joined the ranks of marriages in which commitment provides a bond, but sharing of emotions rarely occurs. Fortunately they saw what was coming and sought a change.

Jennifer and Bob were caught in the win-lose game. Nurtured by a culture of individualism and competition, they could see no other way to relate to each other. They knew they were unhappy, but they did not know why or what to do about it. To find another way, they had to let go of the spirituality of control and dominion; they had to be freed from the win-lose-draw system. They had to come out of Babylon. They found it very difficult, for after eight years they had become very skillful in their win-lose-tie relationship. They were not skillful at sharing feelings just for the sake of understanding each other, nor at listening to each other with empathy or interest. There were very few things they enjoyed doing together, so they needed to develop some new interests.

Coming out of Babylon

To "come out of Babylon" means to recognize that personal worth does not depend on winning. Winning and losing are both frauds. There is a better way: a way of listening to the other, not out of curiosity or for the sake of gaining power, but in reverence, rejoicing, and wonder; a way of gratitude that gives thanks for what the other gives without feeling under obligation; a way of rejoicing in the successes of the other and satisfaction over all the talents that makes the other great and glorious. Today Jennifer and Bob are learning. They are on an exodus journey and are discovering an exciting paradox: each is happiest and each is most free when each seeks first to respond to the other.

On the personal level, liberation means walking away from that desire each of us has to win, to be in charge, to have the status of jurisdiction. What does it mean on a corporate level? When Babylon begins to crush and dehumanize people in our society, how can we find liberation?

In the early 1980's this country experienced the most severe recession since the Great Depression of the 1930's.[77] The national unemployment rate rose to 10.8%. This recession was unique, however, in that the brunt of the job losses was borne by a single class of workers, those employed in the production lines of heavy industry. Our entire economy was in a precarious position, but the impact was most severe on those who had been employed regularly since their teens, worked hard all their lives, and had looked down on people who accepted welfare and public assistance.

As a pastor I served a congregation in which a tenth of our working families were receiving unemployment benefits. Our congregation was more fortunate than the Valley Station-Pleasure Ridge Park area as a whole, where the unemployment rate reached over 20%. One out of every five workers did not have a job and did not know when or where they would go back to work. Anyone who did not live in a working class community in this period will have a difficult time grasping

CHAPTER 9

the level of stress, anguish, frustration, and despair which gripped our neighborhoods.

The social structures that we looked to for security and for employment were unresponsive. The unions, which were under attack by government and industry, provided little support. Though workers in heavy industry had helped elect Ronald Reagan, little aid and no new programs were forthcoming from the White House. Federal economic policy seemed to be hurting rather than helping. Private employment agencies, which help workers with specialized skills who have the potential for payment of reasonably large fees, were of no use to blue-collar workers. The only employment assistance available was from the over-burdened and inefficient state agency located fifteen miles away in the downtown area. The state unemployment system may have been set up initially to help people find work, but by 1980 the system existed to provide income for laid-off industrial workers until the company called them back to work. Through the years the system had become the servant of industry, acting to provide an adequate supply of workers for industrial production. The workers were willing participants in this system, which only became destructive when plant closings replaced layoffs. When real unemployment came, the workers had been trained to expect others to provide assistance, and feelings of hopelessness overpowered them.

We formed an organization to provide a support community for the unemployed. Composed of a couple of members from my congregation, myself, representatives from two or three other congregations, concerned persons from the newly opened community college, and two or three other community leaders, we offered seminars on how to live on less income. We tried workshops on stress. We offered free breakfasts for job hunters as an inducement to meet to provide mutual support and to share job leads. Very few came to any of these programs. Getting depressed people together to talk about how depressed they are is depressing, not helpful.

Finally we held a seminar on "How to find a job." The response was overwhelming, and the space we had reserved was too small for everyone who wanted to come. After a year and a half of work, we finally grasped the obvious: people wanted help, not sympathy. Finding a job is a skill that must be learned, and the working people of our community did not know *how* to find a job. So our group accepted the task of teaching job-finding skills and incorporated under the name "Get That Job, Inc."

We hired a program director and fund-raiser. Through hard work, research, and the good fortune of having Bernard Haldane in Louisville at the time, we developed a program consisting of a one-week training seminar based on Haldane's ideas and approaches.[78] By trial and error we arrived at a position that has since become axiomatic in my theology: we learned to see the world from the point of view of divine economy rather than from the world's way of viewing economic life.

In first-year economics courses one learns that the availability of resources for goods and services is scarce and an economic system is the means that a social order uses to apportion the scarce resources among its competing members. The world bases its economic systems on this premise of scarcity: we are all in competition for a limited amount of goods and services. The economics of scarcity is the economics of Babylon, the economics that forms our vision of the world.

The economics of scarcity states that if I have something, then another person cannot have it. In terms of the unemployed, this view becomes translated as: there are very few jobs available. I need a job. No one is going to give up a job for me. I hope I can get one, but experience shows me I need "connections" or luck. I don't know how I can survive after unemployment runs out. Unable to find a job, unsuccessful applicants evaluate themselves as useless and worthless. As long as the focus remained on the scarcity of jobs, despair was the inevitable result, and the despair further inhibited the job seekers. We needed to find a different way; we needed to come out of Babylon.

Jesus told a parable about economics. It is such a strange parable that few people understand it to be about economics; most people give it a "spiritual" interpretation. A man went out to hire laborers for his vineyard. He hired some early in the morning, more at 9:00, more at noon, more at 3:00 and even some more at 5:00 in the afternoon. At the end of the day, he paid them all a full day's wage (Matt. 20:1-15). I believe this parable describes the difference between the human economies and the divine economy. The economies of this world, beginning with the premise of scarcity, say that you only get what you earn. The divine economy begins with the opposite premise, that this is a world of abundance; everything we have is a gift.[79] Thus the laborers in the vineyard do not earn what they receive; they are all given gifts, generous gifts. The householder sums up the parable, "I choose to give to this one as I give to you....Do you begrudge my generosity?"

The divine economy works a different way. God the creator has given each of his children an abundance of gifts. Our task is to know our gifts and to offer them in service to others. Through "Get That Job" we learned to put this theological insight to practical use. The first two days of the seminar were spent in group work, helping the participants identify their gifts and skills. An unemployed boiler-maker had always enjoyed teaching church school classes and was a counselor to many because of his wise advice. One of the air traffic controllers who was fired after striking in 1980 came to our seminar after two years of unsuccessful job hunting. He had an abundance of skill in managing "in-put" and "out-put" of all kinds. An unemployed secretary had previously, on her own, arranged trips for others to the Philippines, to Hawaii, and to various American cities. Her skill of making arrangements and in managing people had gone unnoticed. One can hardly imagine the excitement that fills a room when gifts and employable skills are being discovered among those who two days before felt worthless and dejected. By Wednesday the spirit of gloom and doom was lifted. Participants in the seminar began to smile, to speak with confidence and authority, and to walk with a sense of pride. The spiritual change was physically discernible.

Then we had to take the theology of the divine economy from the seminar room into the market place. Résumés were written that emphasized generalized skills and talents rather than job history, which only consisted of one or two jobs for which there was no longer any market. A networking process was developed that always began with the statement, "I do not expect you to have a job for me, but I would like you to look over this resume." The conversation that followed normally consisted of suggestions of all kinds of employment opportunities that existed for someone who had the skills listed. Contacts and specific names often followed. The emphasis had been taken off the one thing the friend or manager could not do—provide a job—and placed on the individual's skills and the abundant employment opportunities for those skills.

In the midst of 20% unemployment it seemed absurd to talk about abundance. In the midst of personal depression, to share successes seemed an artificial boosting of morale that would soon fall back to even lower levels. The idea that the Lamb can conquer the beast is hard to appropriate. But in practice, it worked. In three years 385 people completed the "Get That Job" seminar and within one month 74% of them had jobs. Almost none came to us before their unemployment payments were about to run out; they had all been looking for a job for almost a year. Three new successful businesses were started. An additional 1,200 people were helped in other capacities. While many of the jobs did not pay as well as the old industrial jobs, some paid more. When people are using well-developed and motivated skills, they will do a better job and their services are worth more. One man moved from a job paying $13,000 a year to a salary of $20,000 and a company car.

CHAPTER 9

The boiler-maker got a grant to attend college to get a degree in teaching. The fired air traffic controller is now a manager in a major trucking shipping department, with a salary commensurate with his old job and a lot less stress. The secretary got another secretarial job, but with higher pay, more responsibilities, and less stenographic duties.

We came to understand that what we were teaching was not a new technique. Those who saw this as a clever way to get a job were never as successful as those who truly began to see the abundance of their own gifts and skills and to discover a new sense of personal worth. We were not teaching a procedure; we were opening people's eyes to see a reality that previously they could not see. By the end of the week we generally knew who would be successful, for it was obvious whose eyes were truly opened and who was still angrily wanting someone to give them a job.

For the unemployed, as for Bob and Jennifer, the system that had promised security, prosperity, and happiness became destructive. Bob and Jennifer felt caught in a pattern of actions and responses they could not control. When they recognized their foolish competition, when they recognized their worth did not depend on winning, they could then see the beastly domination of their culture. The unemployed also saw themselves in bondage. Unable to find a job and feeling like failures, their depression added to their difficulties in searching for a job. But the experience of bondage alone did not bring freedom. In both examples they tried to solve their problems with the solutions of Babylon. Bob and Jennifer learned to end arguments in a tie; the unemployed learned to go weekly to the unemployment service, fill out forms, and blame others for their plight. To discover freedom and new life, Bob and Jennifer had to come out of Babylon and discover a new way based on giving to and honoring one another; the unemployed had to come out of Babylon and discover a new way based on the divine economy of abundance.

Another insight emerged from our work with the unemployed. The job seekers played a supporting role in their victimization through their own blindness. They helped build the prison that bound them, the prison that prevented them from being the person God created each of them to be. The power of the beast comes from the alliance of our fallenness with the spirit of domination. All along they had the resources within themselves to find or even create a job, but they remained unemployed. Clearly they were allowing the domination of the system to destroy their worth as human beings.

But we must be very clear: the part that the unemployed played in their victimization was neither conscious nor intentional. The system that had always provided for them had also trained them to be dependent. All hope was placed on the state unemployment system and on the federal government's developing remedies that would restore jobs. Most employment services also do the work for the client and thus maintained a system of human dependence on an agency. The beast encourages dependence. Because of the seduction and illusions of the beast, they were unable to see the reality that could free them—their own gifts and talents. Generally they came to us hoping we could control and correct the beast, and provide a job for them. They did not expect to be taught how to find a job for themselves.

Since through ignorance the victim normally participates in building prisons, the first step in liberation is to become aware of that participation and to stop cooperating with the beast. Then with a new vision of a different kind of economy, the unemployed discovered within themselves resources for a new job. Given eyes to see a different way and the support to let go of the economics of scarcity, they were liberated to discover human dignity.

God is a generous giver and selfless lover. There is truth in the premise that resources are limited, but God's world also includes abundance that increases through giving as well as scarce resources that dwindle through hoarding. The world teaches us that the way to security and freedom is to get things and to build more and bigger barns in which to keep them. It teaches that the more money we have and the more power we have, the more secure we will be. But in reality, security cannot be bought. Security and freedom are more likely to be found through a change of vision than through the pursuit of money and power. The divine economy refutes the idea that possessions will make one free; freedom comes through giving them away. The world encourages consumption on the premise that one can never have enough; God's economy says, "Be not anxious, there is more than enough." The world says work is a means to achieve identity; in the divine economy, work is one way we exercise our gifts and talents, serve one another, and receive payment for our efforts.

The first beatitude reads, "Blessed are the poor in spirit, for theirs is the kingdom of heaven." Poverty of spirit means freedom from wanting things.[80] It means being free from the bondage of basing our self-worth on our productivity and income. Being poor in spirit means being open to see the abundance of the divine economy.

Biblical faith is not primarily concerned about how much a person possesses, but about one's attitude toward possessions. Possessions tend to possess the owner (Matt. 6:19-21, Lk. 12:32-34). Material poverty, however, does not automatically make one poor in spirit. The poor can covet the power and security that seems to accompany wealth. All John's admonitions in his letters are against the subtle, corruptive influences of worldliness. All the churches except Philadelphia and Smyrna are urged to return to a more single-minded commitment and a purer separation from worldly glories. One can even hear in Babylon's boast, "A queen I sit, I am no widow, mourning I shall never see," an echo of the pride of the church of Laodicea, "I am rich, I have prospered, and I need nothing." Even in the poorest churches, the followers of the Lamb must continue to examine who is lord of their lives: the subtle and seductive power of death or the honest, sometimes painful, healing power of life.

One might assume that coming out of Babylon also means abandoning the economic and political processes, as the Essenes, a first-century Jewish apocalyptic community, believed. Certainly the Christian tradition has spawned a variety of sectarian movements that have sought to isolate themselves from the world. Those to whom Revelation was addressed did not figure in the political or economic spheres. However, coming out of Babylon means letting go of the spirit of domination and self-aggrandizement often incarnate in politics and business, not escaping from the world. Far from removing us from economic and political processes, the freedom that comes from this spiritual exodus impels us into working for economic and political reform.

To come out of Babylon is to embrace a kind of "downward mobility" toward a greater and greater identification with the poor and the outcast.[81] When we discover our personal value in terms of God's love for us, we necessarily recognize a fundamental equality of all people. The inferiority of the "small" and the superiority of the "great" both dissolve. For those who stand above us in or status, unconditional love means we freely accept them on the basis of their humanity and ignore our differences as unimportant. Free from false distinctions, we can relate as vulnerable, needy human beings; that is, unless they are overly impressed with their own importance.

For those who reside on a lower rung of the ladder, however, the situation is more complex. For the well-to-do to preach the unimportance of money to the poor is cynicism. How can we love those who lack the material and spiritual benefits we have, who are denied the power to attain them, and who are treated with less than human dignity, if we do not desire those things for them? Divisions of power and wealth and discrimination on the basis of race, sex, or age become an outrage. To love unconditionally brings a tendency toward solidarity with the outcast and the poor. To love only the well-to-do is to be in bondage to a false set of values. Downward mobility is the way of healthy relationships, of strong personal identity, and of true freedom.

Downward mobility is the way of Christ. "Let this mind be in you which was in Christ who did not count equality with God a thing to be grasped, but emptied himself, taking the form of a servant" (Phil. 2:5f). To share all one has, to resist consumption, to give away wealth and privilege, to accept being misunderstood, to welcome obscurity, to have no personal career goal save the kingdom, leads to an extraordinary degree of freedom and independence which forms the basis of the power of the Lamb.

What does it mean to "come out of Babylon"? It means to live a life no longer dominated by fear. It means discovering the extraordinary freedom of acting for God's will even in the face of acknowledged danger.

In this country a strong majority opposes the nuclear arms race. In 1980 a majority favored a verifiable mutual arms production freeze; in 1987 there was equal support for a test ban treaty. Why have we been unable to make significant progress in the reduction of these weapons? Part of the answer surely lies in the tactics opponents to the arms race have used to counter the arms build-up. Over and over one hears the opponents of nuclear arms describing the probability of nuclear war and the devastating results. Can we not see that using fear to oppose the beast is fighting on the beast's terms? We build bombs because of fear. Fear is our reason for having an overly-militarized economy and continuing to build weapons of mass destruction. Fear is the foundation for the plan to launch a "defensive" space system. Increasing people's fear plays into the hands of those who would have us strengthen the military. The more people fear, the more support there will be for those who claim to provide national security. As long as the battle is fought with the weapons of the beast, the beast will win. We must fight with hope, not fear; with a vision of world order, not of world destruction. We must use the weapons of the Lamb, not those of the beast.

"Fallen, fallen is Babylon the great!"

And the kings of the earth, who committed fornication and were wanton with her, will weep and wail over her when they see the smoke of her burning; they will stand far off, in fear and torment and say,

"Alas, alas, for the great city
that was clothed in fine linen, in purple and scarlet,
bedecked with gold, with jewels, and with pearls!
In one hour all this wealth has been laid waste."

And all shipmasters and seafaring men, sailors and all whose trade is on the sea, stood far off and cried out as they saw the smoke of her burning,

"What city was like the great city?
Alas, alas, for the great city
where all who had ships at sea grew rich by her wealth!
In one hour she has been laid waste."

"So shall Babylon the great city be thrown down with violence,
and shall be found no more;
   and the sound of harpers and minstrels
      of flute players and trumpeters, shall be heard in thee
no more;
   and a craftsman of any craft shall be found in thee no
more;
   and the light of a lamp shall shine in thee no more;
   and the voice of bridegroom and bride shall be heard in
thee no more
      for thy merchants were the great men of the earth,
      and all nations were deceived by thy sorcery.
   And in her was found the blood of prophets and of
saints,
      and of all who have been slain on earth."

"Rejoice over her, O heaven,
O saints and apostles and prophets,

for God has *imposed on her the judgment she passed on you!*"[82]

Is John too happy at the destruction of worldly greatness? Rejoice? Rejoice that the lights are out, that commerce and industry have stopped, that rulers and millionaires have been thrown down, and that there is no singing or music any more? Rejoice!? We protest.

Perhaps John does enjoy retribution a little too much. Perhaps a real hatred of merchants and rulers is showing through John's writing. After all, John was presumably in exile on Patmos. His congregations were poor and harassed. When life is lived under the domination of the powerful, when one is at the bottom of the pyramid of power, antagonism toward those above is a natural emotion. Perhaps John has given vent to his animosity.

Perhaps we ourselves identify a little too closely with those who buy and sell, with those who enjoy the luxury items and the excitement of city life, with those who are blind to the destructive side of our society. Perhaps we have seen so many pictures of starving children, wounded soldiers, and lonely people sleeping on the street that we have become numb to the suffering that goes unheeded in the midst of prosperity. Perhaps John takes more seriously than we do the exploitation of human beings by political, economic, and social systems. Nowhere else in Scripture (which generally is more tolerant of human social systems) is slavery seen as a sin deserving punishment. Perhaps we are offended by John's exultation over the fall of Babylon because we are trapped within her walls.

A careful reading of this entire passage makes it clear that vengeance and retribution are not at work so much as a simple collapse of a structure built on incorrect principles.[83] A primary feature of apocalyptic literature was the symbolic tracing of the rise and fall of nations. Within a tradition that focused on the collapse of principalities, there is an implicit understanding that the powers collapse under their own weight. Built on greed, the system will be destroyed by greed; built on domination, it will be eclipsed; built on exploitation, it will be overturned by the exploited. This insight is equally clear in any age, be the power economic or political. As we learned from the nineteenth century, unregulated capitalism with laissez-faire government does not lead to efficient allocation of resources, but to monopoly and, unless corrective measures are taken, to the collapse of the economic system. And as we painfully discovered in this country, to tolerate slavery may lead to civil war. On a smaller scale, the business that makes large profits by paying low wages has set itself up for labor problems and a racist government provides a seedbed for discontent.

> Render to her as she herself has rendered, and repay her double for her deeds; mix a double draught for her in the cup she mixed. As she glorified herself and played the wanton, so give her a like measure of torment and mourning. Since in her heart she says, "A queen I sit, I am no widow, mourning I shall never see." So shall her plagues come in a single day, pestilence and mourning and famine. (18:6-8a)

The pictures of Revelation are drawn in black and white. This provides strength to the images, but encourages the readers to see themselves and others as either righteous or wicked. A more theological reading of Revelation gives us a slightly different message. There are powers of love, justice and righteousness, and there are powers of greed, corruption and destruction. People give their obedience to one or the other. But that does not mean anyone gives total obedience all the time to the forces for evil or to the forces for good. Generally we human beings have a propensity to look out for "number one" while at the same time seeking to live moral lives. Situations are not clear cut. We live in the beast and the beast in us; we dwell in Christ and he in us. The war in human society is also fought in microcosm within our hearts. How can

CHAPTER 9

we rejoice in the destruction of Babylon when we have at least one foot in that kingdom? We can feel the pain in the lament over Babylon, but how can we celebrate when she provides for our comfort.

In this passage, the emotions are more complex than in other portions of Revelation. Though the hymn calls for rejoicing over the fall of Babylon, the words convey the pathos of a lament: "Alas, alas, for the great city that was clothed in fine linen, in purple and scarlet, bedecked with gold, with jewels, and with pearls! In one hour all this wealth has been laid waste. What city was like the great city? Alas, alas." There is sadness at the destruction of such wealth, but the greatest sadness is that the wealth was wasted in self-glorification. There is sadness that the kings and merchants and sailors have been thrown down, but the greater sadness is that they made their fortunes in slave trade, in selling luxury items while people starved, and in ignoring, even persecuting, those who proclaimed the truth of God. We can lament over the pain and the waste that are produced by Babylon, even if we find difficulty in feeling joy at its possible demise.

When I see the destruction the spirituality of the beast nearly caused Jennifer and Bob, when I think about the loneliness and destruction the break-up of their marriage would have caused them and their children, and when I think of the thousands of thousands of couples who, like Jennifer and Bob, are caught in Babylon, substituting routine for intimacy and outward success for inner growth, then I am able to rejoice in the idea that Babylon will crumble.

When I think of my friends who are under-employed, working in dull, uninteresting jobs at low pay, when I see a family lose their home because of long-term illness and no insurance, when I see the increasing numbers of homeless people on our streets and hear of those who find life so despairing that they willingly destroy their minds with drugs, then I hope for a new system based on caring for all people and on honoring and utilizing the abundance of human gifts.

Coming out of Babylon

When I stop and think about the great danger our world is in under the sword of nuclear threat, when I realize the arms race is fueled by fear and competitiveness, when I remember that my own prosperity is supported in part by military spending, then I know Babylon must fall.

To read this lament and to rejoice at the fall of Babylon may be for us a means of liberation. Babylon is the spiritual enticement for security other than God and prosperity that depends on others' poverty. Yes, we grieve, but if we can also rejoice, then we have begun an exodus out of that great city. Wealth builds a false sense of security that prevents people from seeing greed, cruelty, economic abuse, and injustice in their true light. Wealth encourages people and nations to "lord it over others" as if they were divine. Babylon is the great city of Mesopotamia; it is Rome; it is Washington and Moscow and New York and Beijing; it is the spiritual reality that encourages human beings to use one another in the pursuit of comfort and things; it is prosperity built on fornication. We will know the true joys of the new Jerusalem only when we have come out of the false prosperity and false security of Babylon.

The New Jerusalem

Then I saw a new heaven and a new earth; for the first earth had passed away, and the sea was no more. And I saw the holy city, new Jerusalem, coming down out of heaven from God, prepared as a bride adorned for her husband; and I heard a great voice from the throne saying, "Behold, the dwelling of God is with men. He will dwell with them and they shall be his people, and God himself will be with them; he will wipe away every tear from their eyes, and death shall be no more, neither shall there be mourning nor crying nor pain any more, for the former things have passed away."

And he who sat upon the throne said, "Behold, I make all things new." Also he said, "Write this, for these words are trustworthy and true." And he said to me, "It is done! I am the Alpha and the Omega, the beginning and the end. To the thirsty I will give water without price from the fountain of the water of life. He who conquers shall have this heritage, and I will be his God, and he shall be my son" (Rev. 21:1-7).

Broken pots are what archaeologists find when they dig in ancient ruins. In the early years of archaeology, the excavators searched for beautiful artifacts and often threw away the common pottery. Today we know the importance of pottery for dating each stratum of a dig and for indicating the size of the population and its cultural development. Wherever there were people, there were pots. Go to the Greek exhibit in the Metropolitan Museum in New York City. Here in rooms dedicated to the builders of magnificent temples, graceful statues, and impressive ships, here in exhibits devoted to the founders of philosophy and democracy, we find pots, rows and rows, shelves and shelves of pots. Pottery is an image of the

The New Jerusalem

common life in the ancient world. Life was hard. Life was dull. Most of one's time was spent getting enough to eat, storing some food, preparing meals, eating, and taking care of children. Most people of the first century were among the anonymous millions who used and broke all those pots while pursuing those common tasks necessary for survival.

> Then he showed me the river of the water of life, bright as crystal, flowing from the throne of God and of the Lamb through the middle of the street of the city; also, on either side of the river, the tree of life with its twelve kinds of fruit, yielding its fruit each month; and the leaves of the tree were for the healing of the nations. There shall no more be anything accursed, but the throne of God and of the Lamb shall be in it, and his servants shall worship him; they shall see his face, and his name shall be on their foreheads. And night shall be no more; they need no light of lamp or sun, for the Lord God will be their light, and they shall reign for ever and ever. (Rev. 22:1-5)

Is it too hard for us to imagine that all those people, caught in the hard, dull routine of survival, would long for a time when life would be less difficult? How easy life would be if fruit ripened each month, water were plentiful, and the leaves of the trees would heal any wound!

The image of the new Jerusalem is the image of life as John's fellow Christians might have wished it: relief from the burdens of survival, gold and jewels everywhere, not just in the storerooms of the wealthy, light and sunshine. We easily understand how people whose lives were drab and dreary would dream about an easier, better life. One of the reasons for the popularity of apocalyptic literature must have been the mythic fantasies of journeys through time and heaven.[84] There is nothing drab about the scenes of heaven in Revelation or in other apocalyptic writings. In our own day, thos who love Revelation, Daniel and the other biblical apocalyptic writings are usually from a social sphere where life is marginal and routine. In apocalypse, supernatural fantasy combines with the wish for a better life in response to the needs of people whose lives are surrounded by bleakness.

The new creation does not seem to be a continuation of history, but beyond history, unconnected to the chain of human decisions, actions, and consequences. It appears to come down from God in his own time. The voice from the throne has announced that "the former things have passed away," that "it is done!" The first heaven and the first earth have passed away and the sea is no more. This does not sound like history. Does our journey through Revelation end with escapist hope in a heaven after death, or a future that is brought in by God when he is ready? In the final analysis, does Revelation teach anything beyond an opiate religion that tells people to submit to the suffering imposed by those in power?

> And I saw no temple in the city, for its temple is the Lord God the Almighty and the Lamb. And the city has no need of sun or moon to shine upon it, for the glory of God is its light, and its lamp is the Lamb. By its light shall the nations walk; and the kings of the earth shall bring their glory into it, and its gates shall never be shut by day—and there shall be no night there; they shall bring into it the glory and the honor of the nations. (Rev. 21:22-26)

Revelation may appear to conclude with an escapist vision of heaven, but much evidence suggests a different interpretation. We must remind ourselves of the nature of John's symbolism. His images are rich, multifaceted, and vivid, but they are not descriptions of anything conceivable outside of the dream world. Who can imagine a city wall that in modern measurements is 1,500 miles (yes, *miles*) high and only 200 feet thick? The description of the new Jerusalem shows us how much John enjoyed symbolism and how little he cared for engineering. Why is a wall even needed when the gates are left open all day and there is no night? John's imagery is designed to stimulate the imagination and affect one's feelings; it describes not material realities, but the spiritual realities that inform our present life.

As with other images in Revelation, the new Jerusalem has its roots in the writings of the prophets.[85] The entire passage is filled with allusions to visionary Old Testament descriptions of the restoration of Jerusalem. "Behold, I create new heavens and a new earth; and the former things shall not be remembered...I create Jerusalem a rejoicing and her people a joy...no more shall be heard in it the sound of weeping" (Is. 65:17-19). Isaiah's expectation was related to history; so too may we expect John's vision to intersect in some way with history.

Though this scene derives from the Old Testament, it develops and resolves many of the themes which have been running throughout the book.[86] The abundant use of the number 12 and and its square of 144 point toward understanding this passage as a description of the community of faith—Israel, composed of the twelve tribes, and the new Israel, founded on the witness of the twelve apostles. John's earlier descriptions of the worshiping community indicate that he is imagining the freedom, wholeness, richness, and harmony experienced in the Christian fellowship projected to the highest possible degree. In the worshiping community, one gets a taste of what union with God would be like; the new Jerusalem is a vision of the wedding feast, of full unity with God. What one experiences in worship is a hint of the end point toward which creation is moving.

Further, the new creation does not eliminate the secular by replacing it with the holy. It is a new heaven and a new earth; the holy and the secular become one. The Greek word "new" (*kainos*) connotes "renewed," or "new in kind," not "another."[87] God is making all things new; he is not making all new things.

"If any one is in Christ, he is a new creation; the old has passed away, behold, the new has come" (2 Cor. 5:17). The new Jerusalem is a description of a renewed creation; it is not all that different from Paul's description of the life in Christ in the eighth chapter of Romans. Just as an individual believer finds life dramatically changed and renewed by the relationship with God through Christ, so all of creation will be renewed when estrangement from God ends. Rephrasing the Old Testament description of the covenant relationship, John proclaims that the goal of life is to dwell in unity with God. The "new thing" about the new creation is the dwelling of God with his people: "They shall be his people, and God himself will be with them" (21:3).[88] John then gives us a dramatic image of what that kind of life would look and feel like. The new Jerusalem is a visual picture of Paul's theological description of life in Christ.

The central impact of the vision is an image of what life will be like when unity is restored between God and his people. Nowhere else in Revelation is the relationship between the Christian and God described with such intimacy. There is no temple in the city; there is no need for religion as a bridge to God, no need for a symbol of God's presence; God is in the midst of the city and his glory provides constant light. Ezekiel's description of the restored temple (for Jewish worship) in the restored Jerusalem (open to Gentiles) has become a single reality that reflects the unity of Gentile and Jew in the Christian faith. At last, in a fulfilled, covenanted relationship, the Bride (the church) has become the wife of the Lamb (21:9). Though John never refers to God as our Father, he does hear God declare that those who conquer will be his sons (21:7). John, who fainted upon beholding the glorified Christ (1:17) and could see only the glory of the One seated on the throne (4:2), tells us that God's servants shall actually see his face (22:4).

The new Jerusalem, that holy city, stands in direct contrast with Babylon, that great city. There is a remarkable similarity between this passage and a description in Herodotus of the historical city of Babylon. Babylon, according to Herodotus, was "foursquare" with each side measuring 120 furlongs, its walls were 50 royal cubits in width and 200 in height ("a royal cubit is larger by three fingers than the common cubit"), and its magnificence excelled "every other city that eyes have ever seen."[89] But the description of the new Jerusalem—its size, its buildings made out of gold, the jasper walls, the jewels on the foundation, and the gates of pearl—allow the dreamer to recognize that in comparison the queenly splendor of Babylon is merely gaudy.

Life in union with God contrasts dramatically with life under the dominion of the beast. When we discover our filiation with God, the rule of death and fear is broken. Death no longer has dominion; fear of pain is replaced by healing. Life flows like a river from the throne and the Lamb. In relationship with God, we lose the need to protect ourselves and control others. The gates to the city are opened, even to the nations and the kings of the earth who have been the enemies of the people of God.

In Revelation's picture of the kings entering the gates of the new Jerusalem, we finally find an image of forgiveness. God's purpose for all humanity, including the kings and merchants, is to bring them into the divine unity and to enable them to offer their gifts for the whole. "The treasures and wealth of the nations," the riches of the old creation that have been wasted in Babylon, are an important part of the new. The richness of gold and jewels throughout the city proclaim the divine economy of abundance that is part of life when unity between God and all people is restored.

The new Jerusalem may serve as a picture of life after death, but its image of unity is also a symbol of the goal for life in this world. We cannot know the thoughts, feelings, and motives of those early Christians who stood firmly in their faith in the face of hardship and discrimination. We know they believed Christ's resurrection pointed toward their personal resurrection. Perhaps they endured suffering in the belief that patience would earn them a place in heaven. Perhaps. But in the first twenty-one chapters of Revelation, "faithful witness" and "steadfast endurance" are the means for conquering the beast, for destroying adulterous Babylon, and for making visible the truth that the Lamb has conquered and the world has been

CHAPTER 10

returned to its dominion. Revelation holds that those early Christians suffered in order to change the world, not to get to heaven. The image of the holy city is the vision that gave birth to the future.

The new Jerusalem is a portrayal of life so wonderful that it provides motivation to come out of Babylon and begin the journey through the wilderness. Finding this abundant life is worth the risk of abandoning the security of slavery. As the Israelites who followed Moses carried with them the tent of the Presence, so the worshiping community of the church provides the journeying Christian with an experience of the glory that lies ahead. That glory motivates the worshiper to endure. The new Jerusalem expresses the dissatisfaction with the present, dull and oppressive life, but it is not escapism; it is the dream that transforms the present.

Jesus had a dream; he called it the kingdom of God. The kingdom is not a blueprint for creating the just and perfect society, nor is it an end that provides the basis for a system of ethical decisions. In his teaching about the kingdom, Jesus did not give us a manual describing how to create this reign of God. He taught that the kingdom is like a man who gives a banquet, a woman who finds a lost coin, a father who has two sons. He gave us images of the abundant, forgiving life, a vision of what life will be like when we are truly God's people and God himself is with us. The kingdom is a vision that has changed our world and will continue to change it.

Change begins with the dream. We need a vision of a better life and some hope of moving toward that dream if we are to risk the discomfort entailed in acting for change. Part of our sense of powerlessness is our inability to dream dreams and see visions of a future that is worth making sacrifices to reach. Lamb power is the power to dream God's dream even in the midst of Babylon.

> I say to you today, my friends, that in spite of the difficulties and frustrations of the moment, I still have a

dream. It is a dream deeply rooted in the American dream. I have a dream that one day this nation will rise up and live out the true meaning of its creed: "We hold these truths to be self-evident—that all men are created equal." I have a dream that one day on the red hills of Georgia the sons of former slaves and the sons of former slaveowners will be able to sit down together at the table of brotherhood. I have a dream that one day even the state of Mississippi, a desert state sweltering with the heat of injustice and oppression, will be transformed into an oasis of freedom and justice. I have a dream that my four little children will one day live in a nation where they will not be judged by the color of their skin but by the content of their character. I have a dream today. I have a dream that one day every valley shall be exalted, every hill and mountain shall be made low, the rough places will be made plains, and the crooked places will be made straight, and the glory of the Lord shall be revealed, and all flesh shall see it together.[90]

Even people who know little about Martin Luther King know this speech, which he gave at the march on Washington in 1963. That vision captured the hopes of many citizens of the United States and motivated them to change. That dream expressed dissatisfaction with the present, and became a vision of the future that continues to exert pressure for change. To dream of a time when God's intervention will lift up every valley and make low every mountain and hill is not escapism; it is an image that allows the blind to see a future worth working to achieve.

As we work for justice in our society, we need more than the pictures of injustice; we also need a vision that motivates us to work toward a new order. A basis for developing a new dream is the vision of the new Jerusalem and Jesus' dream of the kingdom of God. Central in that vision is the concept of the covenant community.

The new Jerusalem is the Bride of Christ. The redeemed community is based on the covenant relationship of commitment: for better for worse, for richer for poorer, in sickness and in health, to love and to cherish. In contrast to the temporary character of relationships in the contractual community, relationships in the renewed community are based on the steadfast love (*hesed, agape*) of God.

When John speaks of seeing the heavenly city, twice he speaks of it as "coming down" (1:2,10). Surely it did not come down twice, an event that would presuppose its removal from earth. The descent is not an event that happens once or twice, but is a permanent characteristic of the city.[91] In the midst of the powers and principalities, true community always appears to be coming down from heaven. The covenant community is not created by human beings but depends on the condescension of God: on Sinai, in the nation of Israel, in Jesus the Christ, and in the worshiping community. Community, as understood biblically and in Revelation, is initiated by God and renewed in the experience of worship.

God and the Lamb are at the center of the new Jerusalem. In our traditional understanding of God and of divine power, we see God (the most powerful) residing at the top of a pyramid of power. Yet the Incarnation and crucifixion clarify this picture: though God has the power, he chooses to exercise it from within the midst of his people, not from on high. Community does not result from everyone's obeying the law out of fear of God's judgment, but because of God's commitment to the covenant relationship—he will be our God and we his people.

All the themes of Revelation—in fact, the movement of the entire biblical story—come together in the experience of the covenant community: deliverance, identity, worship, and mission. The covenant community is inaugurated by God, who delivers us from diverse sorts of bondage to freedom. The unity of the community is founded on the covenant relationship, which gives us a new identity as children of God. We are reminded of our deliverance and identity through worship, which transcends the way of the world by focusing on the Transcendent One. Finally we share a common purpose. We are called as a community to participation in the redemptive action of God that gives meaning to history and is moving toward the restoration of creation within a universal order of peace.[92]

Ezekiel described his hoped-for Jerusalem as four-square (Ezek. 45:2, 48:20). Possibly in imitation of the cube-shaped Holy of Holies in Solomon's temple (1 Kings 6:20), John pushed his vision of the spiritual city beyond Ezekiel's by making its height as well as its length and breadth equal. The cube became a perfect symbol of divine presence, wholeness, and equality. In the community of the One who sits upon the throne and the Lamb, the symmetry of the cube connotes a cooperative social structure, an absence of differences in the distribution of wealth and power, and a common identity as children of God. This equality of the cube stands in contrast to the image of the pyramid we used earlier to describe the community of the beast.

Community is God's intention for his world. At the heart of the religious vision in both Judaism and Christianity is the conviction that "human freedom is ultimately meaningful and fulfilling only in a community of love, in which persons live primarily for others because of the power which God has given them for that purpose and because the conditions of their nature which he created can be fulfilled in no other way."[93] Community is "the primary aspiration of all history."[94] This understanding must begin to inform our vision for life in our country if we are to regain a dream powerful enough to motivate change.

Community—unity with God, peace within oneself, and fellowship with others—is not only the end we seek, it is also the means we have to pursue that end. The goal and the medium are one.

When Fred joined Alcoholics Anonymous, he found far more than rules to follow. He found a community where he was accepted and supported in his struggle with this disease. He found a welcome from people who truly understood his thoughts and feelings because they, too, had struggled with alcoholism. Doctor, plumber, homemaker, or teacher—all had shared in a common history. In that community he found a new identity, based not on his position or his performance but on his humanity. Fred's eyes were opened; he developed new understandings about his cunning, baffling, and powerful disease. He discovered that seeking to assert personal control, even over his drinking, was an act of pride that would lead to his loss of control over life. He learned through the experience of the community to take life one day at a time and to depend each day on the support of his group and his higher power. In and through AA Fred's eyes were opened, he received a new identity, he discovered the strength of mutual support, and he found the possibility of a new, sober life of healthy relationships. The community that is AA came first; the twelve steps followed. Take away the community and the steps would be largely ineffective.

When Sue came to the "Get That Job" seminar, she too found a new and liberating community. In that one-week seminar, where all who participated shared a common frustration and a common need, she found a new sense of personal worth based on her God-given gifts. Through the experience of the ongoing community she began to perceive the new economics of abundance, an understanding on which she could build a life. Without it, the skills and insights used by "Get That Job" become merely good advice that people find difficult to follow.

When someone comes to church, too often what is found is a group of people who do not know each other, who have no vision of the new Jerusalem, who are seeking to rise to the highest possible position in Babylon, who are fearful, and who seek answers from the clergy and the Bible to solve their problems and to provide personal support. No wonder clergy feel overworked and overburdened. There is great power in the Word and in the tradition, but remove it from a truly supportive community and the power is dramatically weakened.

John's seven congregations present us with the picture of a cohesive community that is a powerful formative and supportive group for anyone living in a hostile environment. In his letters we find that his primary concern is for unity and commitment. John wants a clear definition of membership; those who would confuse the faith with additional teachings (the Jezebels, Balaams, and Nicolaitans) must be excluded. He expects conformity to group norms. Prosperity increases one's vulnerability to the seduction of the beast and increases the personal cost of following the Lamb. Poverty is honored as an outward sign of the "downward mobility" of the spirituality of the Lamb. A high level of commitment is required when members face discrimination and abuse from neighbors and government, and John expects commitment even to death. The small size of the churches demands a high level of participation by members. Taken together, these factors form a community that can become a locus of power,[95] a community that is both a support to the individual and a formative environment. It enables members to see and to operate within the world from the spirituality of the new Jerusalem.

In a less hostile environment, we can and should decry John's classism and intolerance as falling short of Christian love. What may be necessary in the midst of hostility is often inappropriate in a more tolerant environment. However, we must look at our churches today: What kind of powerful, cohesive, worshiping communities do we find there? The lack of small communities within the churches may well be the major reason for an absence of effective confrontation of the world by Christians. The development of intentional groups that study and pray together seems to be the common factor among the growing and renewed congregations. Such groups are the essential means for the development and support of Christian identity and values in a secular age.

In Latin America the proponents of what has become known as "liberation theology" have centered their renewal of the church and the state through just such small communities for study, sharing, and prayer. They are often referred to as "base communities," grassroots gatherings whose goal is to return to the basic values of Christian living. These groups "are already living the new communion between God and human beings, and between human beings themselves, that constitutes the most essential content of the kingdom. They are living it imperfectly in the chiaroscuro of faith and with sinful defects, but they are living it in a real way."[96] These base communities create "liberation theology," not the other way around.

The covenant community is where we discover the kingdom; it is also where ministry and service occur naturally. As a young minister recently graduated from seminary, I served a small church in the mountains of Bristol, Tennessee. On a typical Sunday morning, we numbered between twenty-five and forty people gathered for worship–counting the children, but not the dogs. That little church taught me much of what I know about community. One example stands out. A parishioner named Sarah was six months pregnant when her doctor told her she would lose the baby if she did hard work of any kind. With two children at home and a husband and a house to care for, this restriction seemed impossible. Members of the church learned of her need; phone calls were made; a rotation schedule developed. For three months, every day, five days a week, someone was at Sarah's home to take care of the children when they arrived from school, to help with laundry and cleaning, and to prepare the evening meal. When the child was baptized, the entire church joined in saying, "We present this child to receive the sacrament of baptism."

In the Book of Acts the church is portrayed as a community that is concerned for the welfare of all its members. Such concern was understood as an essential characteristic of the church's unity and power.

> Now the company of those who believed were of one heart and soul, and no one said that any of the things which he possessed was his own, but they had everything

> in common. And with great power the apostles gave their testimony to the resurrection of the Lord Jesus, and great grace was upon them all. There was not a needy person among them, for as many as were possessors of lands or houses sold them, and brought the proceeds of what was sold and laid it at the apostles' feet; and distribution was made to each as any had need. (Acts 5:32-35)

The experiment in communal possession of goods did not last, as it was too easily abused. However, the community from which John is writing and the churches to which he writes must have had similar concern for all their members. When there is community, ministry naturally follows. When a person is in trouble and needs help and is recognized as a brother or sister, as a part of the family, then the family seeks to respond. At times that response is ineffective and sometimes even counter-productive, but it can be counted on.

Why do we have problems in providing housing for the poor? As a nation we certainly have the financial resources, but the poor have been isolated from the larger community in ghettoes. They do not attend our churches. They wear different clothes, speak a different dialect, and at times a different language. When the poor cease to be seen as "those people" and become a part of our community, then we will devote the resources needed (be they financial or educational or psychological) to enable a better quality of life for all members of the community. The problem of having enough is subordinate to the problem of community; if the community exists, "enough" will be found. Those churches that do bridge the social and racial gaps of our society tend to be more involved and concerned with healing the pain caused by our social inequalities. The covenant community is the goal, the means, and the locus for ministry.

The entire world cannot be a mutual, caring community. Even a congregation of two or three hundred members is too large for all members to enter into mutual relationships of healing and growth with all the other members. However, the spirit of unity includes an openness to all God's children, and community can spread beyond the boundaries of personal contact when its members intend to honor anyone who comes. To intend anything less than the inclusion of all who come to the community in the church is to exclude some from relationship. To exclude anyone means to restrict the capacity for love and to establish a norm of works and status for membership.[97] The church cannot be the covenant community unless it is inclusive; in God's community there can be no lepers, no outcasts.

It was the first Sunday of our regular fall and winter program in the church I serve in downtown Buffalo. We had special events planned: a luncheon after the service and a musical presentation by our children's choir. Shortly after the service began, a Native American entered the church. Shabbily dressed and smelling of alcohol, he walked down the aisle and took his place in the front pew. Whispers and furtive glances indicated the congregation's discomfort. By coincidence, the topic of my sermon was the importance of including all persons in the community of faith. After the service our visitor was warmly greeted and invited to the luncheon in the parish hall. He was a full-blooded Sioux Indian, with papers to prove it, heading for South Dakota. He loved the children's presentation. He ate a hearty meal. Then he played the piano for us. He brought us a gift of pleasure. He left with a gift of dark glasses from my daughter. I was accused of planting him for the sake of my sermon, but I will not take credit for providence.

Living in a hostile environment, the churches of Revelation had little experience of a community outside of their own small congregations, but in the vision of the new Jerusalem, we see a vision of inclusiveness. The old enemies, the kings and the nations of the earth, are entering the gates and bringing their glory into the holy city. The foundation of the city rests on the twelve apostles and on the gates are the names of the twelve tribes of Israel; both faiths are included in the city's structure. In Ezekiel's vision of the restored temple, which is one source for this vision, the Gentiles and uncircumcised are excluded (Ezek. 44:7, 9); in John's, there is no such exclusion. Inclusion is essential to the theology of grace that frees us from Babylon, bringing life and strength to the church's mission in the world.

Where community does not exist, deliberate inclusion must form the basis of our ministry. When prosperous, educated, middle-class Christians reach out to solve the problems of the poor, they are likely to get their hands slapped. When we treat another person with dignity and respect, when we expect to receive as well as serve, then we are more likely to develop a relationship. At a soup kitchen in downtown Buffalo, the clients are referred to as "guests" and the kitchen as a "dining room." When the guests arrive, they are offered coffee and doughnuts and are seated at tables decorated with flowers. Those who work in the dining room serve the guests at the tables—between two and four hundred each day.

We also have a food pantry where food is given out to persons in need, each of whom must have a referral and some identification. A record is kept and each person is checked against the record to prevent one person from receiving too much food. We have great difficulty recruiting workers for the food pantry; burnout is a constant problem. Yet at the dining room we have plenty of workers, many of whom have served four and five years. For ministry to be informed by intentional community makes a measurable difference to both server and served.

Finally, community is one way we have of confronting oppressive powers. As I defined power earlier, it comes out of the relationship between the strength of the one who would wield power and the resistance of the recipient. When the recipient has little or no power, resistance will be more effective if a community of resistance can be formed. The stories of the women's suffrage movement, of the formation of labor unions, of the civil rights struggle, and the protest against the war in

Vietnam are dramatic examples of effective group action to overcome strong wielders of power. A woman in a man's world, the single employee who could easily be fired, a black person in the white world of legal segregation, one student facing the draft—all are extremely vulnerable and powerless. But united in their refusal to cooperate with evil, each of these communities has made significant contributions to the transformation of our world.

As we seek to go beyond the Book of Revelation in understanding the power of Christ, we may define Lamb power as the power that enables covenant community. It is "relational power." Relational power is dramatically different from the power to exercise control. Linear power operates in one direction; it is the power to influence, and it is based on differences in power. Relational power involves giving and receiving; it is the capacity both to influence and to be influenced.[98] Relational power strives to create circles of equality and unity.[99]

Differences in innate abilities will always exist. However, where competition does not reign and inequalities are not used to dominate or control, differences act to enhance the whole. They do not make one person better than another; they make people different. In the environment of trust and creative openness, differences help define gifts that may be used to enhance the whole.

Because our ideas about power are formed by the structures of linear power, we have difficulty seeing true power as the capacity to be influenced by others. If we use the almost synonymous term "strength," we understand that great strength is required from someone who nurtures the caring community.

Jane and Mary, two high school seniors, were both on the basketball team and the track team. Mary was the better athlete—the star basketball player and holder of several city records in track. It was appropriate for the coach to appoint Mary captain of the basketball team, as basketball was the sport she cared about the most. But the track coach decided to name Jane captain of the track team and announced the appointment on a day Mary was away from school.

I saw Mary that evening, and she was angry. "I should be captain. I'm the better runner. Jane doesn't hold a single individual record. It's not fair. Well, I don't have to congratulate her; she never congratulated me for being made basketball captain."

Mostly I listened to Mary vent her anger, but I knew her well enough to respond. "I don't think that's a good idea. I think you know that rivalry and fussing between team members will hurt the basketball team and the track team. It was petty and small of Jane not to congratulate you. But you're a bigger person than that; you're strong enough to swallow your pride and congratulate her."

I found out later that Mary did congratulate Jane on her appointment.

To nurture community requires strength. We often speak of such strength in terms of size—a "big" or a "small" person. Strength is required for a person to swallow pride and return kindness for rudeness, or to receive criticism without getting defensive. Openness to another's influence and willingness to change one's ideas or actions, while at the same time not losing one's own sense of identity and responsibility, is a sign of strength. The insecure, fearful person is incapable of such openness. I remember a seminary professor telling us that if we wanted to be leaders of our congregations, then we must be willing to accept responsibility for all failures and to give credit and praise to others for every success. I do not believe that is precisely true, though leadership often seems that way. Strength is required to accept blame for failure honestly and to share praise for success. Such strength is the power of the Lamb, a power that makes truly mutual relationships possible and encourages development of healthy, supportive communities.

The good that results from such a community is neither a preconceived ideal nor the goal of a single person. The good emerges from the relationship, with each member making a contribution. Attempting to control the relationships obstructs the possibilities. Results coming from truly cooperative communities are creative, mutually satisfying, and unifying.

If you were the new minister in a small working-class congregation that in its twenty-year history had had nine different vicars, and which raised only $7,000 of its $25,000 budget, would you raise money to buy a pipe organ? The question may sound absurd, but when I went to St. Peter's in Louisville in 1975 that was its condition and that was the first action we undertook. I arrived at St. Peter's with all sorts of ideas about stewardship and evangelism and community service. I asked the board to go away for a weekend planning retreat. When the weekend was over, the top priority determined by the board was to improve the music program. We found an old organ in a closed church in Indiana, bought it for $500, moved, and installed it ourselves. The total cost was less than $2,000, which we raised in less than one month. If we were going to be a community, then our goals had to come from the community, not just from the clergy. In retrospect, I believe that decision was absolutely correct. Before we could worry about evangelism or stewardship we needed to learn to sing together.

Saul Alinsky, the pioneer of community organizing, taught that upon entering a neighborhood, you must first listen to the issues and concerns of the people who live there. Then build community by connecting people who have the same concerns. The people who live in the neighborhood have a better sense of what irritates them and what is possible for them. The action, if it is to build a sense of community, must emerge from the community.

In the real world mutuality must persevere through all sorts of good and bad times, through moments of true understanding and communion and moments of hostility and isolation, through times of sorrow as well as joy, through hardship and abundance, through frustration as well as the creative emergence of new possibilities. Unless there is true commitment to the relationship of collaboration as well as to the other individuals, mutuality will be lost. The energy and strength needed to persevere in commitment to true equality can be enormous. The cross is the symbol of the cost of sustaining mutual relationships and the covenanted community.[100] The ability to endure suffering for the sake of a larger purpose is a decisive mark of maturity. The ability to endure suffering, even great suffering, for the sake of others' welfare and fulfillment is a decisive mark of the Lamb.

When Jesus said the meek shall inherit the earth, surely he did not mean the submissive people who serve as doormats for the powerful. Rather, the meek who will inherit the earth are those who are able to endure suffering in the cause of encouraging mutual relationships and nurturing cooperative communities.

The image of the new Jerusalem reminds us that our faith is in resurrection. Bearing the cross leads to new life, health, and joy. The experience of the truly supportive, worshiping, covenant community makes the cross seem, in retrospect, a light yoke and an easy burden (Matt. 11:29f).

The power of the Lamb is essentially relational power. Known through the worshiping community and leading to the fulfilled community, it is the strength to sustain relationships among all sorts of people and in all kinds of different situations. It is the power that overcomes loneliness and despair, bringing community and empowerment.

CHAPTER   11

Faithful Witness

On Thursday afternoon, December 1, 1955, Mrs. Rosa Parks, a tailor's assistant in a downtown department store in Montgomery, Alabama, got on a bus to go home. She took her seat in the rear, behind the white people's section. When the bus filled up, the driver ordered Mrs. Parks to stand so a white man could sit down. She refused to move. She'd gone shopping after work, and her feet hurt. She couldn't bear the thought of having to stand all the way home. The driver, of course, threatened to call the police. Go ahead and call them, Mrs. Parks sighed. And she thought about how you spend your whole life making things comfortable for white people. You just live for their well-being, and they don't even treat you like a human being. Well, let the cops come. She wasn't moving. Two patrolmen took her down to the police station, where officials booked her for violating the city bus ordinance.

From Rosa Parks's arrest came the boycott of the city buses in Montgomery, and a young Baptist preacher named Martin Luther King, Jr., who only weeks before had declined to run for the presidency of the NAACP in Montgomery, was elected unanimously to head the Montgomery Improvement Association. Quoting Thoreau, King addressed the boycotters with the words, "He who accepts evil without protesting against it is really cooperating with evil."

Mrs. Parks's arrest was not entirely without preparation. For the past ten months the NAACP had been at work opposing the bus segregation laws and practices. Mrs. Parks was familiar with the opposition, having served as the secretary of the Montgomery NAACP. She had met with groups concerned about racial justice; her eyes were open to injustice and her faith in God affirmed her basic dignity. But her arrest was not part of a strategy for starting the civil rights movement or any other movement. She refused to move because she was tired: tired from walking and tired of the accumulated indignities. She remained in her seat on the bus as a statement of human dignity, not as a political action. She left the results in God's hands, and God provided E. D. Nixon and Martin Luther King, Jr.[101]

When faced with apparently overpowering forces, where do we find the motivation to stand up for the truth as we perceive it? How do we bring the power of God to bear on injustice?

There are two terms found in various forms throughout Revelation that we may use to describe John's understanding of the role of the Christian and of the church in the end-time: "faithful witness" and "patient endurance." Through faithful witness and patient endurance the power of the Lamb becomes operative in human life and in history.

The Greek word for "witness" (*martus*) has evolved into the English word "martyr." The supreme witness is, of course, the surrender of one's life for one's faith. Revelation does refer to the crucifixion as the testimony, or witness, of Jesus, and understands that our witness to the Lamb may include martyrdom. However, the basic meaning of the word *martus* in Revelation is rendered accurately by the translation "witness" or "testimony."[102] John frequently connects the term "faithful" to the term "witness." "Faithful witness" is the title given to Jesus in the opening vision of the heavenly court (1:5; see also 2:13 and 3:14). Other uses of the term "witness" connect it with faithfulness to the point of death, faithfulness in not worshiping the beast, and fidelity to the word of God. Simply stated, faithful witness is standing firm for what one believes and for the ethical practices that result from one's beliefs. It will always involve some withdrawal or conflict with the values and actions of this world; therefore such witness always includes taking up the cross of Christ. Only a few, however, are called to the supreme witness of martyrdom.

The term "patient endurance" is a weak translation of the Greek *hypomone*. The term might be more accurately rendered "absolute intransigence." The commentaries translate it with a variety of phrases: "unbending determination," "obstinacy," "the capacity to endure persecution, torture, and death without yielding one's faith," and "perseverance on the basis of the inner victorious sense that all contrary relationships and hostile forces can be overcome."[103] It is part of the vocabulary of the entire New Testament, in which it is found 31 times (7 in Revelation). Within the New Testament and especially in Revelation we must understand the word in a positive sense. In English "patience" and "endurance" may imply simply trying to survive. *Hypomone* is a positive, strong determination that is an important component in the power of the Lamb to overcome the violence of the beast. We are not called merely to endure evil; we are called to confrontation and to victory. The Lamb may appear meek, but in reality he is also the Lion of Judah.

These terms—faithful witness and patient endurance—seek to communicate a style of action that brings the victory of Christ to bear effectively on injustice and destruction in our society. Such action is faithful in that it is true to the style of the Lamb: noncontrolling, truthful, even when the truth appears to hurt one's own cause, undeterred by violence and the threat of violence, vulnerable and unprotective, willing to suffer and to bear the sins of others. It is not a witness to our personal integrity, but to the One who treated lepers with dignity, who fed the hungry, and who beneath the shadow of the sword of the kingdom of Caesar taught about the kingdom of God, refusing to cower before violence.

Faithful witness is a testimony to our experience within the covenant community, where we "come out of Babylon" and discover a fellowship founded on the premise that each person is worth dying for, that each person has important and unique gifts, and that justice demands equal treatment for all human beings. Through the worshiping community we receive the gift of discernment to see the hidden, spiritual realities of oppression. Faithful witness is an action given form by the experience of community. It shows the world that we have experienced a better way and invites it to begin the journey to freedom and dignity.

Faithful witness is a witness to the new Jerusalem, to the vision for human life in unity with God and one another, to a vision of life based on abundance, grace, and resurrection. Both the experience of the victory of Christ and the vision of the holy city are important. To seek the new Jerusalem without remembering the story of Jesus is to believe in a romanticized utopianism; to respond to Jesus without the joyous dream of redeemed society leads to irrelevant pietism or stern justice.

Faithful witness is standing up and expressing your truth, even when—maybe *especially* when—you are powerless. It is living by your truth, even when doing so puts you in a threatened minority. It involves letting go of the *results* of your actions to concentrate simply on acting faithfully, even though the outcome may include your own death or imprisonment. Faithful witness is not necessarily oriented toward a specific result; it seeks to reveal the truth as a way of bringing freedom and change. When achievement of a desired goal seems impossible, faithful witness provides a different motivation for our actions.

I remember a scene from an old movie of a man demonstrating against capital punishment. As I remember it, it was night and raining, and he was standing alone with a sign in front of a prison where an execution was about to take place. A reporter came up to him, forlorn sight that he was, and said, "Do you really think you can change the world?" The man shook his head and said, "Not really; I'm just trying to keep the world from changing me."

CHAPTER 11

We can imagine what would have happened to John's seven congregations had they accepted as their goal the Christianizing of the Roman world or the conversion of the Roman emperors or even, more modestly, the legalization of Christianity. How in the world could such small, almost invisible, churches ever accomplish such grandiose goals? For the Christian in the first-century congregation in Smyrna even to consider converting the emperor would have been laughable. If such goals had been the basis for action, those early Christians never would have persisted in the face of persecution and hardship.

Witness and steadfast endurance describe the motivation of those first Christians. Witness to a vision of human dignity motivated Rosa Parks. Witness to a justice higher than the laws of the state led the demonstrator to endure in front of the prison. The action of faithful witness can transform worlds, but the motive may involve surrendering the desire to transform even one's immediate surroundings.

A vision is not the same thing as a goal. A goal is a statement of what one intends to achieve; a vision is a dream of what life could be. Good goals are measurable, attainable, and specific. Setting goals is an important stage in planning, because it allows for the cohesive action of a community. Without goals that represent the consensus of the group, the power of the community is dissipated. But we must be careful. In a society under the domination of the beast, goals easily become gods, and plans easily become means of control and manipulation, and people easily become means to an end. When planning and goals become ends and people become means, we are operating once again in the way of the beast.

A vision is not easily broken down into goals, objectives, strategies and tactics. One does not achieve the new Jerusalem by following steps (A) through (Q). But as the worshiping community can have a partial and fragmentary experience of the new Jerusalem, when God dwells with his people, so too one can live in the present moment in small ways that reflect the dream. We do not achieve a vision so much as we live the vision by discovering how to express it in the present time.

A friend of mine, a priest in the Episcopal Church, married late in his life. Though he and his wife wanted children, because of their ages they chose to adopt. It was a long process. Finally after almost two years of waiting, they learned they could adopt a baby boy. Jack knew no greater excitement—a son! A football fan, Jack bought his infant son a New England Patriots' sweat shirt. He looked to the future when he would teach his son to throw the football. But soon after they brought their son home, they realized something was wrong. They took him back to the doctor and later received the diagnosis—congenital brain damage. He would never mature intellectually beyond the level of a two-year-old.

As he left the doctor's office and began walking across the Boston Common, Jack was approached by a derelict man who saw the clerical collar. "Hey, Father. Can you spare some change so I can get some breakfast?"

"No," Jack replied. Then he said, "But could you do something for me?" He told the man of his son, and then asked, "Would you pray for me and for my wife and for our son?"

The panhandler stood with tears in his eyes. "Yes, Father, I will. And thank you. No one has asked me to pray for them in years."

Jesus did not give us plans to achieve his dream of the kingdom the way Marx and Engels laid down plans to achieve the "workers' paradise." Jesus did something much simpler: he lived his dream. He took time to feed the hungry when he saw the people were hungry. He invited the poor and the outcast to join him in fellowship at the dinner table. He treated women with the same respect and honor that he gave to men, even though it placed him out of step with his culture. He welcomed children. He boldly challenged his own official religion to make its holy place a "house of prayer for all people." We "seek first the kingdom of God" by living the

CHAPTER 11

dream as Jesus lived it, by doing what we can and leaving the results in God's hands.

Surrendering goals as a motive for action is a great liberator when we must face incredible power. When we examine large goals, like ridding our society of racism or reforming business practices or resolving the problems of unemployment or bringing the arms race to a peaceful end, then the goals seem so impossible that just thinking about them produces feelings of powerlessness. Goal setting makes initial action in the face of massive power seem pointless; even when there is some success, the final goal is never achieved. Goals are important means for accomplishing tasks, but they are means only. To focus only on goals implies that we are responsible for devising the right plan and the correct procedure to produce the kingdom. As long as goals are our primary motivation, we will experience frustration and burnout. Living the dream provides motivation for action even when we cannot solve the problems.

When we look at our world—at the power of big government, big business, big unions, and global economic forces—we forget that the most powerful force in the world is God's dream for his creation. The twelve steps of Alcoholics Anonymous, the Bill of Rights—these are just a few human expressions of God's vision for life. When we get caught by that dream, when we get excited about living the dream here and now, then we become forces in God's acting to transform his world.

Our strongest weapon in this transformation is the Word.

> Then I saw heaven opened, and behold, a white horse!
> He who sat upon it is called Faithful and True, and in
> righteousness he judges and makes war. His eyes are like a
> flame of fire, and on his head are many diadems; and he
> has a name inscribed which no one knows but himself.
> He is clad in a robe dipped in blood, and the name by
> which he is called is the Word of God. And the armies of

heaven, arrayed in fine linen, white and pure, followed
him on white horses. From his mouth issues a sharp sword
with which to smite the nations, and he will rule them
with a rod of iron. (Rev. 19:11-15)

This picture of the climactic conquest of Christ over the
beast and his followers is developed through the images of
power found at the beginning of Revelation. The title "Faithful and True" reminds us of the title for Jesus, "the faithful witness," with which the book began (1:5). The eyes like flames
recall the vision of the glorified Christ (1:14), while the white
horse and the diadems reflect the crowns and white horse of
his nemesis, which pretended to divinity and righteous
authority (6:1-8). What follows in the Word's train is significantly different from war, famine, death and destruction.
The blood on his robe is most easily understood as Jesus' own
blood from his sacrifice on the cross, since the Word on the
white horse has not yet entered into battle. The iron rod
(from Psalm 2) likewise is found in the earlier description
(2:27) and repeated in the description of the child born of the
woman clothed in the sun (12:5). This image of Christ gives
us yet another perspective on the historical Jesus and the
image of the Lamb. Here the focus is on the name "Word of
God" and the sword from his mouth, described in chapter 1 as
a sharp two-edged sword (1:16, repeated in 2:12, 16).

The connection of the Word of God with a sword is found
in the Old Testament and was picked up as one of the stock
images in the apocalyptic tradition. The widespread use of this
image of the Word as a sword is confirmed by its use in
Ephesians and Hebrews as well as in Revelation.[104] Though the
title "the Word" is found in the Fourth Gospel in reference in
Jesus, its use here is different. There it is used in a conceptual
way to describe the nature and origin of the historic Jesus.
Here it is used in a more direct manner to refer to the
prophetic witness, to the witness of the followers of the Lamb
which exposes and disarms the beast, and to Christ—whose
witness speaks so loud that it brings victory over the beast.

CHAPTER 11

When the Word of truth and faithfulness is spoken boldly and clearly, it pierces to the heart and reveals evil in its true light.

One way we witness faithfully to the Word is by supporting responsible agencies that publish the truth, such as Amnesty International and Freedom House, which issue invaluable annual surveys on human rights abuses, terrorist violence, political prisoners and the like.[105] We ought to subscribe to at least one religious magazine or journal that reports on social and political issues, as well as pay attention to newspapers, magazines, radio and television. Clearly these voices have special interests and biases, as well as the need to make money. But in comparison to government information agencies, they are wonderfully truthful. The beast loves darkness and secrecy—secret agreements, insider information, covert operations, executive privilege, and security classification. Part of our faithful witness must be to support freedom of expression, of assembly, and of the press, being on the alert for attempts to cripple those rights.

We should also recognize that the proclamation of the truth is more than mere words. Symbols likewise may confront the beast with its true nature. I have never been one who liked beautiful marble monuments that glorified the cause of a war and whitewashed the depth of human suffering. What a difference it would make to see war from the perspective of the victims instead of that of the victors. The National Vietnam Memorial in Washington, D.C., is such a memorial. To visit that spot is an awesome experience. To read the names of those who died, and to see the people laying down their gifts and then walking down into that dark, grave-like depression in the earth, is to feel a solemn breath of terror and thanksgiving. That monument pays tribute to valor while acknowledging loss, with a reverence and poignancy that transcend the political divisions that surrounded the war and the monument itself.

The truth in that stone has provided healing for more than one person. In the six years since its dedication, about five million people a year have passed by the black granite. It is a dignified, unheroic place of reconciliation, at times international in scope. Recently four Vietnamese doctors from Hanoi, brought here by the Indochina Project, visited the memorial one evening. Two of them had fought against the American forces in Vietnam. All of them had lost family and friends in the war. But they were "moved almost to reverence" by the sight of groups of people using flashlights to locate and touch names on the wall. One of the doctors carefully rearranged a vase of dry flowers that had blown over, replacing several small American flags that had been scattered.[106] The power of truth resides in that monument.

In the beginning of the 14th chapter of Revelation, immediately following the appearance of the dragon and his two companions, we are shown a picture of the Lamb and his people gathered for battle:

> Then I looked, and lo, on Mount Zion stood the Lamb and with him a hundred and forty-four thousand who had his name and his Father's name written on their foreheads. And I heard a voice from heaven like the sound of loud thunder; the voice I heard was like the sound of harpers playing on their harps, and they sing a new song before the throne and before the four living creatures and before the elders. (Rev. 14:1-3a)

What a strange way to confront the beast—by singing a song! Is John suggesting that coercive, deceitful, and seductive powers can be opposed by a hymn sing? In a single word, yes; the power of the Lamb enters the struggle through worshipful singing. This is the first passage in Revelation where the Lamb appears on earth, a scene that includes Zion and the heavenly worship without distinguishing between mundane and spiritual realities. The distinction between the church on earth and the saints in heaven is dissolving, the unity between visible realities and the spiritual reality emerging.

Authentic worship brings an experience of union between the worshiper and God, between the worshiper and the gathered community, and between the present experience of lonely struggle and God's future of wholeness and fellowship. For many, singing brings a foretaste of that union. Every group contains those who talk much and those who talk little, those who lead and those who follow, but when the group joins in song, every member can participate and diversity is blended into a whole. In the face of isolation or oppression, such singing is a witness that, by the power of the Crucified, life does not have to be lonely or despairing. To sing the new song is to be among the "first fruits" of the coming harvest of wholeness and peace (14:5). To leave such worship is to go into the world dissatisfied with the status quo.

The Christian has already seen the new creation and tasted the wedding banquet; the joy of that experience must inform even one's opposition to oppression. Alan Paton, the well-known South African author who spent decades writing and speaking against apartheid, urged others not to take the problems of the world too personally. In 1987 he told a gathering of students, "Your life wasn't given to you to be spent in suffering. It was given to be enjoyed. It is good to fight against injustice, but don't become obsessed by it, for such an obsession—indeed any obsession—will eat away your life."[107]

From the first Christians to whom John addressed his apocalypse to present-day movements for social reform, singing has been an integral part of the group life. The following account is taken from a letter written shortly after the march from Selma to Birmingham, Alabama in 1964 by someone who had not previously been involved in any of the actions for civil rights.

> If I were asked to characterize the march itself, I think I would say that it was like a combination of a football game, a Santa Claus parade, and a Baptist revival. There was a feeling that simply because they were allowed to march and because the march was so strongly supported that victory had already been won. Those Negroes standing along the side of the road who were too old or

> too young to march all had joy on their faces and all
> waved as they would to Miss America had it been she in a
> parade. The freedom songs and cries that were sung in the
> march gave an air of a football game or of a carnival. And
> yet the entire demonstration was undergirded with a real
> religious feeling.[108]

Many of the "freedom songs" from the civil rights movement were developed from the songs used by the labor union
movement sixty years before, while others came from the
tradition of black spirituals. For many the demonstrations and
the singing became an experience of unity and victory that
foreshadowed civil rights laws, voting rights acts, and affirmative action. It is difficult to conceive that we could face down
the coercive, violent, controlling powers of this world by singing, but as we know from our own history, in the battle with
police and dogs and clubs and water hoses and midnight
bombings, the singers won.

We cannot overstate the importance of speaking through
deed, symbol, or song the word of truth and faithfulness.
Blindness to injustice, suffering, and domination characterize
human perception, a blindness that is encouraged by the
beast's use of manipulative symbols to promote its self-
glorification.[109]

In 1966 I spent the summer working in a church in Santo
Domingo in the Dominican Republic, one year after U.S.
troops had intervened to stop the revolution against a military
junta. From the airport on the east, through the downtown
area, and to the fairgrounds on the west, Santo Domingo was a
beautiful city of wide boulevards, white sandy beaches, and
palm trees. The tourist who visited this city during the days of
the dictator Trujillo saw a modern and prosperous metropolis.
I lived north of downtown with a middle-class family. All had
jobs and cars, but we had no running water in the house, and
sewage and kitchen facilities were inadequate. The poor sections of town with unpaved streets and open sewers were un-
believably unsanitary and dreadful. The image projected by

Trujillo for the tourists had little connection with the lives of the Dominican people.

The dramatic example of a dictatorial government should not lull us into thinking that image is unimportant in the United States. It is no coincidence that the most popular president since Roosevelt was an actor. Able to project warmth, concern, and confidence on television, Ronald Reagan maintained high personal popularity ratings in opinion polls even as the arms-for-hostages deal with Iran and the illegal network of funding for Nicaraguan contras were exposed. Every administration, whether it be that of John Kennedy or George Bush, projects images of its successes and hides unresolved problems. But as John, the seer, reminds us, denial of problems does not make them go away. They continue to grow until they become truly destructive.

The power of faithful witness lies in its authenticity. It acts with openness and innocence; it has a straightforward quality that comes not from strategy but from a life centered in worship and service. Such faithful witness reflects the gospels' directive concerning confrontation with persecutors:

> They will lay their hands on you, delivering you up to the synagogues and prisons, and you will be brought before kings and governors for my name's sake. This will be a time for you to bear testimony [*marturion*]. Settle it therefore in your minds, not to meditate beforehand how to answer; for I will give you a mouth and wisdom, which none of your adversaries will be able to withstand or contradict. (Lk. 21:12-15)

Simplicity, genuineness and veracity do not mean, however, that we do not care whether others see our witness. An arrest in the night, unknown to neighbors, or an unacknowledged murder by a death squad in a hidden place, does not confront the despot. The suffering of innocent people, by itself, is not a witness. Lamb power is not primarily about suffering; it is about confronting the forces that enslave and opening the possibilities for freedom. We must plan to make our witness clear so those who see may gain a vision that will free them from the power of the beast. Jesus clearly planned his confrontation in Jerusalem to be during the Passover, a time when the city was filled with people and the religious issue of liberation was paramount. We are sent out like sheep among wolves; therefore we must be wise as serpents while we act as vulnerable as doves (Matt. 10:16). We are called to be truthful and unguarded; we are not called to be foolish and compliant.

Faithful witness does calculate; it intends to be seen and heard, and it works deliberately to reflect the character of the Lamb. A friend related to me her training in preparation for a demonstration against U.S. policies in Central America. In the past, the police had become violent with the demonstrators, so in preparation for the event, they trained with people who role-played abusive and threatening guards. "When you are dealing with an oppressive force and are yourself the product of a violent society," she told me, "it takes careful planning to keep the situation from becoming violent." To act vulnerably as doves requires preparation and training.

True faithful witness will accept apparent defeat rather than complicity with evil; in so doing, it aligns itself with the victory of the Lamb. Many of Martin Luther King's successes came through such apparent defeats. All he needed was an oppressive law officer who would use clubs and dogs and water hoses, so that those who watched could see clearly the nature of the beastly oppression that was normally hidden from view. To be attacked by dogs or beaten with a club or called names and threatened with death does not feel like success. King's greatest problem, always, was to maintain the commitment to nonviolence in the face of such abuse. But when the demonstrators could maintain calm when confronted with violence, then their action became a sign that called a nation to repentance and to justice.

Faithful witness aims to show the hidden spiritual realities of the world so that the world might become free. Such action is designed primarily to reveal the true character of the beast and a vision of life lived in the way of the Lamb. The cross is the epitome of failure, but it is "successful" in that it shows the dark face of religious and political dominion and the forgiving love of God.

The Fourth Gospel interpreted Jesus' ministry with the concept of "signs." Jesus' healing miracles and the feeding of the five thousand were not intended to solve human health needs or to end hunger. His miracles were signs, signs of the presence of the kingdom which brings freedom and empowerment and choice. His parables and actions present a vision in unique images of what life can be like. Engaged and attracted by the signs, we freely choose to follow.

Similarly, our "Get That Job" ministry at St. Peter's in Louisville did not solve the problems of unemployment; it hardly made a dent in the 6,000 or so people who were looking for work. But it was a sign, a sign of God's abundance bringing healing and new possibilities.

Seeing actions as signs rather than as means to an end is another way of describing faithful witness. Whether or not one achieves the goal, the action is still a sign of God's healing and sacrificial love; it is still a witness for justice; it still points to a better way of life. People are able to read the sign and respond out of free choice for justice, for community, and for peace. Thus whether or not the goal is achieved, if the action invites one to come out of Babylon and becomes a sign to others of a better way, it has been successful.

What of the church and its ministry of social action? One could object that faithful witness sounds passive and reactive, while words like "acceptance," "surrender," and "living the dream" hardly seem revolutionary. Are we just to sit around waiting for the opportunity to act? Lamb power is not passive, though it often feels that way. We do need to be actively working for the extension of God's kingdom, but we must be particularly aware of how we work.

When the church accepts a model for Christian social ministry that understands it primarily in terms of using its power for good, and assumes that the forces which really determine history are in the hands of politicians, armies, and economic leaders, then the church has denied her theology. "How inappropriate and preposterous was the prevailing assumption from the time of Constantine until yesterday, that the fundamental responsibility of the church for society is to manage it."[110] In the words of Bishop Desmond Tutu, Archbishop for the Anglican Church in South Africa and winner of the 1984 Nobel Peace Prize,

> The Church is constantly tempted to be conformed to the world, to want influence that comes from power, prestige and privilege, and it forgets all the while that its Lord and Master was born in a stable, that the message of the angels about His birth was announced first not to the high and mighty but to the simple rustic shepherds. The Church forgets that His solidarity was with the poor, the downtrodden, the sinners, the despised ones, the outcasts, the prostitutes, the very scum of society. The Church thinks to its peril that it must sanctify any particular status quo, that it must identify with the powerful and uphold the system which will invariably be exploitative and oppressive to some extent. Woe betide that Church when that system is overthrown, when the powerless, the poor come into their own![111]

The temptation of linear power is the offer of a quick fix. A husband and wife are unable to agree; so, instead of further discussion and investigation, one of them decides. In small matters of minor importance or in emergencies, a one-sided decision-making process may be appropriate. But when this pattern gets established, then a relationship of give and take is replaced by one of dominance and submission. Similarly, top management often works from the assumption that involvement of lower level managers and employees in decisions would take too much time. To be competitive, a business must respond quickly to changes in the market place, so those in charge consolidate decision-making in a few people at the top of organizational structure. No one asks how long it takes to

CHAPTER 11

implement an order from on high when employees disagree with it, nor questions the quality of work under such an authoritarian system. No one asks what happens to labor relations when management gives orders, but is unaware of employee concerns. The seductiveness of a quick solution can produce a system of power distribution so unequal as to produce low morale, poor workmanship, inadequate performance, and labor unrest. This process of power consolidation happens in families, in businesses, in churches, in institutions, and in governments.

Are we to conclude, then, that the church should avoid any involvement in politics or business? Is the church's true ministry to produce a model society which, though small, will be so attractive that the world will be converted to a different way? This sectarian understanding of Christian ministry is a minor but persistent theme running throughout the history of Christianity.

Woven into the accounts of the descent of the dragon from heaven and the appearance of the beast and the false prophet on earth (chaps. 12 and 13) is a strange story of a beautiful woman, clothed with the sun, standing on the moon, with twelve stars in her crown. She gives birth to a male child who is to rule the nations, thereby overthrowing the rule of the beast. The dragon seeks to devour the child, but the child is "caught up to God and his throne, and the woman fled into the wilderness, where she has a place prepared by God in which to be nourished for one thousand, two hundred and sixty days." (Rev. 12:5-6; the full story is found in 12:1-6, 13-18.) The origin of this symbolic woman may lie within pagan mythology, but as she is treated in Revelation, she has become a symbol for the community of faith. The twelve stars in John's system of symbols point to the twelve tribes and the twelve apostles, the old and the new Israel. As the community of faith, this woman gives birth to the Christ. The dragon is unable to defeat Jesus, even by crucifixion, so he turns to attack the community that gave him birth. The woman does not stand, waiting to be destroyed, but flees into the wilderness in order to survive. The 1,260 days is approximately three and one-half years, the symbolic time for the reign of the beast.

One task of the church is survival. In times of persecution, the first duty of the faith community is to survive. Its very existence becomes an opposing of the beast. Under severe repression, of necessity the church becomes sectarian. Then when the time for the reign of the beast is coming to an end, the church is present to give birth to the Lamb. Given their small size, their relative impotence, and the discrimination and abuse laid on the congregations of Revelation, we can understand the sectarian tendency of John's understanding of witness. These churches had to withdraw at least partially from a hostile environment in order to survive.

The situation in the developed countries of the West, however, is not the same. As major corporate bodies possessing large amounts of money, land, and buildings, the churches are part of the political, business, and social structures of our society. They do not have the privilege of asking whether or not they should be involved in politics, business, or social issues. The question is, will the church work to support the status quo or will it work for change?

The wheat and the tares grow together (Matt. 13:24-30). The spirit of community, equality, and cooperation and the spirit of domination, competition, and inequality exist side by side in our world, in our institutions, even within our personal relationships. Though the two are dramatically different, discernment is difficult. For the modern Christian to separate faithful action from the power struggles of politics or the vicious competition of business—because issues are unclear and solutions seem utopian—is to side with the powerful. To leave the results of one's witness in God's hands does not mean to surrender power to those who would abuse it. Our world would not be a better place if all Christians retreated from politics, from positions of authority in businesses or unions, or from support of legitimate use of the military.

CHAPTER 11

This book primarily seeks to address those who feel power-less. To avoid idealistic and grandiose positions, I have generally limited myself to the Book of Revelation and to personal experiences of powerlessness. It goes beyond the scope of this book to develop a theology of Christian ministry. From a reading of the Book of Revelation, I believe that theology is best developed from the concept of vocation.[112]

After our conversation, my friend Jan—the art teacher who took a job in the school administration curriculum depart-ment—decided to return to full-time teaching. Her experience in administration was largely frustrating and unrewarding: she was unable to accomplish her goals and found herself overly critical of others in her office. She is a wonderful teacher who enables children to discover previously untapped potential and to achieve beyond their expectations. Jan did not have a call-ing for administration; her vocation is teaching. Her return to the classroom cost Jan a reduction in salary and a loss of status—there is a price for non-compliance with the beast—but she now enjoys her work and has a strong sense of con-tributing to her students' welfare and development.

I have another friend who is deeply involved as an elected member of the school board. Her commitment to education is expressed through frequent trips to the state capital to talk with legislators about education issues and to obtain funding for special programs. She is stimulated by the election cam-paign, by struggles over busing and integration, and by seeking to improve the quality of education. In the center of school politics, she finds excitement and a sense of fulfillment. Hers is a different vocation.

Like individuals, communities also have a vocation. Each community has a unique history, special gifts, and particular interests. St. Peter's in Louisville, a working-class congrega-tion, was called to minister to the unemployed, to develop a network of working-class congregations in the Ohio River Valley, and to assist in raising such issues within our national denomination. Today I am in a large, old downtown church in

Buffalo. Our history and spirit involve us in a different mission: in housing ministries, in downtown revitalization issues, and in concern over racism and urban poverty.

When Paul talks about gifts and vocation in Scripture, he asserts that if everyone serves in accordance with their call, all the needs of the community will be satisfied (I Cor. 12 and 13). We all have a part to play.

In the state of New York, we have a governor who opposes the death penalty and courageously vetoes the annual bill calling for capital punishment. But his witness requires my witness, too. I am not called to be a politician, but I must speak, write, and teach to help build the consensus of support necessary to sustain his witness for life. The abundance of the divine economy is realized when we are all set free to exercise our giftedness.

Should Christians go out and work in soup kitchens, when by doing so we encourage the government to avoid its responsibilities for the poor? Or should we spend our time lobbying for government food programs? A complex issue like hunger deserves more than a simple response. However, the simple response is that we witness to the hunger of our fellow citizens by ministering according to our personal and communal gifts. Some will work in food pantries, others in soup kitchens, others in education programs, others by lobbying governmental and international agencies, and others by working with the media. Each witness is a response to the need, a response to the vision of a healthier society, and an invitation to others to join in ministry. We will know the new creation when all, especially the poor who are presently so bound, find liberation to express their gifts in service to others.

Faithful witness does not directly address the issue of the church's involvement in political, social, or business issues; it does not specify *where* to witness. Faithful witness provides a model for a style of involvement wherever a person is called to exercise ministry. Faithful witness means living that is faithful to the character of divine love. It means loving one's enemies,

CHAPTER 11

not seeking to overcome them; serving others, not lording over them. It means remaining vulnerable and at the mercy of others, abandoning the claim to superior insight or knowledge, and listening. It means being willing to suffer rather than compromise with evil. Christian action as faithful witness comes out of our experience of a new order of human existence in the person of Jesus of Nazareth. If we are unable to solve a problem, we do not stop acting. Having once experienced the liberating reality of truth, we are driven to invite others into the experience.

Action and Hope in our Apocalyptic Age

When my son was about three years old he was given a toy consisting of a flat board with pegs protruding from it and gears to put on the pegs. When placed on adjacent pegs, the gears would mesh. We would arrange different numbers of gears in a variety of patterns. Then I would ask him, "If I turn this gear in this direction, which direction will this gear over here turn?" One day he took four of the gears, and placing them on the board, said, "This gear is Mom, this one is Daddy, this gear is me, and this gear is Jennifer. When I turn my gear, your gears turn too." I do not know how much he was just playing and how much he really meant what he said, but his demonstration was a simple lesson in family systems. When one person acts, the other members of the family react.

All families develop systems of action and reaction, with patterns of behavior that form a system of rules, roles, limits, and expectations that govern the interaction of the family. When the baby cries, one parent in particular is more likely to get up to care for the infant; another child might take advantage of the moment to gain the attention of the second parent. Such patterns fit together to form a system of behavior.

Of course, the system is not as simple as our gear board. The actions of one member on another are not a case of direct cause-and-effect like the gear teeth; one person's actions influence another's behavior less directly, more like gearless wheels rubbing against other wheels. Nor is the amount of force the same for all members of the family. Some of the wheels are bigger and heavier; they run the family system but are not influenced much by the other members of the family. The degree of connection also differs. Some wheels—such as a child who is leaving home, or a parent whose function is viewed primarily in terms of earning income—are not closely connected with other family members. Whatever the system, one person's behavior affects every other person's, and each member of the family is molded and influenced by the system. A healthy family system provides security, predictability, and a sense of belonging for its members.

The system is actually made up of a variety of sub-systems— pairs of wheels, to continue the metaphor. A sub-system is formed between a parent and a child, between grandparents and grandchildren, between sexes, between two members who assist each other in a common task (like doing dishes or parenting), or between members who share a common interest. The sub-systems also define certain rules of the system: "You are not your sister's parent; we will do the disciplining in this house." In a healthy family the sub-systems act to provide a sense of individual identity.

Just as the family system is composed of many sub-systems, so the family itself represents a sub-system within the systems of a job or school or neighborhood or church. Interaction with peers, with friends, with co-workers, and with acquaintances is greatly influenced by the health and quality of the family system of home. A family system also reaches across time with its influence. Even after leaving home, the family of one's birth is a major influence on adjustment in a marriage, in a job, or in a neighborhood. The wheels are characterized by inertia; they keep spinning in the same direction even after they have disengaged from the original system.

In turn each of these larger organizations—a church, a school, a business, a neighborhood—forms a system that also defines the members' roles, interactions, expectations, and behavior. These systems in turn are sub-systems in still larger bodies, such as a religious denomination, an educational system, a company, a city. Whether the system be that of a family, a prayer group, a political party, a business, a city, or a nation, it will be governed by forces such as fear, coercion, cooperation, truth, deception, anger, or love. The world is composed of systems and sub-systems that form a complex, interlocking and interacting set of rules, roles, expectations, and limits. Our world is a system of systems. Everyone participates in some; everyone is affected by some; every system affects and is affected by other systems.

The biblical image for this understanding of organizations is the body. The church is the body of Christ, a system composed of many smaller systems. When one portion of the church does not function properly (the foot wants to be a hand), then the functioning of the whole body is affected negatively. Similarly, when each part of the body functions well, the whole body can be productive.

Much work has been done regarding families in which one member abuses drugs or alcohol. As the chemically dependent person's illness progresses, the family struggles to control his or her behavior and still maintain family unity. It becomes a central focus of the family. One family member may become the hurt, angry, resentful caretaker of the dependent person. Another may become a "savior," lying for the sick member, covering up unacceptable behavior, and resolving financial or legal problems that arise. One may try the tough guy approach, urging discipline as the solution. Another may disengage, which involves loss of security, of the sense of belonging, and of personal identity. Slowly each member of the family takes responsibility for the dependent person's behavior; roles and rules become rigid; communication of honest feelings becomes unacceptable. When one member of the family becomes sick through chemical dependency, the whole family system malfunctions.

Health may return to the family when either the dependent person seeks treatment or the family seeks assistance. Sue began attending Al-Anon because she could no longer take the abuse constantly dumped on her by her husband. He constantly blamed her for the family's problems: they didn't have enough money because she did not shop wisely. She didn't know how to handle the kids. She never wanted go out with him any more. She tiptoed around hoping to avoid criticism. Everything she did was controlled by fear of his anger.

In Al-Anon, with the support of others, Sue learned to stop cowering. She began to let go of her resentments and anger. She began to see that she could have a healthy and satisfying life with the children even if her husband was not at home; she did not have to spend her time worrying about his behavior. As she began to develop healthier attitudes, the family patterns also improved. Each member began to exercise responsibility for their own behavior while granting more freedom and tolerance to others. As the family system began to heal, Sue's husband started to feel pressure to take responsibility for his actions and his addiction. Two years after Sue entered Al-Anon, her husband went to his first AA meeting. It is difficult and painful for one wheel to spin in a direction contrary to the family system.

When we act to change our society, we tend to think in terms of a technological model and not in terms of systems. Operating on the premise of cause and effect, the technological model tells us that if we can figure out the correct actions and controls, then we can produce the desired results. This model invites us to set goals, develop necessary strategies, and seek control of people if we believe our goals are right. It also tempts us to evaluate our ministry on the basis of our success—a method that leads to setting small, "safe" goals, if not to outright failure.

The world is composed of circles, small and large communities, that form this interlocking system of systems. The lie of linear power is its assumption that long-term, effective healing can be achieved through manipulation of one part of the community while ignoring the rest. For example, simply forcing the alcoholic to stop drinking rarely works; neither the alcoholic nor the affected family is healed. The malfunctioning family system's obsession with the dependent person's behavior continues. The rules become even more rigid. Communication of honest feelings becomes even more difficult.

Similarly, our national effort to end alcohol use through Prohibition was a tragic failure. Rather than curing the problem of alcohol abuse, Prohibition inaugurated and established the new problem of organized crime. Social systems are too complex to respond to simplistic, coercive solutions. We seem to be repeating the same fallacy in our current war on drugs by focusing our energy and resources on reducing the supply and preventing the sale of drugs. We must also focus on the social conditions that encourage drug selling and use, on drug education programs, on rehabilitation programs, on providing hope for a better future for drug users, and on our society's attitude toward addiction and gratification. Systems do not respond to simplistic cause-and-effect analysis.

The style of ministry pictured by faithful witness and steadfast endurance is a more appropriate way of ministering in our world of interconnected systems. It frees us from the need to achieve a specific goal. To begin the process of healing, Sue had to let go of the desire to stop her husband's drinking; she had to focus on responsibility for her own behavior and on the health of her family. Her new behavior was based on a sense of her inherent value as a human being; it was not designed as a subtle way to force her husband to stop drinking. When one person finds healing, the systems surrounding that person must change for the better. When any system becomes healthier, the people affected by that system will also be influenced. The healthier Sue's family became, the more pressure there was for her husband to become responsible for his illness and to seek help. Sue's involvement in Al-Anon also supported other men and women coping with addiction in their families. In our world of interlocking gears and wheels, one wheel can have an affect on several small systems, which in turn affect others. As one wheel endures, several sub-systems are changed. As sub-systems are changed, larger systems are pushed. Unlike simple solutions, patient endurance by its constant pressure has power in a world that is a system of systems.

What is true of ministry for the individual is also true for a larger community. In the world of systems, a community founded on a covenanted relationship and willing to endure hardship and suffering steadfastly and faithfully is one that exerts great power. Community is the means we have as well as the end we seek.

When we think of the civil rights movement, we think first of Martin Luther King, the strength of his commitment to nonviolence and the power of his words. But we do not diminish King's importance by pointing out the vast numbers of supporters, leaders, workers, and demonstrators that were required to dismantle the legal framework of segregation. Nor is the importance of the Montgomery bus boycott diminished by noting that bus segregation was ended not by the boycott, but by the U.S. Supreme Court in its decision on the case of Rosa Parks filed by the NAACP. The larger and more entrenched is a system of injustice, the larger the community must be to change it.

Nor can we say that the United States resolved the problems of racial injustice with the passing of the civil rights legislation. These laws mark a victory, but many battles must still be fought. In recent years, affirmative action and school desegregation programs designed to begin correcting the abuses of two centuries of racism have come under attack. Blatant discrimination continues, and economic injustice still has a racial bias. Laws are signs of a system's values, and legal changes indicate movement in a social system, but systems do not change because laws change. To bring full racial equality and justice into the American system will require generations of workers. The community of faith—black and white—must pursue equal rights for all people with steadfast and faithful determination.

Actions do not have to be strategically correct or effective to have an impact. As witnesses, as "signs," they affect the corporate spirit—even if they are naive or futile. Such an insight should not encourage us to ignore effectiveness; rather, we should find in this the freedom to act boldly. In almost any situation we can respond with suffering, servant love. Such love will affect those around us and the systems in which we participate, and it represents the power of the Lamb. Our actions will always make a difference. No action controls a social system; all actions affect the system. Next to the temptation to take the short, "easy" way of linear power, the greatest seduction of the beast is to convince people they are impotent.

In the early 1950's a prison chaplain became concerned about the number of prisoners who were approved for parole but could not be released from prison because they had no approved place to live and no job on the outside. In Illinois, a prisoner who had no friends or family to make such arrangements could not get out of jail on parole. The lack of outside support meant a longer term. The chaplain decided to attack this injustice by taking two particular prisoners into his home, convincing the parole board to approve his home as a dwelling and a job. Within a year there were six ex-cons living with the chaplain, his wife, and their two children. When people asked if he was afraid, he responded that not only was he unafraid, he and his family felt very well protected.

But the need was greater than one family and one house could fill. Our chaplain raised funds, bought an old house, provided a room for a resident manager, and used it as a residence for paroled prisoners. Thus was born the first halfway house. From that responsive, faithful action came a concept that is important today not only in prisoner rehabilitation but also in work with the emotionally disturbed, with alcoholics, and with many other groups that seek to help individuals reenter society from institutions.

CHAPTER 12

God calls us to open our eyes, to see the world as it is, and to act in response to the injustice we see and the good we can do. He does not call us to save the world or to establish the kingdom. God is leading; we follow with faithful action.

To see the world as a system of interlocking systems is to understand that every action makes a difference. As a part of one body, we either contribute to the health of the body by our actions or we hurt it. Everything we do either supports the status quo or works for change.

When Elie Wiesel accepted the Nobel Peace Prize in 1986 for his efforts in keeping the memory and horrors of the Holocaust alive, he said,

> We must always take sides. Neutrality helps the oppressor, never the victim. Silence encourages the tormentor, never the tormented. One person—a Raoul Wallenberg, an Albert Schweitzer, one person of integrity—can make a difference, a difference of life and death. As long as one dissident is in prison, our freedom will not be true. As long as one child is hungry, our lives will be filled with anguish and shame. What all these victims need above all is to know that they are not alone; that we are not forgetting them, that when their voices are stifled, we shall lend them ours, that while their freedom depends on ours, the quality of our freedom depends on theirs.

Much of the power of the beast is based on fear. When confronted with fortitude, its power is diminished; when confronted with silent submission, its power increases. The power of evil is directly related to our willingness to give it power.

John's call for single-minded commitment reflects the truth that we are in a battle and we are called to confront evil. Hymns like "Onward Christian Soldiers" have become unpopular today because of their military images and message. If those hymns encourage self-righteous, triumphalist attitudes that we are superior to others and should force them to be like us, then they should be expunged from the Christian tradition. But if our dislike of military language reflects our desire to smooth over the reality that we are in conflict with evil, then we are being seduced by the beast. We are not called to go on "witch hunts," seeking out evil to confront; it will find us when we open our eyes. We are called to stand firm when justice and truth are threatened. Faithful witness does not call us to attack and destroy human beings; it does call us to resist evil when and as we see it, that we might liberate people from its control. There is no middle ground.

John's call for commitment also reflects the need for personal conversion. It is God's victory we seek, not our own. To be empowered by the Lamb, we must shift from self-seeking to seeking God's will. We are not the builders of the kingdom on earth; we are looking for signs of God's kingdom, which is perpetually coming.

To seek God's will does not mean figuring out the solution to a puzzle and then carrying it out regardless of the amount of human suffering such action requires. Doing God's will is a process of study, worship, dreaming, and action. We are not called to perfect performance; we are called to enter the process.

To seek God's will does not mean we know the truth or that we see reality as it is, because we are still seduced by the images the beast uses to confuse and defeat us. Learning to discern the will of God does not even mean that we agree with others in our worshiping community. We are still sinful. We do not see the world as God sees it; we see everything from the perspective of our personal histories and our social and economic status. Yet at times we do see reality as it is, and unless we speak out boldly, the truth that we see may not be heard and seen by others. Knowing our fallibility, we must work for truth as we understand it, and we must seek goals that from our perspective incarnate that truth.

One could hardly construe Revelation as a tract for toleration. John's call for single-minded commitment in worship of the Lamb is so urgent that there is absolutely no tolerance of any false doctrine within the faith community. Yet within

John's perspective lies the foundation for a positive commitment to pluralism of ideas.

Few writings have a stronger sense of God's wholly otherness than the book of Revelation. None of our ways of understanding God or the world, none of our ways of serving God or others is, strictly speaking, God's way. To do God's will, then, means to be in relationship with God, to seek to see the spiritual realities of this world more clearly, and then to act boldly. We are called to absolute trust and commitment to Christ the Lamb; we are called to faithfulness and perseverence in our action, but we are not called to be infallible.

Triumphalism, absolutism, and illusions of certainty have no place before the Lamb and the One who sits upon the throne, nor in the actions of those who follow the Lamb in this world. To insist on one's own view or way—as though it were God's view or God's will—is arrogant and dangerous. Our differences ensure that in this world we will have conflict; intolerance sets our inevitable conflicts on a course for destruction. The goal and dream for human society is true community. When groups come into conflict, the way to community is through compromise. Until we reach the kingdom of God, we will be called to responsible compromise again and again. To reject compromise is to put oneself in the place of God. Absolute commitment to the will of God does not deny the virtues of pluralism.

At the same time our witness is faithful, obstinate, and resolute. Commitment to the point of self-sacrifice seems to be necessary in order to effect true social change. But a commitment that acknowledges the worth of every human being also embraces an honest pluralism. Such commitment says, "Here I stand. I firmly believe that I am right. But only God is God and only God knows who is right." Such a commitment to pluralism is far more positive than a tolerance that, while acknowledging the right of others to have a voice in our society, would seek to relegate that voice to inferior status. Revelation provides an understanding of doing God's will that lies be-

tween passivity and intolerance. Refusal to speak the truth
boldly is a denial of one's God-given value, as well as fear of
failure; refusal to speak the truth *humbly* is a denial of others'
God-given value and a blasphemous arrogance.

There is a "market place" dynamic in faithful witness that
over time brings it into conformity with God's will. The
process of doing God's will leads to bold and even obstinate
action, but it does not attempt to control the results. Witness
leaves the outcome in God's hands. The personal act of doing
God's will becomes part of a corporate process through which
God's will is done. Many refer to this as the test of Gamaliel.
Arrested for preaching the resurrection of Jesus and com-
manded by the high priests to cease their preaching, Peter and
the apostles responded, "We must obey God rather than men."
The council in anger expressed the desire to kill the apostles,
but Gamaliel spoke and carried the day. "Take care what you
do with these men," he said. Then he told of Theudas and
Judas the Galilean, both of whom made messianic claims and
developed a following, but after their deaths their followers
were dispersed and the movements came to nothing. "So in
the present case," Gamaliel continued, "I tell you, keep away
from these men and let them alone; for if this plan or this un-
dertaking is of men, it will fail; but if it is of God, you will not
be able to overthrow them. You might even be found opposing
God!" (Acts 5:27-39)

This noncoercive aspect of faithful witness is part of what
brings it success. Our task is to witness to the truth as we perceive it, not to create the kingdom. Instead of rigidity and
control, one discovers creative change and cooperative working together. The good emerges from, through, and toward the
covenant community. God guides the process of bringing the
kingdom. Lamb power is based on the ability to let go of the
need to control, to surrender to God's will, to accept the world
as it is—not as we would have it—and to stand firm with and
for others. We each have our gifts to offer, humbly, for the
good of the whole.

CHAPTER 12

In the popular view, apocalyptic hope is pure escapism. As Revelation, Daniel, and other apocalyptic writings are read and interpreted, hope means waiting for God to bring in the kingdom. The world is out of control. Human beings can do nothing to stop things from getting worse. Our only hope is for God to intervene by destroying the wicked and establishing the kingdom. "In case of Rapture, this car will be driverless," reads the bumper sticker. If the driver's only hope is the "rapture," that bumper sticker is a statement of defeat. To base hope solely on God's deliverance from this "vale of woe" is to surrender to despair and escapism. Though perhaps justified in the Book of Daniel, this popular view fails to read Revelation carefully.

John gives us a different view. True, the world seems out of control. We think there is nothing we can do to bring justice and peace. But John's understanding of power challenges such feelings. The more vulnerable we are, the more powerful the power of the Lamb becomes.

In John's structure of Revelation, the five accounts of strife accelerating to conflict, each followed by God's victory, reflect an understanding of history as recurrent.[113] History is moving toward God's end; however, at each point in history one can discern a pattern that repeats the kinds of decisions that have gone before, and a future that is moving in a particular direction. John is not unique. Tracing the pattern of history is a common characteristic of apocalypse, and it makes possible the fundamentalists' use of Revelation to predict the future. It is a short step from tracing the rise and fall of the ancient empires (Assyria, Babylon, Persia, Greece and Rome) to applying the same images to the Holy Roman Empire, the British Empire, and the U.S. and Russian empires.

Within this apocalyptic understanding of history, as conflict builds, as the future looks bleak, as we approach an impending Armageddon, that is the time of hope. The dragon rages with great wrath because it knows its time is short. Hope for John is based on the common apocalyptic premise that as times grow worse, the time for God's power and glory to be known on earth approaches.

The picture of history as moving in cycles is not foreign to our experience. We recognize the rise and fall of powers as the normal way history moves, but what we fail to see is that the time of pain and conflict is often the time of hope. For the family suffering from the disease of alcoholism, conditions must get bad enough for members of the family to seek help either through AA or Al-Anon. Education and intervention allow people to find help for alcoholism before they "hit bottom," but education will not prevent the disease. Similarly, many married couples in conflict come to the counselor for help only after they have spent years caught in a cycle of tension, fighting, and resolution that leads to renewed tension. The growing chaos of the relationship, though painful, provides the desire to seek help to change. A couple must desire change more than they fear it before they will seek help. The popular understanding of hope implies that we can be hopeful only when life is peaceful and prosperous, never when life is hard and threatening. John's picture of history gives us a different view. The moment when life seems hopeless is the moment when hope may be born anew.

Earlier we defined an apocalyptic age as an age when many believe themselves to be powerless before mammoth controlling forces. It is an age of great danger; in ours, we could destroy the world. For the faith community, however, an apocalyptic age is also a time of hope. In feeling powerless, we must look for alternative understandings of power and for different ways of acting. Without such searching we remain blind; looking for alternatives is how we begin to exercise the power of the Lamb.

In the story line of John's apocalypse, the people's actions are directly related to the coming kingdom. Following the fall of Babylon and preceding the final victory of Christ the Word, we read:

> "Let us rejoice and exult and give him the glory, for the marriage of the Lamb has come, and his Bride has made herself ready; it was granted her to be clothed with fine linen, bright and pure"—for the fine linen is the righteous deeds of the saints. (Rev. 19:7-8)

The church, the Bride of Christ, has come out of Babylon. Because of her own weaknesses, Babylon has fallen. The church has made herself ready; she has put on a gown created by the faithful actions of the witnesses who have gone before, including the martyr witness of Jesus. The action of the church is one factor that makes possible the wedding feast of the Lamb.

We find this same understanding of the role of the church in the vision of the martyrs in heaven. When the fifth seal was opened, John saw under the heavenly altar the souls of those who were slain for the word of God and for the witness (*marturia*) they had borne (6:9-11). Their cry of "How long?" is answered, "Until the number of their fellow servants and their brethren should be complete, who were to be killed as they themselves had been" (6:11). The martyr witness of the saints makes a difference. The time between now and the full reign is shortened by the faithful actions of the Christian.

Two other passages point to this role of the faithful. In the exultation at the defeat of the dragon (12:7-12), the voice in heaven proclaims that "the salvation and the power and the kingdom of our God and the authority of his Christ have come .... They have conquered him by the blood of the Lamb and by the word of their testimony (*marturia*), for they loved not their lives even unto death." In the cryptic passage about the two witnesses (*martus*) in Jerusalem (11:3-13),[114] the beginning of the end time waits until "they have finished their testimony."

Perhaps even more telling than any particular passage is John's placement of scenes of the worshiping community in his narratives. As each narrative reaches a climax of the woes and plagues, just before the destruction of the forces of evil and the establishment of the kingdom, John stops the action and presents a scene of the redeemed community.[115] When the faithful witnessing community appears in the narrative, the reign of evil ends and the story concludes. The story of Revelation begins with the premise that the Lamb has defeated the beast. But the war is not over; it is all the more fierce because the beast knows its time is short. The final battle will be fought by the faithful witnessing of the saints.

This narrative skillfully and carefully walks the line between salvation by works, which is destructive to human integrity, and determinism, which would destroy human motivation. It provides both the foundation for Christian hope and the motivation for Christian action. If the future consummation is assured no matter what we or our community of faith does, then our action is irrelevant. Any suffering we must accept becomes meaningless except as some sort of individual and personal refinement by fire. Since our action makes no difference, God's delay in bringing the kingdom is irresponsible. Then God is a toying potentate who does not care about human suffering.

If our actions literally bring in the kingdom, then the load we must carry is oppressive, even hopeless. If God's triumph depends on our right action, then we had better not make a mistake. If my actions might prevent the ultimate fulfilling of God's will, little room remains for failure, forgiveness and grace. Faith and relationships become secondary to performance, and our hope depends on faith in human goodness.

God brings the kingdom through the power of the Lamb. The beauty of the new Jerusalem is so appealing, the power of truth so invincible, and the persistence of God's love so strong that John cannot conceive that God's purposes for creation could fail. But the faithful witness of the covenant community is crucial in order for the victory of the Lamb to become operative in the world. In the death and resurrection of Jesus the relative strengths of the beast and the Lamb have been tested. The beast has been dealt a mortal blow, and the vic-

CHAPTER 12

tory has been won. But the time still to elapse between that victory and the fulfillment imaged in the new Jerusalem depends on the faithful witness of the church.

Faithful witness shortens the time in two ways: by confronting the beast and by revealing a better way of life. Empowered by the self-sacrificing love of Christ and in witness to his steadfast confrontation, the Lamb's followers stand undauntedly before the beast. The refusal to cower shows the world the beast's true nature. The followers of the Lamb need not develop the battle plan nor seek to win the war; their task is to confront evil as faithful witnesses of Christ and to leave the rest in God's hands. Faithful witness brings judgment, which does shorten the time between the past fulfillment and the future promise. Action is important, but forgiveness and grace are assumed: failure to act will not produce a crucial defeat; another time will soon arrive for witness. The Lamb's people have been empowered; the kingdom awaits their use of that power.

Faithful witness also invites others to discover a new vision of life. One cannot see the holy city from Babylon. By leaving Babylon and being faithful to self-sacrificing, servant love, the church prepares for the wedding feast of the Lamb. The church does not create the kingdom; the kingdom "is at hand." The work of the church is to look actively for the coming kingdom, to see the descending city of God, to look for where God is at work in our world, and then as allies work with and for that action of God.

Like John's first readers, we do not need to achieve our goal to keep hope and motivation alive. We need only see the possibility, experience small victories, and know that we are being led forward toward God's future. Just as their small, faithful actions transformed the Roman world and Christianized the West, so our small faithful actions will play a similar role in the future of our world.

The changes we seek for our families, our communities, our businesses, and our governments are not small changes. We seek a major shift in thinking and in world view.[116] To make such a positive change requires effort by many, many people. It requires prophetic leadership that boldly speaks the Word of God, and hundreds of communities of faith where people are experiencing a new way of living.

One hundred and fifty years ago, this country was an agrarian society. The change we seek in values is every bit as great as the change from such a society to an industrialized economy. The change will come about in the same way: piece by piece, change in one community and then in another, one shift encouraging another, until one day people look back and recognize what has happened. The change will not be the result of centralized planning, but will emerge from thousands of thousands of faithful actions by ordinary people.

In 1935 Bill W., a New York stockbroker who had found sobriety from alcoholism as a result of a religious experience, met Dr. Bob, an Akron, Ohio physician, himself an alcoholic. Out of that meeting the doctor found sobriety and together they discovered that one alcoholic could affect another as no one else could. When these two men decided the best way to maintain their sobriety was to work with the alcoholics who arrived at the Akron City Hospital, Alcoholics Anonymous was founded. Four years later there were two groups, one in Akron and one in New York City, and a few other small groups trying to get started. With a total membership of about a hundred, they published the first edition of *Alcoholics Anonymous*. By 1983, less than fifty years later, there were about 50,000 groups in 110 countries, and over two million people had found sobriety. Through the faithful witness of these two men and the covenant community of AA, the world of the alcoholic has been changed.

In Revelation the church is the central player in the struggle against oppressive domination. Here in the covenant community gathered in worship before the Lamb and the One who sits upon the throne, we are rendered humble. Through genuine relationships we are changed. Here we are given new identities, eyes to see, and ears to hear what the Spirit is saying.

If the churches are to be agents to change the social structures, it will come about because they will become truly inclusive communities. I believe the future of our world may well depend on how open the churches can be. The greater diversity we have gathered around God's altar, the greater our witness to the truth. The greater the representation from different social structures there are included in the circle of worship, the more readily we will recognize our neighbor's different needs and concerns and the more likely we are to respond. The more open we are to all people, the freer we will be from the dominion of the beast. The power of the Lamb will enter our society through the church in direct proportion to the downward mobility of the churches. John's approval of Philadelphia and his correction for Laodicea were designed to shorten the time between the resurrection and the coming of the new Jerusalem.

In a world composed of millions of interconnected systems, to bring change we must trust the power that would transform these systems into true communities. When we see clearly the deceptions of the beast, when we enter the covenant community based on our common humanity, when we sincerely intend the inclusion of every person, then the church becomes a sign of the coming kingdom and a force for healing in our world. By the faithfulness of our witness as we gather week by week to break bread together, we will confront the world with our care for one another. The change comes about through persistent struggle, through a supportive and redemptive community, and through faith that God will guide the process. We dare hope that some day the world's system of systems may become a community of communities.

Apocalypse: Literature of the Powerless

The traditional definition of apocalypse focuses on certain common characteristics of these writings: bizarre, stereotyped symbols; the esoteric claim of disclosure of divine, secret knowledge; a view of history that sees the approach of God's intervention; and pseudonymous authorship. The traditional definition is found in D. S. Russell's study, *The Method and Message of Jewish Apocalyptic* (1964), but this view has been challenged by more recent works such as Christopher Rowland's *The Open Heaven: A Study of Apocalyptic in Judaism and Early Christianity* (1982) and Paul Hanson's *The Dawn of Apocalyptic* (1979). Paul Hanson convincingly demonstrates that the sources of apocalyptic are certain groups in Judah that became dispossessed following the return from exile in Babylon. When we strive to define the genre more closely, however, the traditional definition slips away.

I believe a more productive approach begins by focusing on the type of community that would produce and preserve such writings. Who looks forward to the destruction of the present age and the dawning of a new social order with hopeful anticipation? Who desires to see the present rulers—kings, merchants, landlords, the wealthy—thrown down from their exalted positions in punishment for their cruel oppression? Who sees the poor and downtrodden as the more righteous segment of society?

Certainly the answer to these questions is not "the upper class." A central characteristic of apocalyptic literature is its pessimistic view of the present age, including hostility toward the ruling classes and belief that though the lower classes may be oppressed, they are the faithful of God. I believe we best understand apocalyptic literature if we recognize it as the literature of the underclass rather than as a particular genre. There are several other characteristics of apocalyptic literature that also reflect the lower class setting. The word "apocalypse" means revelation. The apocalyptic writings purport to reveal divine truth through visions and secret information. Such an understanding of revelation allows the believer access to saving information without the need for scribes, education, or erudite clergy.

Apocalyptic literature is frequently characterized by flights of fancy into the world of angels, multiple heavens, and fantastic beasts. Fascination with such fantasy is a common escapist tactic, and escapism is more popular among those whose lives are dull and difficult.

The combination of determinism and pessimism found in apocalypse is also easily understood as an expression of the feelings and views of the powerless. As apocalypse views history, the world is in bad shape and is getting worse. No one can do anything to change the situation. Such a view reflects the condition of those who have no power to influence events. The world is hurting them and their only hope is divine intervention. Still, determinism does not affect the eternal fate of individuals. In the midst of powerlessness, apocalypse calls for the believer to decide for God.

In tracing the development of apocalypse from the Old Testament prophets, Paul Hanson proposes that these writings emerge from the prophetic tradition when the gap between reality and vision becomes unbridgeable (pp. 1-26, 431-434). The vision of the prophetic writings focused on the divine plan for Israel, and through Israel, for the world. The prophet's task was to translate that plan into historical, political, and individual terms. On the basis of their vision, the prophets called upon the rulers and people to turn from injustice and idolatry to follow God's laws.

After the exile, Israel had little control over its political life. We see the impact of realism in the prophetic tradition of Haggai and Zechariah, who wedded their calls for obedience to the plans to build the Temple. The prophetic, ethical vision of life was submerged in the harsh realities of post-exilic life.

With the loss of political capacity by the religious community, the prophetic ethic was abdicated for the hope that God would bring the kingdom despite all historical evidence to the contrary. Apocalypse was born when the vision of God's rule of justice and peace became an impossible dream for the community of faith. The mythic vision of God's plan served as an escape from reality as well as a way of preserving the prophetic vision. Thus hope was kept alive, the people of God were encouraged to remain true to their dream, but the importance of individual action in the world was diminished.

When the country was under the domination of an outside power, apocalypse expressed the hope and the resistance of the people. When the political establishment became a hierocratic group, authoritative and legalistic, then apocalypse became the possession of the poor and the outcast. This picture is important for our understanding of Jesus' ministry. When Jesus appears on the scene speaking of the coming "kingdom of God," his use of apocalyptic terminology immediately identified him with the poor and the underclass. To speak of the coming of the kingdom of God to the rulers of the kingdom of this world was to speak in revolutionary language.

If it is true that in our day the religious community also feels the tension between the realities we see in the world and the biblical vision of justice, then apocalypse becomes a literature relevant to our situation. Apocalypse, and especially the Christian apocalypse, Revelation, expresses our frustrations, our hopes, our powerlessness, and above all our faith that God is the God of history and that through our actions we can ally ourselves with the dream for God's rule now and tomorrow.

Interpreting Revelation

Then I turned to see the voice that was speaking to me,
and on turning I saw seven golden lampstands, and in the
midst of the lampstands one like a son of man, clothed
with a long robe and with a golden girdle round his breast
. . . in his right hand he held seven stars, from his mouth
issued a sharp two-edged sword, and his face was like the
sun shining in full strength. (Rev. 1:9a,10,11a,12-13,16)

One need not read far in the book of Revelation
before the meaning becomes obscure! With a beginning like
this, no wonder most people forego further reading in Revelation. Time seems better spent on less obscure texts. The images are difficult to picture. Even the figure of the Lamb is
more complex than we usually remember: "And between the
throne and the four living creatures and among the elders, I
saw a Lamb standing, as though it had been slain, with seven
horns and with seven eyes"(5:6). How easily one forgets the
seven eyes and the seven horns when picturing the Lamb!
And how can it "stand as though it had been slain"?

In recent years two basic approaches have developed as
means for understanding this strange and irrational book: the
literal/fundamentalist interpretation and the interpretation
that derives from the tools of historical/literary criticism.

The fundamentalists interpret Revelation as prediction of
future events. Depending on a few verses in the last chapter
that indicate the book was written to predict the future (22:7,
12, 20), they search the images for ways to relate them to current events. They may be right; perhaps Christ is about to
return, perhaps the word "soon" does not have the same meaning in the Bible that it has elsewhere. To date, however, those
who would use Revelation to predict future events are batting

0.000. Historically, the evidence is clear; using Revelation to predict the future does not work. Personally I approach works like Hal Lindsey's best-selling *The Late Great Planet Earth*, which uses Scripture to predict the end of the world, as interesting, fanciful speculation that is essentially fiction. Furthermore, this approach implies Jesus was wrong in telling his followers to be watchful and alert, because no one can know the hour or the time the householder comes. If the prediction approach is correct, one need not be watchful; rather, one should be clever and figure out the hour.

More is at stake, however, than the ability to derive predictions from Revelation. If this approach is correct, it leads to some unfortunate conclusions about the nature of God. Since the end has not yet arrived, the events that indicate when the end will come did not occur during the first 1900 years of the Christian era. God then is a god who has intentionally misled and confused devout Christians with a book that no one could possibly understand until the 20th century (or the 21st or the 28th) because the events referred to in the text had not occurred. Much about God is unknowable, but do we wish to assert that divine revelation purposely misleads those who seek to know God and God's will?

My reservations about the literalistic-prediction approach go beyond these specifics to a more fundamental point: this approach removes the believer from dialogue with God through the Word. The reader or listener becomes a passive recipient of the authority handed down from on high. Elsewhere in the Bible the vitality of the Word engages the believer in an encounter that leads to self-examination, new insight, growth, and confrontation with the person of God. The parables of Jesus nag at our minds and pull us forward in our spiritual quest. When Paul wrestles with the issues of law and grace, we too struggle to understand our relationship with the God who loves us so freely. Surely a book as mystifying as Revelation invites us to participate in dialogue with God at the levels of imagination and feeling.

APPENDIX B

The other approach to interpreting Revelation comes from the historical-critical point of view. While this perspective avoids the pitfalls of literalism, it also misses the vitality of Revelation. The historical-critical conclusion that Revelation was written to encourage Christians to remain faithful to their beliefs in the face of persecution by the Emperor Domitian is widely accepted, but it has many difficulties. The primary objection comes from history itself. Present historical knowledge indicates any persecution by Domitian was sporadic, not aimed at Christians, and restricted to the environs of Rome. The lack of evidence for a Domitian persecution led G. B. Caird to postulate that John anticipated such a persecution. The primary evidence for the Domitian persecution is the Book of Revelation!

A second difficulty with the traditional historical-critical approach is the assumption that persecution provides the motive for apocalyptic writings. Vast amounts of apocalyptic literature have survived to the present day, most of it outside of Scripture. Must we assume some persecution as the motive for the writing of each of these works? Or may we more safely assume that apocalyptic writings were popular writings of the disenfranchised who normally saw authorities as threatening? The connection of apocalypse with specific persecutions cannot be maintained in the face of so many apocalyptic writings.

Further difficulty for this approach comes from the text of Revelation itself. Systematic persecution is not one of the concerns expressed in the letters to the seven churches (chs. 2-3), where John is concerned about complacency and pagan influence. The discrimination and hardships described sound very similar to the kinds of troubles Paul had in his journeys and in his congregations. Nor does John urge his readers to "hold on"; instead, he urges them on to victory.

Finally, by identifying Revelation with an official persecution, the historical-critical approach tends to encourage neglect of this book by the modern reader. In practice many students of the Bible make the implicit assumption that a book written for first-century, persecuted Christians is not very relevant to twentieth-century Christians living under a government that does not interfere with religion.

These two ways of interpreting Revelation leave us with an unhappy choice: Either we reduce the book to a puzzle about the future or to an irrelevant, historical document. We need a third approach.

The basis for an alternative method of interpretation used in this book is to approach Revelation as a literary work that expresses the thoughts, dreams, hopes, and pain of first-century Christians. We come to understand the work through the tools of literary criticism, supported by the insights from the historical approach. We understand the message less with our rational, intellectual and analytical faculties and more with our emotional, artistic and intuitive processes. Both traditional approaches suffer from being too rational and analytical. They look for a message that can be understood by the intellect alone. The rational faculties cannot comprehend the imagery, the kaleidoscope of sounds and emotions, nor the fluid changing of the symbols found in Revelation. The imagery is designed more to affect the emotions than to communicate a clear message. Literary analysis allows a more productive reading of the Book of Revelation.

Endnotes

1. The "method of correlation" as a method for theological thinking is developed by Paul Tillich in *Systematic Theology*, vol. 1 (Chicago: University of Chicago Press, 1951), 59-66.

2. Dale Anderson, "Introspective Baez Surprises Fans," *Buffalo News*, 7 July 1985.

3. Two ways of interpreting Revelation and other apocalyptic writings have dominated: the fundamentalist-predictive approach and the historical-critical method. A fuller discussion of these two approaches is found in Appendix B. In this book a third approach is used, based on reading Revelation primarily as a literary work.

4. This same approach to interpreting Scripture was used in my previous book, *Job: A Vision of God* (New York: Seabury, 1975), 134-146. This manner of interpreting Scripture also allows for the fact that the faith community determined what books would form the Bible and that the people of God at different times and in varying situations perceived God's call and purpose in differing ways. Thus we need not seek to reconcile contradictory sections of Scripture to affirm that the Bible is the divine revelation of God given in and through the relationship of God with a particular community.

5. For a fuller discussion on the definition and characteristics of apocalyptic literature, see Appendix A.

6. The structure of the seven letters uses the following elements: (a) A phrase taken from the vision of the Son of man in chapter 1 identifies the speaker. (b) He says, "I know [your situation]," and proceeds to make an evaluation of the congregation. (c) Words of commendation or chastisement follow based on the analysis. (d) Then comes the formula, "He who has an ear, let him hear what the Spirit says to the churches." (e) The letters close with a promise to the victors. From the fourth letter on, the order of the last two elements is reversed.

7. The most frequently given date depends on a passage from the writings of Irenaeus of Lyons (ca. 180), which states that Revelation was written by John the Apostle during the persecution of the Emperor Domitian. Scholars almost unanimously reject the idea of apostolic authorship, but without other early data, many accept the date and the Domitian persecution. Unfortunately, in the many records contemporary with Domitian's rule there is no evidence of an official persecution of the church. Internal evidence from the Book of Revelation is equally inconclusive. Any interpretation that depends on or assumes a persecution or a late date is suspect. As suggested in Appendix A, it is safer to see apocalypse as a type of literature popular among the underclass rather than seek to tie each work to some specific conflict.

8. G. B. Caird, *The Revelation of St. John the Divine* (New York: Harper & Row, 1966), 51-53. The argument here is persuasive that John looks for the conversion of the Jews and not their humiliation.

9. A wide variety of structures have been proposed by commentators. Most focus on the number 7; those who focus on the hymns discern a liturgical pattern; others take the three woes as the key to the structure; still others develop complex interplays between the seven letters and the rest of the text. The three-fold grouping proposed here is not so much an attempt to delineate John's structure as it is a simple way to assist the person who is not a scholar of Revelation to be able to read the book.

10. We know there were more than seven churches in the province of Asia. The New Testament names three more: Troas (Acts 20:5f), Colossae (Col. 1:2), and Hierapolis (Col. 4:13). Later writings (Ignatius) would suggest even more. The number 7 was possibly selected because of its symbolic value as a symbol of wholeness and belonging to God. 3 1/2 and 6 are numbers symbolic of the beast.

11. P. S. Minear, "The Cosmology of the Apocalypse," *Current Issues in New Testament Interpretation*, ed. W. Klassen and G. F. Snyder (London: SCM, 1962), 23-37; P. S. Minear, *I Saw a New Earth* (Washington: Corpus Books, 1968), 272-278; J. P. M. Sweet, *Revelation* (Philadelphia: Westminster, 1979), 16.

12. This problem is more technical than most lay students of Scripture wish to pursue. Representative examples of these two common approaches to understanding this central section of Revelation are presented by Vernard Eller and Elisabeth Schuessler Fiorenza. Vernard Eller in *The Most Revealing Book of the Bible: Making Sense out of Revelation* (Grand Rapids: Eerdmans, 1974) presents a convincing outline of the structure that has five accounts of the conflict, each ending with the victory of Christ and each with seven parts: (1) the seven seals, 6:1-8:1 (interrupted by chapter 7); (2) the seven trumpets, 8:2-11:19 (interrupted by 10:1-11:13): (3) a free-hand sketch of the end, 12:1-14:20; (4) the seven bowls, 15:1-16:21 (interrupted by 16:15); and (5) the final description of the end, 17-20:3.

Elisabeth Schuessler Fiorenza in "Composition and Structure of the Book of Revelation," *Catholic Biblical Quarterly, 1977 (39)* 344-368, [reprinted in Schuessler Fiorenza, *The Book of Revelation: Justice and Judgment* (Philadelphia: Fortress, 1985)], contends the story is a single telling, beginning at 4:1 and concluding at 20:15. In this story are "pre-announcements" of the final outcome (*e.g.,* 11:14-19; 14:6-20; 16:17-21), interludes that are visions, auditions, and hymns anticipating the eschatalogical future (7; 11:15-19; 12:10; 14:1-5; 15:2-14; 19:1-9; 20:4-6), and intercalations that are scenes placed between two units or episodes that essentially belong together (*e.g.,* the eating of the scroll and fate of the church, 10:1-11:14, is inserted between the sixth and seventh trumpets, and then in a double intercalation, the seventh trumpet, 11:15-19, is between the scroll and fate of the church and persecution of the church, chaps. 12-14). Schuessler

Fiorenza makes the point that John does not divide the book into sections, but joins sections by interweaving themes and episodes.

13. John is expanding the received understanding of evil. The Jews were not a seafaring people. From the creation story through Daniel, the sea is a place of chaos and a source of evil, a notion probably deriving from their unfamiliarity with the sea and the fearfulness of its storms. John expands the *locus* of evil beyond the sea to heaven and earth in his trinitarian image.

14. The identification of Christ's victory with the mythological fall of Satan is attested elsewhere in the New Testament, see Luke 10-18, and John 12:31-33, 14:30, and 16:11. Satan is the prosecuting counsel in the heavenly court (Job 1, Zech. 3, Jude 9) who demands justice with a vengeance. Michael is the council for the defense (I Tim. 3:6, I Peter 5:8, Jude 9, and many non-biblical Jewish texts). Through Christ's death and resurrection, the mercy of God becomes the moral basis for judgment of sinners. There is no longer a need for a prosecutor. Christ's death not only changed the course of history, but also revised the spiritual realities that lie beneath the chronology of events. Satan is the deceiver of the world (12:9) by virtue of his position that vengeful justice is a proper spirituality rather than mercy. See Caird, *Revelation*, 153-157 and Sweet, *Revelation*, 198-200.

15. Though the idea of the sea as an image of chaos and as part of a trinity seems to predominate in this section, we should not exclude this detail as an additional layer of symbolism pointing toward Rome. Rome comes to Asia Minor from the sea through Ephesus. In 2 Esdras 11:1, Rome is an eagle appearing from the sea. Revelation 17 describes the seven heads as symbols of the seven hills of Rome and as symbols of seven emperors (vv. 9f); the emperors are also symbolized by the ten horns (v. 12). There are many good reasons to assume portions of this chapter (with 13:18) are interpolations by a later scribe seeking to clarify the beast's identity with

Rome and to point to a particular emperor as the epitome of evil. Only 13:18 mentions the number 666. Elsewhere when the mark of the beast is mentioned, the number is omitted. If we omitted 17:9-11 as a later addition, Babylon, not the beast, would be a clear image of Rome. 17:18 identifies Babylon as the city which has dominion, and chapter 18 depicts Babylon as close to the sea—true for Rome, but not for the historical Babylon. Understanding Babylon as Rome would also preserve the symmetry between the three-fold evil one and its kingdom, and the three-fold God and his church. Even if 17:9-11 is an addition, it still confirms the statement that the early Christians would identify certain aspects of the description as allusions to Rome. See R. H. Charles, *The Revelation of St. John* (New York: Charles Scribner's Sons, 1920), 67-75 and Eller, *Most Revealing Book*, 159-167.

16. In Daniel the horns represent the kings of the Seleucid dynasty that succeeded Alexander the Great. The ten horns were found on the fourth and most horrible beast which represented the Greeks (Dan. 7:2-8). That John understood the horns on his beast to symbolize kings is affirmed by the diadems on each horn. The time of the beast's reign (42 months or 3 1/2 years) is also found in Daniel 7:25, 9:27, and 12:7. The beast's warring against the saints and conquering them is a quote from Daniel 7:21 (also see 7:25 and 8:24).

17. William Stringfellow, *An Ethic for Christians and Other Aliens in a Strange Land* (Waco, TX: Word Books, 1973), 78.

18. Eller, *Most Revealing Book*, 131.

19. Caird, *Revelation*, 173. The identification of the mark with the number 666 may be a later addition to the text.

20. The mark of the beast contrasts with the sealing of the Lamb's people by the angels (chap. 7). This sealing may be a reference to the signing in the name of the Spirit in baptism. That the mark is given by the third member of the malevolent trinity supports the association with baptism. Though the idea is speculative, I wonder if the word *charagma* (mark) was chosen as a pun on *charisma*, the gift given by the Spirit in

baptism. John consistently identifies the faith community as composed of Jews and Christians. That the mark is placed on the forehead and the right hand may represent a parody of the Jewish practice of wearing phylacteries on the forehead and the left hand (Charles, *Revelation*, 362-3). The mark of the beast is a symbol of allegiance in contrast to the signs of membership in the faith community: baptism and the wearing of phylacteries.

21. Max Weber, *The Theory of Social and Economic Organization*, ed. Talcott Parsons (Glencoe, IL: Free Press, 1957), 152.

22. This "commonsense" definition of power comes from several sources and has been refined by students in classes taught on power. Two articles were particularly helpful in developing this definition and the model of social interaction which follows: Bernard H. Loomer, "Two Kinds of Power," *Criterion* (Winter, 1976), 11-29; Dean Brackley, "Downward Mobility: Reflections on Ignatius' 'Two Standards,'" a privately circulated paper dated May 17, 1979.

23. Frank G. Kirkpatrick, *Community: A Trinity of Models* (Washington: Georgetown University Press, 1986), 13-60.

24. "Downward Mobility," 4-6.

25. "Two Kinds of Power," 14-15.

26. Jerry Sullivan, "Michael Mania," *The Buffalo News*, 27 May 1989.

27. "Two Kinds of Power," 16.

28. Ann Landi, "When Having Everything Isn't Enough," *Psychology Today* (April 1989) 27-30.

29. "Downward Mobility," 14.

30. Paul Tournier, *The Strong and the Weak*, trans. Edwin Hudson (Philadelphia: Westminster, 1963). This book argues that those who desire to be strong and those who feel themselves weak both operate primarily out of insecurity and fear.

31. In the analysis that follows I depend heavily on the work of Walter Wink: *Naming the Powers* (Philadelphia: Fortress, 1984), 104-148; *Unmasking the Powers* (Philadelphia:

Fortress, 1986); *Engaging the Powers* (Philadelphia: Fortress, 1987). Other important works are C. B. Caird, *Principalities and Powers* (Oxford: Clarendon Press, 1962) and William Stringfellow's *An Ethic for Christians and Other Aliens* and *Conscience & Obedience: The Politics of Romans 13 and Revelation 13 in the Light of the Second Coming* (Waco, TX: Word Books, 1973).

32. Wink, *Naming*, 110

33. John Howard Yoder, *The Politics of Jesus* (Grand Rapids: Eerdmans, 1972), 193-214, contains an excellent discussion of Romans 13, which places it in context and argues persuasively that Paul did not mean the Christian should surrender moral independence.

34. Most commentators seek to connect the worship of the beast to some sort of emperor worship cult. Unfortunately, there is almost no evidence for such a cult, nor that anyone was put to death for refusing such worship in the first century. A much simpler explanation comes from the many references to the Book of Daniel throughout Revelation. Historical evidence is abundant for Antiochus IV's erection of the image of Zeus in the Temple in Jerusalem and of his forcing the Jews at the point of the sword to worship the image. Echoes of Daniel 3, the story of the fiery furnace written to oppose the actions of Antiochus Epiphanes, are clearly heard in Revelation 13:15. The observance of Chanukah and the popularity of the names of the Maccabean heroes (such as John) indicate a vivid memory of that event. Antiochus stands out as a symbol for the blasphemous arrogance of demonic tyranny.

35. John L. McKnight, "Regenerating Community," *Social Policy* (Winter 1987) 55-56.

36. Charles, *Revelation*, 164.

37. Caird, *Revelation*, 295.

38. "All Things Considered," National Public Radio, 26 February, 1988.

39. Kirkpatrick, *Community*. The first section of this book traces the "atomistic/contractarian" model of community from

the Sophists to present-day economic and social understandings.

40. *Ibid.*, 52. See also Robert N. Bellah, Richard Madsen, William M. Sullivan, Ann Swidler, and Steven M. Tipton, *Habits of the Heart: Individualism and Commitment in American Life* (New York: Harper & Row, 1986). This important study develops the thesis that because of its stress on individualism, American culture is losing the concept of community and the language for expressing the values of community life.

41. In the first century no definition of the canonical books of the Old Testament had yet been set. While the Law (Torah) and the Prophets (Nebim)—the first two sections of the Jewish scriptures—were set, additional scrolls were used by devout Jews. Some of these additional writings became part of Scripture in the section of the Old Testament called the Writings (Ketubim), others were included in the Greek Old Testament and became part of the Apocrypha of the Christian Bible, and others are known to us as the Pseudepigrapha. The "Apocalypse of Ezra" (sometimes called "4 Ezra" in collections of the Pseudepigrapha) is found in the Apocrypha in 2 Esdras, chapters 3-14 and is usually dated in the first century B.C.E. Allusions to earthquakes may be found in Ezekiel 37:19-20 and 2 Esdras 5:8, 9:3. The last two psalms from the Psalms of Solomon (dated 70 - 40 B.C.E.) predict the coming Messiah who will cleanse Jerusalem, punish sinners, subdue the nations hostile to Israel, and rule in righteousness. 2 Esdras 11:37-12:34 tells of a savior, a lion, that destroys the eagle from the sea (symbol of Rome), which was the last of the four beasts (empires) to rule the world.

This description of the life of the church in Philadelphia is based on historical and archaeological evidence as well as Revelation 3:7-13, 6:10.

42. C. H. Dodd, *Apostolic Preaching and Its Developments* (Grand Rapids: Baker, 1980).

43. In the RSV the last line of the song to the Lamb is translated with most manuscripts, "they *shall* reign on earth."

The variant reading of the present tense here followed is to be preferred, as it is the harder reading. A scribe with millennial ideas would naturally change the present tense by adding a single letter, but no motive is apparent for changing the future to the present. Also the present tense is similar to John's usage elsewhere in Revelation, *e.g.*, 11:15, 17.   Present or future tense, the reader must still include in the interpretation the phrase "on earth." As Caird points out, even to translate this line as future tense does not mean that the reign will occur at the millennium, when the martyrs reign, or in the new Jerusalem, which is not "on earth." The Lamb has made his followers kings and priests. They are empowered. Their reign will begin no later than the immediate future. Sweet, *Revelation*, 130-131; Caird, *Revelation*, 76-77; Charles, *Revelation*, 148.

44. Massey H. Shepherd, Jr., *The Paschal Liturgy and the Apocalypse* (Richmond: John Knox, 1960), 77-78, and P. Prigent, *Apocalypse et Liturgie* (Delachaux et Niestle, 1964) 61-76.   One need not argue that John is intentionally describing first-century worship, only that the worship he knew informed the context of his vision.

45. There is no clear evidence to indicate the origin of the figure of the Lamb as a symbol for Jesus. The evidence cited by J. Massyngberde Ford in *Revelation*, The Anchor Bible (New York: Doubleday, 1975), 15-16, 30-31, that the Lamb is based on an apocalyptic, conquering lamb who will appear in the final days and destroy evil, is very weak. Dodd's note is merely a surmise; the lamb in 1 Enoch 90:38 is not a messianic figure; and the passage in the Testament of Joseph 19:8 is highly suspect as a scribal interpolation.   There is stronger evidence that the symbol comes from the association of the crucifixion with the Passover. In I Cor. 5:1, "Christ our Passover is sacrificed for us," Paul associates the crucifixion, Passover, and sacrifice. It seems a small step to move from this association to associating the crucifixion with the Paschal lamb and sacrifice, and then associate sacrifice with deliverance and

redemption. I Peter uses *amnos* to refer to the sacrificial lamb that is a ransom (Passover reference) and in 2:24 paraphrases Isaiah 53:7 ("Like a lamb that is led to the slaughter"; also see Acts 8:32) in speaking of Jesus as bearing our sins that we might die to sin and live to righteousness. The connection seems simple; the problem is, how did the word "lamb" change from *amnos* to *arnos* and, in Revelation, to *arnion*? (*Cf.* Luke 10:3 and John 21:15, the only other NT uses) In other OT references in Revelation, John does not seem to be using the Septuagint. Perhaps he was translating from the Hebrew or using a different Greek translation. *Arnion* may well be an equally good translation of "paschal lamb" (*sheh*) as *amnos*. In Revelation the image of the Lamb develops in contrast to the beast, a striking image in apocalyptic literature. The strength of Vernard Eller's commentary, *The Most Revealing Book of the Bible*, is his development of the image of the Lamb and his consistent application of the image. On this passage, see 78-82.

46. In the New Testament *arnion* is found only in John 21:15, "Feed my lambs," which is paralleled in 21:16-17 with "Feed my sheep" (*probaton*). In Revelation the word is found 28 times. In the Greek translation of the Old Testament (LXX), the word is found in only three places: Psalm 114, in which the hills skip like *lambs* at the presence of God; Jeremiah 11:19, "like a *gentle lamb* led to slaughter"; Jeremiah 50:45, a passage in which the Lord, as a lion, will destroy Babylon and "drag away the *little ones* of their flock." All of these uses point to a young, vulnerable animal.

47. This passage in Luke may well reflect the Septuagint, where in Isaiah's vision of the peaceable kingdom the wolf and the lamb shall dwell together (Is. 11:6; 65:25). Here the image of the lamb is clearly one of defenselessness and corresponds to other LXX uses of *arnos*.

48. Schuessler Fiorenza, "Redemption as Liberation: Apocalypse 1:5f and 5:9f," Catholic Biblical Quarterly 1974 (36) 228 [reprinted in *The Book of Revelation: Justice and Judg-*

ment]. The connection of the crucifixion with the paschal lamb is an early Christian theme largely because of the occurrence of the crucifixion at the time of the Passover (1 Cor. 5:7, 1 Peter 1:18). In the Gospel of John the crucifixion occurs on the "day of preparation for the Passover," the day the paschal lambs were killed. Other references to the Exodus found in Revelation include:

The plagues brought upon Egypt to force Pharoah to free the Hebrew slaves form the basis for the plagues of the trumpets (8:6-12) and the plagues of the bowls (16:1-9).

15:1-5 pictures those who have won the victory over the beast standing beside a sea of glass and fire singing the the song of Moses and the Lamb. (*cf.* Exod. 15) This passage is followed by the image of the tabernacle, the Tent of the Presence, filled with the smoke of the glory of God (15:5-8).

The woman robed with the sun (12:1-6), an image of the faith community, escapes the dragon by fleeing into the wilderness and barely avoids drowning in a river of water from the dragon's mouth (12:14-16).

The phrase "kingdom and priests" found in 1:6 and 5:10 and mirrored in 20:6, which describes martyrs who reign as priests, echoes the phrase "kingdom of priests" of Exodus 19:6.

The presence of God leading the Hebrew people through the wilderness as a pillar of fire by night and a pillar of cloud by day may be the origin of the description of the angel in 10:1-2; it is wrapped in a cloud, has legs like pillars of fire, has one foot on the sea and the other on land, and delivers a scroll, a possible symbol of the law.

The prophet known as Second Isaiah proclaimed a new exodus out of Babylon. In Revelation, Babylon is a symbol of oppression and the call to "come out of Babylon" is a call for a new exodus led by the Lamb.

49. Because of the large number of citations that follow, they have been omitted from the text. The references for each point are as as follows:

The Lamb's horns (5:6), the beast's (13:1, 11-12; 17:12); the beast's healed mortal wound (13:3, 14-15); the beast's coercion through fear and might (6:4, 8; 12:12, 17; 13:4, 7); the call for commitment in the letters (ch. 2, 3) indicates the Lamb's followers must choose (see also 14:12; 19:7-9; 22:17); the Lamb attracts followers through sacrificial love (1:5-6; 5:9; 7:17); the Lamb liberates people from bondage, bringing life (1:5; 2:7, 11; 3:6; 7:9-17; 20:4-6; 22:1-3); the beast kills people, drinking their blood (14:8; 16:6; 17:6; 18:24); the Lamb gives his blood to raise people to new life (1:5; 5:9; 7:14; 12:11; 19:13); the beast's people make short-term gains, but the cost is spiritual death (14:9-11); the beast's sword (6:4,8; 13:10) and the Lamb's (1:16; 2:12,16; 19:15, 21); the beast makes war on the saints (13:7; 19:19) while the Lamb and his people celebrate victory with song (5:9-10; 14:1-3; 15:2-4; 19:6-8); the beast numbers people (13:16-17); the Lamb gives his followers his name (7:3; 13:12; 14:1) and invites them to his wedding feast (19:7-9; 21:2; 22:7); the Lamb is a shepherd (7:17); the beast seduces people with images and half-truths (13:13-15; 17:4-5; 19:10; 20:8; 22:15); the Lamb's title is "faithful and true" (3:14; 19:11) and his people speak truth (14:5; 21:27); Babylon (ch. 17, 18) contrasts with Jerusalem (21:2-22:5); the beast blasphemously claims allegiance and and worship (13:1, 5-8, 15; 17:3; 19:20); the Lamb and his people worship God alone (4:1-11; 5:9-14; 7:9-12; 15:2-4; 19:10; 20:4; 22:9).

50. The six victory scenes are Rev. 8:1; 11:15; 14:6-11; 16:17-21; 18:1-8; 19:20, 21.

51. The victory of the Lamb is also proclaimed in 1:5, 18; 2:27; 5:5, 9f; 11:17f; 12:5, 11; 15:4; 17:14; 19:15. In addition to the numerous references to the followers of the Lamb as "conquerors," the conquest and rule of Jesus' followers is also proclaimed in 1:5; 2:26f; 3:21; 5:10; 12:11; 17:14.

52. Caird, *Revelation*, 70-73; Sweet, *Revelation*, 122-124.

53. Thomas B. Woodward, *Turning Things Upside Down: A Theological Workbook* (New York: Seabury, 1975), 74-75.

54. We must take seriously Jesus' refusal to seek political power in his temptation in the wilderness (Matt. 4:8-10, Luke 4:5-8) and his refusal to be made king by the people (John 6:15). Jesus was not called to exercise political power. We must take seriously the seductive control that political power exerts over those who seek to exercise it. However this does not mean Christians should avoid political office; the desire for power, not the position of authority, controls the politician.

55. The variant "it" [the cross] in Col. 2:15 is preferred as the more difficult reading; however, the meaning changes little when the passage is translated using the pronoun "him" [Christ].

56. For a detailed analysis of the New Testament message of Christ's victory over the powers and principalities, see Wink, *Naming the Powers*, 39-96, and J. Christiaan Beker, *Paul the Apostle: The Triumph of God in Life and Thought* (Philadelphia: Fortress, 1980).

57. Alcoholism affects all societies. Though there are many biological and social factors that play a role in alcoholism, the more competitive and individualistic the culture, the greater the power of the disease to victimize the alcoholic. A useful resource is Dr. Barry Leach's paper, "Treatment Psychology," presented at *Alcoholism: The Dynamics of Intervention and Recovery*, a seminar for clergy and others concerned with the problem of alcoholism, sponsored by Department of Health, Physical Education and Recreation, University of Lousiville, 1 June, 1977.

58. Martin L. King, Jr., *Stride Toward Freedom* (New York: Harper & Row, 1958), 80. Also see King's summary of the philosophy of nonviolence in the same work, 83-88.

59. King's universal message on Negro nonviolence from the time of the Montgomery bus boycott, is recorded on *I Have a Dream* (cassette) and partially quoted in Stephen B. Oates, *Let the Trumpet Sound* (New York: Plume Books, 1982),

236. This speech is frequently referred to under the title "To our white brother."

60. For a full account, see David Lampe, *The Danish Resistance* (New York: Ballantine, 1960); also John Danstrup, *A History of Denmark* (Copenhagen: Wivel, 1948), 173-195.

61. For a convincing comparison of violent revolution with nonviolent revolt, see Walter Wink, "Violence and Non-violence in South Africa," *Sojourners* (January 1987) 30-31.

62. Yoder, *Politics*, 238-245.

63. The literature on early Christianity is vast, but two recent studies are illustrative. Robert L. Wilkin, *The Christians as the Romans Saw Them* (New Haven: Yale University Press, 1984), focuses on the strength of non-Christian beliefs and groups, and supports the thesis that Christianity spread largely because of the commitment of believers in the face of civic harassment, mob violence, and elaborate official efforts to destroy the Christian movement. Ramsay MacMullen, *Christianizing the Roman Empire* (New Haven: Yale University Press, 1984), while helping to temper some of our idealized views of the early Christians, fails to provide any serious explanation for the spread of the faith other than the witness of the early Christians.

64. Romano Guardini, *The Lord* (Chicago: Henry Regnery, 1954), 476-479.

65. There are many different proposals for outlining the structure of Revelation, but all acknowledge the importance of John's use of the number seven. Vernard Eller outlines five tellings of the story of the end, each told in seven steps plus an interlude. When one adds the seven letters the result is six septets. The passage on the new Jerusalem makes a seventh part that closes the book. Austin Farrer, *The Revelation of St. John the Divine* (Oxford: Clarendon, 1964), defines fours septets: the letters, the seals, the trumpets, and the bowls. Each septet is related to the letters: the first letter setting the theme for the letter septet, the second letter, the theme for the seals, etc. Jacques Ellul, *Apocalypse: the Book of Revelation* (New

York: Seabury, 1977), defines five septets, including the four defined by Farrer and adding a fifth, chapters 19-22, which repeats "then I saw" seven times. Elisabeth Schuessler Fiorenze, in "Composition and Structure of the Book of Revelation," develops a structure of seven parts based on the three identified septets (not including the letters) and the two scrolls enclosed within the letter septet and the final parousia/new Jerusalem scenes.

66. Ford (*Revelation*, 21) identifies seventeen different hymns. Schuessler Fiorenza, "Composition and Structure," 349, lists sixteen hymns.

67. See Appendix B.

68. For example, he recounts the final victory of God and Christ five times (8:1, 11:14-19, 14:14-20, 16:17-20, and 19:11-20:3) before the full description of the final judgment and the new Jerusalem (20:7-22:5).

69. The scenes of worship are 1:12-19; 4:1-11; 5:8-14; 7:9-12; 11:15-19; 12:10-12; 14:1-5; 15:1-8; 16:5-7; 18:20; 19:1-8.

70. Massey Shepherd (*Liturgy and the Apocalypse*, 77) presents the thesis that "the plan according to which the visions unfold is possibly—we would say probably—laid out in a scheme that follows the order of the Church's Paschal liturgy."

71. John Gager, *Kingdom and Community* (Englewood Cliffs, NJ: Prentice-Hall, 1975), 49-57.

72. David L. Barr, "The Apocalypse as a Symbolic Transformation of the World: A Literary Analysis," *Interpretation* (January 1984) 47.

73. *Ibid.*, 50.

74. The reader may recognize the insight of Immanuel Kant in this paragraph. Since Kant, we have understood explicitly that the mind is an active participant in forming and systematizing one's perception of reality, but this insight is known intuitively by anyone who seeks to influence opinion. Every child knows that the way its mother perceives a request depends partly on her frame of mind at the time of asking.

Similarly, artists know that the way in which one perceives a work is an important part of what one perceives. John's symbols are clearly designed to change the readers' natural perception of the glories of pagan Roman culture and of the apparent insignificance of the Christian community. The call to come out of Babylon (see chapter 9) and into the new Jerusalem (see chapter 10) points toward a conclusion that John knew implicitly: the community that one is part of will nurture one's values and emotions, which in turn will influence one's perception of the world.

75. Schuessler Fiorenza, "Redemption as Liberation," 220-232.

76. I have referred to this clear connection between John's understanding of salvation and the Exodus in chapter 5; see note 48.

77. In December, 1982, the unemployment rate hit 10.8%, which was the highest it had been since the beginning of World War II. 20% of the unemployed had been out of work 27 weeks or longer; the mean duration of unemployment of 18 weeks was also the highest since World War II. The total number of unemployed, 99.1 million, was the largest number in the history of this country, surpassing the Great Depression. Most of the job losses were in transportation, construction, and manufacturing. The unemployed rate was 17.0% for durable goods manufacturing and 16.2% for blue collar workers. *Employment and Earnings*, U.S. Department of Labor/Bureau of Labor Statistics, January, 1983.

78. The primary book used to design the seminars was Bernard Haldane and Jean M. Haldane, *Job Finding Power* (New York: Office for Ministry Development, 1984).

79. Tilden H. Edwards, ed., *Living with Apocalypse: Spiritual Resources for Social Compassion* (San Francisco: Harper & Row, 1984). Henri Nouwen's essay, pp. 15-17, talks about the need to put off the "mentality of scarcity" and put on "the mentality of abundance."

80. A great amount of nonsense has been written and preached in establishment churches that equates being "poor in spirit" with having spiritual needs. Jesus' teaching about money and the power of money to corrupt ("Where your treasure is there your heart will be also," "You cannot love God and mammon") together with the parallel in Luke 6:20, "Blessed are you poor, for yours is the kingdom of God," makes clear that the message of Matthew 5:1 regards our spiritual attitude toward money.

81. *Downward Mobility,*" 8.

82. Rev. 18:2b, 9-13, 15-18, 19bcd, 21c-24, 20. I have edited the text this way in order to make the passage shorter and more fluid to our contemporary ear. The italicized portion of verse 20 follows Caird's translation in *Revelation,* 229-230.

83. Some commentators interpret the angel's dropping of the millstone as the action that destroys Babylon. The text clearly states that Babylon will die of violence as surely as a millstone sinks in the water (18:21). The weight of the millstone causes it to sink; the violence of Babylon leads to its demise.

84. Christopher Rowland defines apocalyptic literature largely on the basis of this distinctive feature. Apocalypse are those books in which God discloses the mysteries of heaven and earth, past and future, to a privileged seer who takes a heavenly journey where supernatural events mirror events on earth. There is a motive to explain God's purposes for the present, but there is also a delight in the supernatural. The Book of Enoch demonstrates this characteristic of apocalypse well. *The Open Heaven: A Study of Apocalyptic in Judaism and Early Christianity* (New York: Crossroad, 1982).

85. For a detailed discussion of the Old Testament sources the reader is referred to the commentaries. Three important visions used by John are Isaiah 65:17-25; Ezekiel 40:1-43:12, chapters 47 and 48; Zechariah 14:8-21.

86. Not only does the vision of the New Jerusalem bring the story to its conclusion, but John also makes references to many

of his earlier images. The title "Alpha, Omega" was used in 1:8, the destruction of death and the wiping away of tears is almost verbatim from 7:16-17, and the phrase "to him who conquers" is from the seven letters, which also contain references to the tree of life (2:7) and the New Jerusalem (3:12).

87. Sweet, *Revelation*, 297.

88. The Old Testament references to these phrases are too numerous to list. The term dwelling (*skene*) has a long theological development, beginning with the tent which was the symbol of God's presence in the midst of Israel in the wilderness and eventually becoming a term for the divine presence. "They shall be his people" is the promise first made in the covenant at Sinai (Lev. 26:12, Jer. 7:23, 11:4), which was renewed in the prophets' writings (Hos. 1:23, Jer. 30:22, Zech. 8:8), realized in the name Emmanuel (Isa. 7:14), and ratified when the title Emmanuel is given to Jesus (Matt. 1:23). Ezekiel 34:30 and 37:23, 27 contain the combination "God will be with them and they shall be his people." Caird, *Revelation*, 263-265.

89. *Ibid.*, 274.

90. Oates, *Trumpet*, 260-261.

91. Caird, *Revelation*, 271.

92. Paul D. Hanson, *The People Called: The Growth of Community in the Bible* (San Francisco: Harper & Row, 1987), 467.

93. Kirkpatrick, 138.

94. Martin Buber, *Paths in Utopia*, quoted in Kirkpatrick, 198.

95. James B. Nelson, *Moral Nexus: Ethics of Christian Identity and Community* (Philadelphia: Westminster, 1971), 74-75.

96. Ronald Munoz, "Ecclesiology in Latin America," *The Challenge of Basic Christian Communities*: Papers for the International Ecumenical Congress of Theology, ed. Sergio Torres and John Eagleson, trans. John Drury (Maryknoll: NY Orbis, 1981), 156.

97. Kirkpatrick, 195-197.

98. "Two Kinds of Power," 20.

Endnotes

99. "Downward Mobility," 8.

100. "Two Kinds of Power," 28.

101. Oates, *Trumpet*, 64-69; King, *Stride Toward Freedom*, 28-52.

102. Allison A. Trites, "*Martus* and Martyrdom in the Apocalypse: A Semantic Study," *Novum Testamentum* 1973 (15) 72-80.

103. Wink, *Naming*, 128-129.

104. Ephesians 6:17 and Hebrews 4:12, though both of these use *machaira* while Revelation uses *rouphaia*. Old Testament references include Isaiah 11:4; 49:2; Hosea 6:1-5; and Wisdom 18:15-16. In the Pseudepigrapha we find references in the Psalms of Solomon 17:26f, 39 (17:24 & 27 combine the sword with Isaiah 11:4, where the descendent of Jesse smites the earth with the rod of his mouth and slays the wicked with the breath of his lips) and in I Enoch 62:2.

105. Amnesty International, Room 64, 200 W. 72nd St., New York, NY 10023, and Freedom House, 20 W. 40th St., New York, NY, 10018.

106. Leon Howell, "No Escape from the Vietnam War," *Christianity and Crisis*, 10 October 1988: 331.

107. "Alan Paton Dies," *The Living Church*, April 17, 1988: 8.

108. The author to the Rev. and Mrs. Kenneth Morris, March 29, 1964.

109. The false prophet creates the image, and through manipulation, marvels, and coercion leads the people to worship the beast and its image (13:14f; also see 14:9, 11; 15:2; 16:2; 19:20; 20:4).

110. Yoder, *Politics*, 248.

111. Desmond M. Tutu, *Hope and Sufferering: Sermons and Speeches* (Grand Rapids: Eerdmans, 1983), 85.

112. Bellah et al., *Habits of the Heart*, 65-71, 287-290. This study develops the thesis that if our society is to continue to hold together, we must reduce the punishment of failure and the rewards of success. Then work can be pursued for its in-

trinsic value (vocation) and the good of others, rather than as the means to one's own advancement.

113. John's structure reflects his view of history. The point does not depend on whether John is telling the same story five times (the fireman's ladder) or one story with five similar chapters (the spiral staircase). At any point in time we can discern a pattern to history moving in a direction that has been foreshadowed. There is a sense in which something similar has happened before, and we know where it is taking us.

114. The simplest explanation of the two witnesses is that they represent Moses, who turned the waters to blood, and Elijah, who caused a drought. Together they stand for the Law and the Prophets (as reflected in the Transfiguration). The Bible tells of Elijah's ascending to heaven and one apocalyptic tradition holds that Moses also ascended. John is only partially, if at all, reworking Jewish apocalypse as he uses the witnesses to represent the necessary work of the faith community.

115. Chapter 7 pictures the worshiping church on earth and in heaven just before the opening of the seventh seal. Chapters 10 and 11 interrupt the seven trumpets with the eating of the scroll so that the prophet can prophesy concerning "peoples and nations and tongues and kings" (10:11) and the account of the witnesses (the faithful community). Then comes the final trumpet and the shout of victory, "The kingdom of the world has become the kingdom of our Lord and of his Christ, and he shall reign for ever and ever"(11:15). Following the descriptions of the trinity of beasts in chapters 13 and 14 comes the scene of the Lamb standing on Zion and singing with his people (14:1-5). Then comes the angel announcing that the hour of God's judgment has come and that Babylon has fallen (14:6-8). Finally the announcement of the wedding of the Lamb with his Bride, the church (19:6-9), precedes the final scene of evil's defeat by the Word of God (19:11-16).

116. Bellah et al., *Habits of the Heart*, 275-296.

Biblical References in Text

Biblical References

Index

Index